FIREFLY ENCYCLOPEDIA
of the
Vivarium

FIREFLY ENCYCLOPEDIA

of the

Vivarium

David Alderton

FIREFLY BOOKS

A FIREFLY BOOK

Published by Firefly Books Ltd. 2007

Copyright © 2007
The Brown Reference Group plc

First printing

Publisher Cataloguing-in-Publication Data (U.S.)
Alderton, David, 1956-
    Firefly encyclopedia of the vivarium : keeping amphibians, reptiles, and insects, spiders and other invertebrates in terraria, aquaterraria, and aquaria / David Alderton.
[224] p. : col. photos. ; cm.
Includes bibliographical references and index.
Summary: A reference for reptile and invertebrate vivarium setup and maintenance, and on reptile and amphibian feeding, breeding and health matters. Includes a directory of snakes, lizards, tortoises, turtles, frogs, newts, salamanders, spiders and other invertebrates.
ISBN-13: 978-1-55407-300-9
ISBN-10: 1-55407-300-6
1. Reptiles as pets. 2. Amphibians as pets. 3. Insects as pets. 4. Invertebrates as pets. 5. Vivariums. I. Title.
 639.39 dc22   QH68.A434   2007

Library and Archives Canada Cataloguing in Publication
Alderton, David, 1956-
    Firefly encyclopedia of the vivarium : keeping amphibians, reptiles, and insects, spiders and other invertebrates in terraria, aquaterraria, and aquaria / David Alderton.

Includes bibliographical references and index.
ISBN 978-1-55407-300-9

    1. Reptiles as pets. 2. Amphibians as pets.
 3. Insects as pets. 4. Invertebrates as
pets. 5. Vivariums. I. Title.

QH68.A43 2007   639.3'9
            C2007-900820-8

Published in the United States by
Firefly Books (U.S.) Inc.
P.O. Box 1338, Ellicott Station,
Buffalo, New York 14205

Published in Canada by
Firefly Books Ltd.
66 Leek Crescent,
Richmond Hill, Ontario L4B 1H1

The Brown Reference Group plc:
(incorporating Andromeda Oxford Limited)
8 Chapel Place, Rivington Street,
London EC2A 3DQ
www.brownreference.com

For the Brown Reference Group plc:
Editorial Director: Lindsey Lowe
Project Editor: Graham Bateman
Editor: Virginia Carter
Design Director: Steve McCurdy
Design: Martin Anderson

Printed in China

Photos
Page 1: Red-eyed Tree Frog (*Agalychnis callidryas*).
Pages 2–3: Panther Chameleon (*Furcifer pardalis*).

Cover Photos
Front: Main Image: White's Tree Frog (*Litoria caerulea*); PhotoDisc, Alan & Sandy Carey. Inset: Green Tree Python (*Morelia viridis*); Shutterstock, Brad Thompson.

Back: (clockwise from top left): Eastern Painted Turtles (*Chrysemys picta picta*); Shutterstock, Matthew. Burmese Python (*Python molurus*); Shutterstock, Vladimir Mucibabic. Green Anole (*Anolis carolinensis*); Shutterstock, Eric Lam. Tarantula; Shutterstock, Frank B. Yuwono. African Reed Frog (*Hyperolius marmoratus*); Shutterstock, EcoPrint.

Spine: Spurrell's Leaf Frog (*Agalychnis spurrelli*); Chris Mattison

CONTENTS

▼ *Leopard gecko (Eublepharis macularius)*

INTRODUCTION

Interest in keeping reptiles, amphibians and invertebrates in the home has grown greatly over recent years. This is partly a reflection of our changing lifestyles. Increasingly, we live in smaller homes, particularly in cities, where keeping traditional pets such as dogs and cats can be very difficult and even unfair on the animals. Fewer of us tend to be living in familiy units, and more people now live alone. Organizing a regular routine to care for pets can be difficult, especially if you have to work long or unpredictable hours.

Caring for reptiles, amphibians or invertebrates is straightforward by comparison. You do not need a large space to accommodate many species adequately, nor will it generally matter if you do not always feed them at exactly the same time each day. Looking after them is relatively simple, and cleaning their quarters is not particularly time-consuming.

Most species are not noisy by nature and will therefore not annoy the neighbors; nor do they have to be taken out for exercise. There is, however, plenty of scope for interaction with some of these creatures. The Bearded Dragon has become the most popular pet lizard for this reason, with hundreds of thousands bred annually in the United States alone. Especially if you obtain them as hatchlings, these lizards can become very tame and learn to interact with their owner, proving to be true companions. The same is true of tortoises and turtles. It is even possible to tame many amphibians sufficiently to feed from your hand.

As far as accommodation is concerned, it is not just possible but also often desirable to create a naturalistic setting for these animals, and a vivarium can become an attractive focal point in a room. This group of creatures has an undeniable appeal, linked to their exotic and often colorful appearance. You may even be able to persuade many species to breed successfully, gaining a fascinating insight into their varied lifestyles.

Selecting an Animal

There are certain guidelines to follow when deciding which species you want to keep. One of the most critical is its likely adult size. This needs careful consideration. In particular, certain reptiles can become very large, and accommodating them in the average home can be difficult. Amphibians and invertebrates, on the other hand, will attain a much smaller adult size.

Another aspect to consider is behavioral needs. Some species burrow, remaining hidden for long periods, while others are nocturnal and appeal essentially to the specialist. Some live in water, and others live mainly off the ground. These behaviors have led to a range of different terms being used to describe their housing.

"Vivarium" has become the umbrella description for housing used for reptiles, amphibians and invertebrates. "Terrarium," meaning earth enclosure, is generally a subdivision that relates to the needs of those living on or below the land. Other groups include semiaquatic species, for example, many turtles; they therefore live in what is known as an "aquaterrarium." There is also a relatively small number of popular species in the hobby that are totally aquatic—notably amphibians—and they require an "aquarium."

Reptiles and amphibians are sometimes known collectively as herptiles, and their care and breeding as herpetoculture. These names stem from "herpetology," the term used for many years to describe the study of these animals in the wild.

Modern equipment has now simplified all aspects of keeping these creatures in the home. With little difficulty you will be able to create conditions that replicate those of a variety of natural habitats, from a dry desert environment through to a lush tropical rain forest with a correspondingly high level of relative humidity.

Dietary requirements may be another significant factor in deciding which animals to keep—a number of species need to be fed on invertebrates, while others are essentially herbivorous or will happily be kept on prepared diets. Studies of the dietary needs of this group of creatures have led to the development of a range of specially formulated foods, particularly for the most widely kept species. The availability of such foods has greatly simplified their care.

Precautions in the Home

You will probably have to change certain aspects of your domestic routine, however, when opting to keep herptiles or invertebrates in the home. Be particularly careful with sprays of any kind, and avoid using them in the room in which the animals are housed, because some chemicals can be potentially fatal to them. Bug killers of any kind are likely to cause death to invertebrates that are exposed to them, and amphibians are

also at risk. Furniture polish sprays and carpet cleaners or fresheners may prove equally dangerous.

The domestic environment can become dry, particularly when central heating is operating, and this can endanger the health of land-dwelling amphibians in particular. Be prepared to mist their vivarium regularly, keeping a close eye on the relative humidity in the tank.

When you go on vacation it can be easier to find a carer for herptiles or invertebrates than for other pets. The easiest thing is to move the vivarium to your friend's home. Leave sufficient food, along with detailed written care instructions and the name of your veterinarian in case of an emergency while you are away.

Herptiles and the Law

Laws controlling the keeping of various species can be complex. They are governed by international, national and local regulations, and the situation changes frequently. Regulations tend to fall into three broad categories: prevention of smuggling; control of the removal of wild specimens from their native habitats; and prevention of the release of non-native species into an alien eco-system. The keeping of reptiles that are considered dangerous, such as crocodilians and venomous snakes

▲ *Bearded Dragons (Pogona vitticeps) are popular pets in North America.*

(which are not covered in this book), may require a special license.

Your local supplier should be a valuable source of information on such matters, but remember that ignorance of the law is no defense. Ensure that where necessary—for example, when dealing with specimens listed on CITES Appendix I—you obtain proof at the time of purchase that animals are being sold legally.

Naming

Naming the creatures covered in this book has been problematic, since many have several different common and scientific names. You will find in many cases that we give both the newest scientific name currently accepted by scientists and the historically well established name. This is because it can often be easier to find more information about these particular species by using the well established scientific nomenclature rather than the newest. In any event, the introduction of a new name does not necessarily invalidate the old one, and many suppliers still use the older names.

The Natural History of Vivarium Animals

▲ *All reptiles such as this male Green Iguana (Iguana iguana) have tough scaly skin and can live in a wide range of habitats.*

The aim of every keeper of herptiles and invertebrates should be to keep their pets in the best of health. The vivarium itself must imitate as near as possible the natural conditions from which the animals originate. Some understanding of the background natural history and biology of vivarium animals is therefore important.

INVERTEBRATES

Invertebrates represent the largest group of animals on Earth, and it is impossible to quantify with any accuracy the number of species that exist. Only a tiny percentage of them, however, are kept in vivarium surroundings. These creatures represent a lineage that extends back to some of the earliest forms of life on the planet, which first emerged more than 600 million years ago. The most distinctive feature that links this diverse group is the absence of a vertebral column—in fact, the lack of any type of bony skeleton.

Invertebrate Types and Biology

Members of the invertebrate phylum Arthropoda are the most significant group as far as this book is concerned. They include crustaceans such as crabs, arachnids such as spiders and scorpions, and insects, which represent the largest category of invertebrates. There may be in excess of 10 million different species of insects alone, of which barely one-tenth have been classified. What sets arthropods apart is the power of locomotion, which derives from their jointed limb structure. They can walk, swim or even fly—some having mastered this skill at an earlier stage than any other animal group. The number of legs varies widely: Insects have three pairs, spiders have four, while other arthropods, such as millipedes, may have hundreds of legs, albeit fewer than their name suggests.

Many arthropods are predatory by nature, often hunting down fellow invertebrates and occasionally small vertebrates. Their relatively small size allows them to hide away in burrows and similar retreats, while some have opted for camouflage in the open as a way of protecting themselves. This can be seen in the amazing array of walking sticks (stick insects) and leaf insects that live mainly on plants.

The way in which arthropods grow is through shedding (molting) their skin. They anchor themselves in place in a secure locality, and the old skin splits along the back. The arthropod can then step out from it. The new skin is soft and can be easily damaged, so it is not a good idea to try to handle the animal at this stage.

Although many invertebrates are short-lived, with a life expectancy varying from a few days through to a year, there are some that can live potentially much longer. Female tarantulas may live for almost half a century, approximately 10 times as long as the males.

Defensive Strategies

Invertebrates are not without means of defending themselves from predators. Crabs, for example, possess pincers that can give a painful nip. Others have more deadly ways of seeking to ensure their survival if necessary and of overcoming prey. Some scorpions have the ability to inflict a very severe sting from the tip of the tail, which can be fatal to humans, although thankfully these animals are not likely to be encountered in the pet trade.

Tarantulas—in spite of their fearsome reputation—are generally not capable of inflicting a life-threatening bite. Its impact is likely to be rather like that of a wasp sting. The hairs covering the spider's body represent a less well documented hazard, however: They can cause intense irritation, especially if they enter the eyes.

If you need to handle these arachnids, therefore, always wear protective gloves and never hold them close to your face. The same applies in the case of centipedes and of giant millipedes, which may be able to spurt venom at you from openings on the sides of the body. In all cases, it is worth remembering that invertebrates are essentially creatures to look at in the vivarium rather than to handle frequently. Be especially careful if you are sensitive to insect bites, since the effects of a bite could become far more serious.

▶ *A TARANTULA REARS UP OFF ITS LEGS IN A DEFENSIVE POSTURE.*

Escape Artists

Many invertebrates have a prodigious reproductive rate, producing hundreds or even thousands of eggs. This helps explain why they can easily become pests under certain circumstances in the wild. Huge swarms of locusts, for example, regularly sweep across parts of Africa and elsewhere in the world, decimating crops. As a result, the sale of locusts as live food for herptiles is banned in some areas, because of fears over what could happen if any escaped into the wild.

It is very important to prevent the escape of all nonnative species, not just invertebrates but also herptiles, in case they start to become established in the area and upset the local ecosystem. Allowing these animals to do so is often a criminal offense because of the potentially very serious environmental consequences.

AMPHIBIANS

It is thought that amphibians (class Amphibia) were the first group of land vertebrates—animals with backbones. The word "amphibian" translates as "a being with a double life," referring to the way in which these creatures generally leave land and return to water at the start of the breeding period. Nevertheless, there are still some amphibians that remain in water throughout the year. Others may breed on damp patches on the forest floor.

Breeding

One of the most remarkable recent discoveries about the biology of amphibians is that some species display parental care toward their eggs and offspring. A notable example is that of the dart frogs, found in parts of Central and South America. They carry their tadpoles to the water-filled cups of bromeliad plants growing in their rain forest homes. The females then return to these cups to deposit infertile eggs, providing food for the growing tadpoles. Some amphibians, including various North American salamanders, are even known to protect the eggs, remaining with them until they hatch into tadpoles. Tadpoles are often described as the larval stage in the amphibian life cycle. They live in water and extract oxygen by external gills present on the sides of the head just behind the eyes.

In some cases, however, usually at the margins of their distribution where environmental conditions may be less conducive to breeding, some populations of amphibians may not lay eggs. Instead, they either produce tadpoles or

◀ *THE BRIGHT COLORS OF THE STRAWBERRY DART FROG (DENDROBATES PUMILIO) INDICATE TO POTENTIAL PREDATORS THAT IT IS POISONOUS. THIS FROG IS CARRYING A TADPOLE TO THE SAFETY OF WATER-FILLED BROMELIADS.*

miniature versions of themselves. Such behavior may be seen in the Fire Salamander *(Salamandra salamandra)*, typically those occurring in northerly parts of the species' range and in mountainous areas. The eggs are simply retained within the female's body and develop there. Unlike in mammals, there is no placental connection between the female and her offspring. The young produced in this way are only likely to number one or two individuals, whereas adult females in other areas may lay 30 or more eggs.

Many other amphibians may lay thousands of eggs at a single spawning. Communal egg-laying is not uncommon in certain areas, so ponds can rapidly become filled with huge quantities of eggs arising from multiple spawnings in the spring. From the outset the tadpoles will face many hazards, not least from fellow amphibians as well as other aquatic creatures, ranging from predatory invertebrates to fish. In particular, newts, which return to ponds to breed at the same time as frogs and toads, are ruthless hunters of frog tadpoles. As the tadpoles themselves grow, the larger individuals are likely to start preying on their smaller, weaker companions, with cannibalism being common in many cases.

◀ *A PAIR OF ORIENTAL FIRE-BELLIED TOADS (BOMBINA ORIENTALIS).*

▼ *THESE CAECILIANS (TYPHLONECTES NATANS) REPRESENT THE OTHER GROUP OF AMPHIBIANS (APART FROM FROGS AND TOADS). THEY ARE RARELY KEPT IN VIVARIA.*

Amphibian Defensive Capabilities

Many adult amphibians can protect themselves by unpleasant skin secretions of varying toxicity. Bright body coloring often acts as a warning to would-be predators. If an amphibian protected in this way finds itself under threat, it will often twist its body to emphasis these brightly colored areas, displaying what is often described as the "Unken" response, or reflex.

Amphibians are found mainly in areas of freshwater. They are not equipped to survive in saltwater of any kind because of their porous skin. This would cause water to be lost from the body into the environment, soon resulting in dehydration and death. A few species can adapt temporarily to brackish surroundings, but only the Crab-eating Frog *(Fejervarya cancrivora)* from mangrove swamps in Southeast Asia can live in this type of environment.

In a few cases, notably the caecilians, limbs are absent entirely. These amphibians have a decidedly wormlike appearance. They also have a keen sense of smell, which helps them find food underwater and on land. Their eyes, in contrast to those of most amphibians, are tiny.

Skin and Breathing

The relative thickness of amphibian skin varies markedly and has a direct impact on the animal's lifestyle. Those with thicker skin, such as bufonid toads, can wander farther from water, since they are at less risk of dehydration. Yet the skin also plays an important role in the breathing process. The respiratory system of amphibians is less efficient than that of mammals, simply because they do not have a diaphragm. (This acts like a pair of bellows, drawing air in and out of the lungs.) Without a diaphragm, breathing has to be much more passive. In order to supplement their oxygen uptake, many amphibians also respire through their moist skin and the mouth. They expel carbon dioxide from the body by the same route.

REPTILES

Reptiles (class Reptilia) are thought to have developed as a lineage from the amphibians about 340 million years ago. They evolved a much tougher skin and are therefore far less likely to suffer from dehydration. Indeed, the outer layer of the reptile's body is covered in protective scales, formed within the skin. These scales are particularly evident in snakes. Because they are set in the skin, they have a degree of flexibility and do not form a rigid protective barrier. The snake can move with considerable agility, while still being protected against dehydration and attack. Other reptiles such as tortoises and turtles enjoy additional protection in the form of a shell.

Reptile Groups

Tortoises and turtles (order Testudines) were well established by the time the dinosaurs disappeared from Earth

▲ *ALL REPTILES PERIODICALLY SHED THEIR SKIN AS THEY GROW. HERE A BOA CONSTRICTOR (BOA CONSTRICTOR) IS IN THE PROCESS OF MOLTING.*

some 65 million years ago, and were largely unaffected by this mass extinction. Crocodilians (order Crocodylia) also survived and, like chelonians, they have altered surprisingly little in appearance since their early days.

Members of both these orders can be found in freshwater haunts and in the sea, although there are no surviving crocodiles that are totally marine. Today there are 23 crocodilian species, with members of the group represented on all continents apart from Europe. As with venomous snakes, their care is not covered in this volume, however, because their ownership is generally either prohibited or permitted only under strict license.

Snakes and lizards (order Squamata) developed at a relatively late stage in the history of reptiles. There is a close evolutionary link between snakes and lizards, in spite of the fact that snakes look very different, owing to the absence of functional limbs. In some species, such as boas, however, signs of vestigial limbs can be seen as spurs toward the rear of the body.

The fourth order (Rhynchocephalia) within the reptiles consists of the tuataras (*Sphenodon* species), which originate from New Zealand. Although they are superficially similar to lizards, they differ in various anatomical respects. For example, they lack eardrums and a middle ear but possess a so-called third eye, which is located in the center of the forehead and which responds to light. Tuartaras are strictly protected on the few offshore islands

◀ *A CRESTED GECKO (RHACODACTYLUS CILIATUS) USES ITS TONGUE TO CLEAN ITS EYES.*

▶ *RED-FOOTED TORTOISE (GEOCHELONE CARBONARIA). LIKE ALL CHELONIANS, IT HAS A SHELL FOR PROTECTION.*

where they occur, and they are not represented within the vivarium hobby.

Reptile Breeding Habits

The reproductive behavior of reptiles is variable. Although the majority lay eggs, some species of lizards and snakes give birth to live young, while others produce eggs with a parchmentlike shell, rather than a hard calcareous casing. These soft-shelled eggs are more susceptible to dehydration. In cases when live young are born, they may have been nourished by a primitive type of placental arrangement prior to birth, although more commonly the eggs are retained in the reptile's body, where they develop.

Parental care is most evident among crocodilians—females not only guard the nest but also frequently carrying the hatchlings to the relative safety of water and even watch over them here. There are few other examples of maternal behavior in reptiles. Female pythons incubate their eggs, however, and certain lizards, such as Monkey-tailed Skinks (*Corucia zebrata*), care for their offspring.

Reptile Survival

In common with amphibians, certain reptiles have the ability to survive under adverse environmental conditions by becoming inactive. Hibernation is the best known example. It is associated with reptiles from temperate regions and is triggered by the fall in temperature at the onset of winter. The reptiles seek out suitable retreats, sometimes hibernating communally, as in the case of various garter snakes (*Thamnophis* species). In warmer climates, faced with a shortage of food and water, reptiles such as African monitors and African Spurred Tortoises (*Geochelone sulcata*) may react in a similar way by undergoing a period of estivation. They become active again once environmental conditions are more favorable.

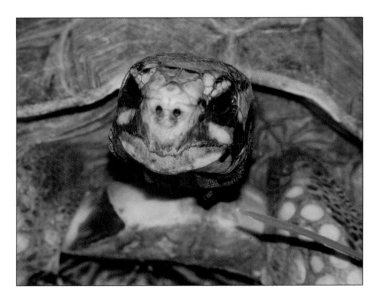

VIVARIUM SETUP AND MAINTENANCE

▲ *Tropical forest vivarium*

VIVARIUM HOUSING

The type of housing for herptiles and invertebrates depends on a number of different factors, not least the environment in which they normally live. This is partly a reflection of the fact that these creatures are all ectothermic (meaning they rely on an outside source of heat to regulate their body temperature rather than using internal metabolic means). Yet simply keeping them at a suitable temperature will not be sufficient in many cases. Other environmental factors, such as the relative humidity and the lighting, are also vital to their well-being, especially over the long run.

The layout of their quarters must reflect their wild habitat, since most species are relatively shy by nature and will require suitable retreats. Without adequate cover, herptiles can become very stressed and may fail to eat, the result being that their health will soon suffer. Some are terrestrial, whereas others are likely to be at least partly arboreal. This has a bearing on the shape of enclosure they will require. There is no universal type of housing that is applicable to all species, so from the outset you will need to design the accommodation with your chosen animals' needs in mind. It is also important to be aware that a number of reptiles in particular can attain a large size—it will therefore be a waste of money to start with a small enclosure that will soon be outgrown.

◄ *STAINLESS STEEL LIGHTING AND HEATING HOOD FITTED TO A GLASS VIVARIUM.*

the tanks. They usually have a sliding panel to give easy access to the interior, and space for an incandescent light bulb. Such hoods have fallen out of favor, however, largely because of the lighting arrangement—a typical incandescent light bulb, for example, tends to make the enclosure too warm for many amphibians. In addition, these hoods do not afford the benefits of sunlight, notably from the ultraviolet part of the spectrum, which is an important feature of modern lighting devised for use above vivaria. A secondary heat source is therefore needed, otherwise the light bulb will have to be switched on continuously to provide heat. This is likely to be detrimental to the occupants, effectively exposing them to constant artificial light.

Converted aquaria can be useful, however, for housing temperate invertebrates or amphibians, which can be maintained in the home at room temperature without requiring additional lighting. Acrylic rather than glass tanks are preferable because they are much lighter to move and are less likely to be broken. A low-wattage light can be incorporated, simply to allow the occupants of the tank to be seen.

▼ *GLASS VIVARIUM WITH SLIDING FRONT DOOR AND FLOOR TRAY, CONTAINING ARTIFICIAL PLANTS AND WATER BOWL.*

VIVARIUM TYPES

The basic enclosure used to house reptiles, amphibians and invertebrates is often described as a vivarium, sometimes abbreviated to "viv." Where dry land is present, the alternative description of "terrarium" is often used. There are a number of different options to consider when researching these types of enclosures.

Converted Aquaria

Traditionally vivaria are made from adapted aquaria. Special hoods containing lighting units are available, allowing a basic tank to be modified. The hoods themselves are sold in various sizes, corresponding to that of

◄ ACRYLIC UNITS WITH VENTILATED HOODS,
PLACED ON A SINGLE HEATING PAD.

Acrylic Units

Several manufacturers now offer clear acrylic units in a range of sizes, with ventilated hoods. Depending on the shape, they are suitable for terrestrial and arboreal species. The lid can be separated easily from the base, and there is a clear service hatch for feeding purposes. This avoids the need to remove the lid, which increases the risk of the occupant escaping. However, the small size and usual lack of lighting preclude the use of these units with many reptiles, which generally require more spacious, well lit surroundings. It is possible to provide heat in these units by means of heating pads (see page 22), typically placed beneath the unit.

When acrylic units are used to accommodate small invertebrates such as walking sticks, remember that they may be able to escape through the spacing of bars in the hood. To avoid this, cover the hood with plastic wrap that has holes punched in it for ventilation, until the

invertebrates are too large to slip through the spaces on the roof.

The larger acrylic units are ideal for housing various newts and salamanders that require an area of relatively shallow water and an area of land. They allow good visibility of the occupants and are invaluable for rearing tadpoles. They should be filled with water and decorated with places where the young amphibians can clamber out of the water for periods as they start to breathe atmospheric air.

Melamine Constructed Vivaria

Many vivaria used for reptiles tend to be constructed from melamine-fronted board, which can be wiped clean very easily. This material also allows holes to be drilled to incorporate overhead sources of light and power within the unit, along with a heating pad. Furthermore, the boxlike design gives the occupants privacy. However, large designs—while relatively robust—are heavy. It is possible to build these vivaria in blocks so that a number of creatures can be accommodated relatively easily in a tidy unit. Melamine vivaria can be constructed to form either a rectangular or a vertical shape.

Gaps in the framework should be sealed with silicone aquarium sealant. Not only will this keep dirt from accumulating in the cracks, but more importantly it will stop parasites such as snake mites becoming established. It also ensures that only the melamine is exposed to water, and not the baseboard, which the melamine will peel away from if the base becomes wet.

The viewing area at the front is usually made of glass. This is easier to keep clean and will not bend at all, unlike plexiglass, which sometimes warps, particularly in a large vivarium. The glass may slide on runners to give easy access to the interior, but in such cases it is very important to have a special vivarium lock on the front. This will prevent the occupants from escaping, which can easily happen if the sliding panel is not completely closed. Lizards and snakes especially can squeeze out through just a small gap and can be very hard to locate in a room. If an amphibian slips out of its quarters, there is a real risk that it could dehydrate rapidly without access to water. In species such as geckos, which can be very quick and can run up vertical surfaces, it is safer to attend to their needs through a small access door in the side of the vivarium, hinged to open outward, rather than using the front panel of the unit for this purpose.

A HOMEMADE VIVARIUM

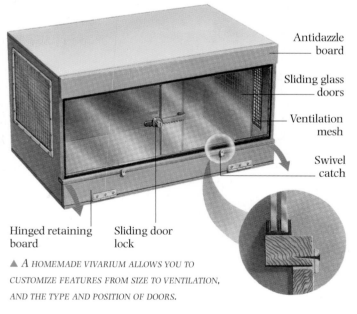

Antidazzle board

Sliding glass doors

Ventilation mesh

Swivel catch

Hinged retaining board   Sliding door lock

▲ A HOMEMADE VIVARIUM ALLOWS YOU TO CUSTOMIZE FEATURES FROM SIZE TO VENTILATION, AND THE TYPE AND POSITION OF DOORS.

▶ *MOLDED POLYETHYLENE TERRARIUM UNITS CAN BE STACKED,*
PRESENTING A TIDY SOLUTION FOR KEEPING A RANGE OF
TERRESTRIAL AND ARBOREAL LIZARDS.

A useful addition to the vivarium is a sliding tray on the floor below the glass front. It can be removed to clean the vivarium floor. But once again, beware of escapees. Spot cleaning is best carried out through the side door. When you need to clean the entire vivarium, it may be better to catch up the occupants first, so you can carry out this task without any fear that they might escape.

Molded Vivaria and Kits

It is not especially difficult to construct a vivarium from scratch, but as an alternative, vivaria are available in kit form—the components simply need to be screwed together. For smaller species, lightweight molded vivaria are also available, made of materials such as polyethylene. Since they are constructed in a single unit, there is little opportunity for dirt to accumulate here.

These units are completely waterproof and should also be resistant to damage by ultraviolet light. Some designs incorporate recessed areas in which you can place heaters and light sources, the advantage here being that these items are then unobtrusive and can be easily screened from the vivarium occupants. It also means that there is little risk of arboreal species in particular coming into direct contact with them and getting burned.

Mesh Enclosures

Fine black-mesh cages, often with a zipper for access, are frequently used as an alternative to acrylic containers for arboreal invertebrates, particularly walking sticks. Such cages are usually cylindrical and can be suspended from a suitable vantage point. By providing significantly greater height than a tank, they are ideal for these large invertebrates, giving them a site from which to hang while molting. The mesh also gives them a suitable surface on which to clamber around their enclosure.

Mesh is also used with great success to create large enclosures for housing chameleons. Although these lizards are not very active by nature, the majority of species are highly territorial when adult, and it is not usually possible to house a pair together in a conventional vivarium, because the weaker individual is likely to be bullied. More spacious surroundings with adequate screening have helped overcome this problem to a large extent. They are also partially responsible for the fact that a number of chameleon species are being bred on a much wider scale than in

◀ *CHAMELEONS SUCH AS JACKSON'S CHAMELEON*
(CHAMAELEO JACKSONII) ARE BEST KEPT IN FINE
BLACK-MESH CAGES.

the past. For chameleons heating is of less significance than lighting, but both can be suspended outside the quarters. Mesh enclosures also provide much-needed air circulation. Enclosures of this type can be made easily by attaching the mesh to wooden frames.

Tortoise Tables

Young tortoises used to be reared almost exclusively in vivaria, but today there is an increasing tendency to accommodate them in specially designed tortoise tables. It has been suggested that they are less vulnerable to respiratory infections in these surroundings, and this accommodation also allows for much closer interaction between these friendly pets and their owners. Studies have shown that they can clearly recognize individual people, and it is easy to tame a young hatchling to feed readily from your hand. It will also allow you to stroke the top of its head without withdrawing into its shell.

There are a number of different designs of tortoise table but, as their name suggests, they are basically in the form of a table with raised sides, supported on legs at a height that gives the owner a good opportunity to interact with the tortoise. It is important that the sides are sufficiently high so there is no risk of the tortoise gaining a foothold over the top edge and clambering over the side. If it did, it could tumble to the floor and injure its shell. Some tortoises can prove very determined to do this, however. Equally, the decor must not be positioned so as to allow the tortoise to reach the edge of the table and climb out. This is more likely to happen as the tortoise grows bigger.

Tortoise tables are sold on the Internet by specialized suppliers, often in kit form. Choose a design that is relatively large, to give your tortoise sufficient space to roam.

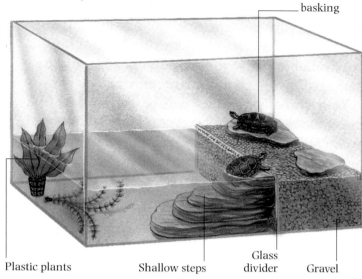

A DIVIDED AQUARIUM

Thin, flat stone for basking

Plastic plants   Shallow steps   Glass divider   Gravel

▲ *A DIVIDED VIVARIUM/ AQUARIUM ALLOWS FOR BOTH AN AQUATIC AREA AND A LAND AREA, WHICH IS IDEAL FOR TURTLES.*

Melamine-fronted chipboard can be used for tortoise tables, and is easy to keep clean. The spaces between the sheets will need to be filled in using aquarium sealant, since tortoises can produce copious volumes of urine, which may easily penetrate into the table or even drip down onto the floor. Melamine can be a slightly slippery surface for a tortoise to walk on, so a suitable substrate is advisable. If ordinary wood is used, check that other types of sealant present, such as varnish, will be safe for the tortoise, and allow sufficient time for it to dry thoroughly before the tortoise is introduced.

Heating needs to be incorporated into the design of the table, together with suitable lighting suspended above the table, the whole effect being to create a thermal gradient. Check whether heating and lighting have already been included in the design of the table if you are buying a kit, or whether you will need to add the appropriate units yourself. Since tortoises generally spend long periods basking in the sun, an ultraviolet light source is especially important for maintaining their health.

Aquatic Vivaria

A wide range of predominantly aquatic reptiles, amphibians and invertebrates are popular pets. Their housing needs to be radically different from that of their terrestrial counterparts. In many cases an aquarium will need to be set up for them, but it is likely to require a dry area as well, allowing

▼ *A TORTOISE TABLE MADE FROM ACRYLIC SHEETING ALLOWS FULL VIEW OF THE OCCUPANTS.*

the creatures to emerge onto land. The water level will generally need to be significantly lower overall than that of a fish tank.

The likely size of the species when adult must be considered, so that the accommodation can be planned accordingly from the outset. In the case of reptiles, for example, some mud turtles may grow no larger than 4 inches (10 cm), even when adult, while other species can attain an adult shell length of over 12 inches (30 cm). A 48-inch (120-cm) aquarium will be suitable for the mud turtles.

Glass aquaria can be used, but do not opt for a bare-framed design, which is more likely to be damaged when moved, unless its edges are protected with plastic. Large acrylic tanks are better because turtles are significantly messier than fish, particularly as they grow larger. The tank therefore needs to be stripped down regularly, which is likely to mean moving it. With glass-framed aquaria there is also a slight risk that a large turtle's sharp claws could damage the silicone sealant holding the panes of glass together, causing a leak.

Usually there is a need to partition the tank to create an area of dry land for the occupants. This can be achieved by using a piece of plastic, cut to the appropriate height, stuck in place with aquarium sealant. Check that it is watertight before filling the chamber behind—it is important that the dry area does not become wet. Alternatively, floating platforms—attached to the sides by suckers—allow turtles to climb in and out of the water easily. These can be purchased from specialized reptile stores, but are more suited to young animals that weigh less than adults. The dry area should be located beneath a basking light, replicating conditions in the wild, where turtles emerge onto land to warm themselves up in the sun before diving back into the water.

The area of dry land can be built up by tipping gravel into the space behind the partition, but this makes the tank very heavy to handle. A better option is to cut a block of polystyrene to fill the space. Cover it with tiles that can retain the heat from the light above. The effect will be to mimic the way in which these reptiles often bask on rocks warmed by the sun. For a breeding pair, cut out an area of the polystyrene block to accommodate a container for egg-laying purposes.

Many amphibians will need a suitable retreat in the land area. Moss makes a good floor covering into which the amphibians will burrow, but it needs to be sprayed regularly to keep it from drying out. Heating should be provided by a heating pad, which can warm the water without the risk of burning the occupants. Amphibians do not bask, so a heat lamp is not needed. Some amphibians, such as fire-bellied toads (*Bombina* species), are unlikely to require auxiliary heating if kept in the home.

Crabs are likely to require a setup similar to that of amphibians, but with an even lower water level. In the case of land hermit crabs, the area should be predominantly dry. A small platform or a secure stack of rockwork in the water will provide an easy way for the occupants to move in and out.

Aquatic vivaria are normally covered with a hood that incorporates a viewing light. Covering the tank in this way prevents water from evaporating too quickly, which can easily happen, particularly in centrally heated rooms where the relative humidity may be low. A hood also ensures that the humidity in the vivarium itself remains high, and keeps amphibians such as newts from escaping—if they were to get out, they would probably die all too quickly from desiccation.

A HOMEMADE RAIN CHAMBER

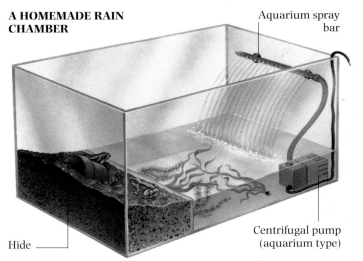

Aquarium spray bar

Centrifugal pump (aquarium type)

Hide

WATERFALL CONSTRUCTION

Gravel

Rock (real or plastic)

Pump

Flowback to pump

Glass divider

Water level

▲ ◀ *Two types of water features can be added to aquaria.*
Above: A rain chamber simulates a tropical rainy season and may stimulate frogs to spawn.
Left: A waterfall can be made from cork bark, driftwood or a pile of stones.

◀ *SPECIES SUCH AS THE DIAMONDBACK TERRAPIN (MALACLEMYS TERRAPIN) REQUIRE SLIGHTLY SALTY (BRACKISH) WATER IN THEIR AQUARIA.*

WATER REQUIREMENTS

Household water is generally not recommended for aquatic herptiles and invertebrates, since the chlorine or, increasingly, the chloramine that is added to domestic supplies is harmful to these animals. Before adding water to the tank, it must therefore be treated with a suitable product to neutralize these chemicals.

For a number of animals originating from brackish rather than freshwater habitats, particularly crabs and the Diamondback Turtle (*Malaclemys terrapin*), salty water is needed. If kept in freshwater, these animals are susceptible to fungal infections. Salty water can be created easily using sea salt (as sold for saltwater aquaria) and making up a solution of appropriate strength as recommended for species from brackish water. When topping up for water that has evaporated, always use dechlorinated freshwater, otherwise the water will become increasingly concentrated and may be harmful to the tank occupants.

The pH (relative acidity) of the water and its hardness can be significant. Acidity (pH) is measured on a log scale, and so even small changes reflect marked alterations in water chemistry—a pH reading of 7.0 being neutral. Rainwater is typically neutral, since it has not acquired any dissolved substances, for example, calcium carbonate, which makes the water alkaline (higher pH), or organic matter, such as peat, which makes the water more acidic (lower pH).

In hard-water areas it may be beneficial to some species to run their water through an ion-exchange column—removing the dissolved salts and making the water closer in composition to fresh rainwater. This is especially helpful for rain forest species that breed in water, such as poison dart frogs (*Dendrobates* species). Deionized water has the added benefit that fine sprayers will not become blocked by deposits of calcium carbonate.

HEATING

A heating system is vital to the well-being of most herptiles and invertebrates. It is important to be aware of the natural environment of each species, which will dictate their temperature requirements. Many reptiles originate in the tropics, where the temperature is relatively constant all year around, but those from temperate areas experience significant changes during the year. Reptiles respond to such changes by undergoing a period of dormancy, often known as hibernation, which affects their breeding cycle. As a result, the temperature in their quarters needs to be adjusted to reflect the seasonal changes in their natural surroundings.

◀ ▶ *LEFT: HEATING PAD ATTACHED TO THE SIDE OF A PLASTIC REPTILE BOX.*
RIGHT: A RANGE OF DIFFERENT HEATING PADS.

Even reptiles found in very hot environments such as deserts do not require uniformly hot surroundings. Although the temperature rises very significantly in the desert during the day, it also drops back dramatically at night, often almost to freezing point. Species such as dab lizards (*Uromastyx* species) originating from this type of habitat should therefore be exposed to a diurnal shift of this type in vivarium surroundings.

Many amphibian species originate from temperate areas and, on the whole, they need to be kept at lower temperatures than reptiles. They too will experience seasonal changes in temperature, which are known to encourage breeding behavior.

Thermoregulation

When heating a vivarium, it is important not to have the enclosure at a constant temperature throughout. Instead, you should attempt to achieve what is known as a thermal gradient running across it. This allows the occupants to bask under the main heat source at one end and then, as they warm up, they can move away from this area into a cooler part of the vivarium. That is how reptiles thermoregulate naturally, keeping their body temperature within defined limits. In the wild during the morning, when the air is relatively cold, they seek out the direct warmth of the sun; as their body temperature rises, enabling them to become more active, they move to a cooler spot.

It is not just the direct heat from the sun that provides reptiles with warmth. They will also seek out sources of radiant heat. In areas where reptiles are common, one of the best places to spot them is on a road shortly after sunrise. The warmth of the road's surface, which retains the heat from the sun, very effectively provides them with a warm basking area. By lying on the road and absorbing some of its radiant heat, the reptiles are able to raise their body temperature.

▲▼ *HEATING OPTIONS. ABOVE: A RANGE OF INFRARED BULBS. RIGHT: AN ARTIFICIAL ROCK WARMED BY HEATING ELEMENTS WITHIN.*

Methods of Heating

There are several ways of providing heat in vivaria. Ordinary incandescent light bulbs are generally unsuitable as heat sources because, as the light is turned on and off, the heat produced will be intermittent; in addition, the quality of light is not ideal. A more effective way of providing heat is to use an infrared lamp that emits heat rather than light. They are available in different wattages to suit the size of the enclosure and are surrounded with a metal heat reflector to concentrate the warmth.

To provide heated surfaces artificial rocks are available with a heating element in their core. A separate thermostat should be used to avoid overheating and possible burns to a reptile's skin. Always position a heated rock away from the main heat source. An ordinary rock, such as a piece of slate, on the vivarium floor beneath the heat source will also absorb heat and provide a basking spot.

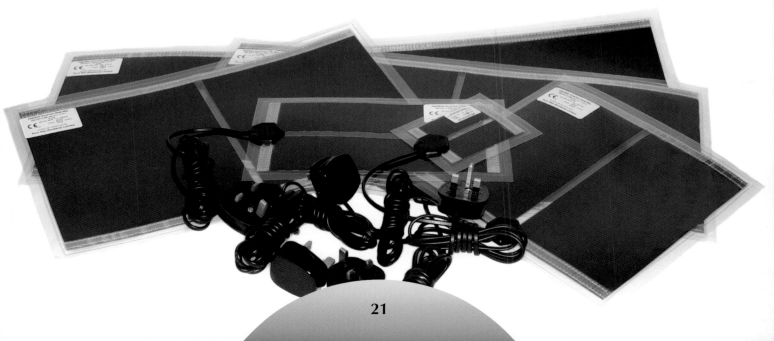

In many vivaria two separate heating sources are usually included (infrared and a heating pad). The infrared heater is placed in the roof and should be shielded in a mesh cage to prevent arboreal species from coming into contact with it and suffering fatal burns. This effectively serves as a daytime heater, mimicking the sun.

A slimline heating pad acts as a secondary heat source. Available in a variety of sizes, these sealed units are little thicker than a sheet of cardboard and can be placed beneath the floor of a vivarium or onto one of the sides—although they look rather unattractive in this position.

These heaters can be used effectively for aquatic vivaria, radiating heat through the glass or acrylic sides of the tank, but they must not be placed in the water itself. A major advantage is that the heater is not likely to be damaged, unlike a typical glass heaterstat in an aquarium, which could be knocked by a large turtle. Nor is there any risk of the tank occupants being burned.

Although installing a special heater guard to a heaterstat should give protection, it may not be sufficient with amphibians, whose front limbs may still come into direct contact with the heater. Also, since aquatic vivaria are only partially full of water, a heaterstat has to be positioned almost horizontally and will occupy a large part of the floor area, encouraging occupants to rest on it, with the risk of burning themselves. Large turtles may dislodge it, even forcing it up and out of the water while it is switched on, which is potentially dangerous if there is no cutout device that switches the heater off out of water.

LIGHTING

Lighting can provide a source of heat, but it is usual to keep heating and lighting separate, but associated, in a vivarium, partly to ensure that the temperature in what is a relatively confined space does not rise too high, endangering the occupants. It is also critically important for their well-being to provide the correct spectrum of light.

The spectrum describes the actual wavelengths of light. Most vivaria now incorporate fluorescent bulbs. The most obvious feature is that they give off a whiter light compared with ordinary incandescent bulbs which produce a yellowish appearance. So-called daylight

◄ *A FULL-SPECTRUM LAMP THAT PRODUCES UVA AND UVB LIGHT,*
IMPORTANT FOR ACTIVE REPTILES AND AMPHIBIANS.

bulbs are highly recommended, since they mimic the various wavelengths of sunlight, incorporating rays from the ultraviolet part of the light spectrum, which are key to the health of the occupants.

Ultraviolet Lighting

Ultraviolet light has two elements, known as UVA and UVB. Both are vital to the health of reptiles and some amphibians. UVA encourages activity, particularly hunting and feeding, and is also important for breeding purposes in the longer term. UVB has a different role, triggering the process that leads to the synthesis of vitamin D3 in the body. This fat-soluble vitamin, which is stored in the liver, plays an important part in regulating the body's calcium stores, in association with phosphorus (see page 34).

The requirement for ultraviolet light varies among different groups. It is highest in lizards, turtles and tortoises but seems to be less significant in the case of snakes. Young, rapidly growing reptiles are most at risk of showing signs of a deficiency, simply because they require more calcium to support the growth of their skeleton. The absorption of calcium into the body from the intestinal tract is controlled by vitamin D3. While this vitamin can be supplied through the diet, most species generally appear to do better if supplied with an ultraviolet light above their quarters.

In order to be effective, lighting must not be screened behind a barrier of glass, which will block off the passage of the ultraviolet rays. Equally, for maximum benefit the reptiles need to be able to get close to the light source (to within about 10 inches/25 cm for fluorescent tubes and up to 36 inches/90 cm for mercury vapor lights). Finally, the level of beneficial ultraviolet illumination declines even before such time as the light ceases to work. Depending on the manufacturer's recommendations,

therefore, the light source should be changed about every nine months to a year.

Other Lights

It is quite normal to have two fluorescent strip lights above the vivarium, only one of which is a source of ultraviolet light. The other can be a brighter light, which will allow better observation of the vivarium occupants. Brighter lights are more important for desert-dwelling species that are naturally exposed to intense sunlight than for forest-dwelling species that live in a dimmer envronment in the wild. Special night lights are available that allow the vivarium occupants to be seen after dark, as if under moonlight. Control of the lighting can also be set so that it switches on and off automatically, using a 24-hour timer for this purpose.

HUMIDITY

High humidity is a feature of a number of natural environments, particularly rain forests. However, even in more arid environments, such as inside the burrow of a tarantula, there can be localized high humidity. Within a vivarium this can be replicated and dehydration avoided simply by spraying the entrance to the burrow. For rain forest species significantly higher humidity will be necessary throughout the vivarium. Special humidifiers, which puff very fine droplets of water into the atmosphereare, are available for this purpose.

It is important in hard-water areas to check that the nozzles do not become blocked by deposits of limescale, reducing the unit's efficiency over a period of time. Relative humidity within the enclosure can be monitored with a hygrometer, which can be acquired from garden centers as well as pet stores specializing in herptiles. Good ventilation is especially important in a rain forest vivarium because, with such high humidity, molds can develop rapidly, causing live plants to die and harming the overall health of the occupants.

► *RIGHT: A TWIN THERMOSTAT CONTROL*
UNIT THAT ALLOWS TWO HEATERS TO BE
CONTROLLED SEPARATELY TO CREATE A
HEAT GRADIENT.
FAR RIGHT: A UNIT THAT CONTROLS DAY
AND NIGHT LIGHTING.

◄ *A VIVARIUM UNDER CONSTRUCTION,*
SHOWING INFRARED AND FLUORESCENT
BULB UNITS IN THE HOOD.

THE FLOOR COVERING—SUBSTRATE

Often referred to as the substrate, the floor covering in the vivarium is very important for both the health and well-being of the vivarium occupants. There is no universal floor covering that is suitable—the choice will be influenced by the heating system being used and the species being kept. If a heating pad is used beneath the floor of the vivarium, it is important to choose a floor covering that will not act as an insulator and prevent the heat from being able to reach the occupants above.

Careful Selection

In some cases bedding can be dangerous for certain types of herptile, which may accidentally ingest substrate material when they grab their prey or if it sticks to their vegetable food. This can accumulate and create an obstruction in their digestive tract. Wooden shavings are particularly dangerous for this reason, as is gravel in some cases.

Some bedding manufacturers have taken advantage of the way in which certain species ingest their bedding. There are now various fine calcium carbonate sand substrates available. They are intended to break down in the reptile's body, thereby supplementing the animal's intake of this vital mineral, which is often lacking, especially in live-food diets.

In some substrates, such as coarse wood chips, invertebrate live foods can hide away out of reach of the animal. On the other hand, some herptiles and invertebrates need a substrate in which to burrow. They are especially vulnerable to respiratory problems if the substrate is dusty, which is partly why sawdust should never be used as a floor covering in a vivarium. Furthermore, the original wood used for sawdust or shavings may have been treated with preservatives or other substances that could be harmful, especially if ingested. It is much safer to stick to bedding options that are designed and sold specifically for use with herptiles.

Cleanliness

Ease of cleaning is also an important factor in the choice of bedding, and spoiling is more apparent in some types of herptiles than in others. Some substrates—sand, for example—are relatively absorbent and are also easy to spot clean. It is a good idea to choose a relatively sterile bedding, which is why soil is very rarely recommended—although soil that has been specially treated is sometimes

◄▲ *A RANGE OF SUBSTRATES: 1 SHREDDED ASPEN WOOD; 2 WOOD CHIPS; 3 HEATED CORN COB KERNELS; 4 WOOD FLAKES; 5 ARTIFICIAL HIGHLY ABSORBENT MEDIUM; 6 VERMICULITE; 7 SPHAGNUM MOSS.*

used in rain forest environments for growing plants. Alternatively, plants can be set in pots, which in turn can be easily disguised with moss.

Newspaper

The frequency of cleaning is also a significant factor to consider as far as the choice of substrate is concerned. Newspaper is still sometimes used for tortoises in vivarium surroundings, simply because it is an absorbent, cheap material that can be easily changed. It does, however, look very unattractive compared with other, more naturalistic floor coverings.

Newspaper is also useful in dealing with a reptile that you suspect is sick—it makes it much easier to keep a watch on the animal's urinary and fecal output. For example, after deworming, any parasites that have been passed can be seen clearly.

However, should any of the newsprint be ingested by the reptile, there is a risk of toxicity caused by the ink in the newspaper. Ordinary paper towel may be a better option. Paper pellets are used for reptiles such as snakes and in environments such as desert-type vivaria, in which the relative humidity needs to be kept low.

Artificial Turf

A naturalistic green appearance can be obtained with a covering of artificial turf. Artificial turf liners are available to suit a particular cage size, or they can be cut to fit. They are relatively hygienic, since they are easily scrubbed off and even disinfected as required. Two pieces are ideal— one in use, the other being cleaned. They do, however, have a relatively harsh texture, which means they are less suitable for amphibians with their sensitive skins. Artificial vivarium turf is also useful for covering the basking area of turtles, for example, because it is unaffected by short-term exposure to water and normally dries off readily.

Moss and Gravel

Sphagnum moss is a favored medium for many amphibians, thanks to its moisture-retaining properties— although other types of moss can be used. Moss is a suitable medium for certain burrowing reptiles as well.

For an aquaterrarium, gravel is preferable to sand because it is less inclined to cloud the water, but it will need to be washed thoroughly first to remove all traces of sediment. Ordinary aquarium gravel is ideal, but avoid colored gravel, even if you are certain that it is colorfast, since it distracts from the natural colors of herptiles. Another major advantage of using gravel rather than sand is that it is possible to install an undergravel filter, with the gravel itself acting as a filter bed.

DECOR

Aside from the substrate, a vivarium should incorporate suitable retreats in which the occupants can hide. This will help them settle in unfamiliar surroundings with minimal stress, reducing the likelihood that they will succumb to illness at this stage. The choice of decor will be influenced

▲ *A NATURAL ENVIRONMENT FOR SPECIES SUCH AS THIS FIRE-BELLIED NEWT (CYNOPS ORIENTALIS) IS ACHIEVED WITH WATERWEEDS AND ROCKS.*

by practical considerations, including the type of backdrop, and also by the nature of the species concerned. In the case of tortoises, for example, there is little point in adding items that will be displaced by the reptile's bulk as it moves around its quarters. In contrast, raised decorations are essential for arboreal snakes and lizards.

Planting

Living plants can be incorporated in vivarium surroundings, but they may not always thrive in this environment. Avoid including potentially dangerous plants, such as cacti with sharp thorns or plants that may have irritating leaves or sap. There is also little point in putting live plants in a vivarium housing herbivorous species, which will simply treat them as food. Realistic artificial plants are available for these setups. They do not require maintenance in terms of watering or care and will not outgrow

◄ *DECOR ACCESSORIES: 1 CORK TUBES; 2 SEASONED BRANCH; 3 LOG HIDES; 4 GRAPEVINE; 5 CORK BARK; 6 SEASONED LOGS.*

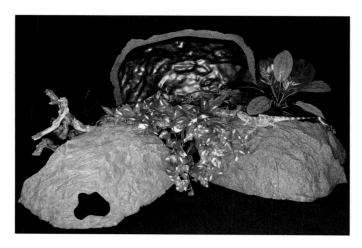

▲ *ARTIFICIAL HIDES AND PLANTS FOR VIVARIUM USE.*

▼ *TOP: ARID COUNTRY (DESERT) VIVARIUM WITH DAB LIZARD (UROMASTYX ACANTHINURUS).*
BOTTOM: TEMPERATE WOODLAND VIVARIUM WITH CORN SNAKE (ELAPHE GUTTATA).

the vivarium. If they become soiled with the droppings of the inhabitants, they can easily be washed off. Another advantage is that artificial plants do not need to be set in pots, but can be weighed down in the substrate, even if it is relatively shallow.

Artificial vines can be strung up in the vivarium, creating a natural effect. They are particularly useful for any arboreal species, allowing them to move around their quarters with ease. For glass vivaria the natural impression can be reinforced by adding a suitable backdrop. These are available in various designs from deserts to rain forests and can be easily affixed to the sides of the enclosure.

If live plants are used, they should mirror as close as possible those found in the natural habitat of the species being housed in the vivarium. Bromeliads, with their central cup of rainwater, are common throughout the rain forest areas where poison dart frogs (*Dendrobates* species) are found, and play a vital role in their breeding cycle. In more temperate amphibian setups, the relatively high humidity required is likely to result in sphagnum moss substrate growing; additional decor, such as small ferns, will do well in these moist surroundings.

Aquatic amphibians will also thrive in a planted environment, and spawning will often take place among the submerged vegetation. By contrast, turtles, with their broad bodies and active natures, are likely to uproot any plants growing in the water. However, a small amount of floating vegetation may be useful to supplement their diet.

Retreats and Ramps

An important requirement for most aquatic species is a rockwork ramp that will provide them the opportunity to emerge easily onto land. As in the case of terrestrial vivaria, it must be carefully positioned so it cannot be accidentally displaced and cause serious injury to the vivarium occupants.

Retreats for invertebrates are more easily arranged, because of their smaller size. A clean clay flowerpot broken in half can make an ideal burrow for a tarantula that would normally spend much of its time underground. Broken flowerpots can be equally useful in an aquaterrarium, acting as a cave in which newts can shelter.

BASIC VIVARIUM TYPES

Arid Country Vivaria

Arid country vivaria are suitable for dab lizards, desert iguanas and Mexican red-kneed tarantulas. This type of environment is characterized by a relatively high daytime temperature—up to 104°F (40°C) under a spotlight—which drops back significantly at night for desert-dwelling species. A reduced temperature range of 75–86°F

(24–30°C) will suit species that occur in savanna. As befits the natural habitat, the substrate should be arid. Vivarium sand is ideal for this purpose, because it retains heat well. Rockwork in a corresponding color helps blend in harmoniously and provides basking opportunites.

The floor space of arid country vivaria is important, since inhabitants are likely to be active by nature, although most will not climb to any significant extent. A shallow bowl of water should be incorporated, as well as suitable retreats in which they can hide.

Tropical Rain Forest Vivaria

Tropical vivaria are suitable for green tree pythons, emerald tree boas, poison dart frogs, Asiatic horned toads and emperor scorpions. A rain forest vivarium is characterized by a relatively constant temperature up to 90°F (32°C), dropping back slightly at night to 75°F (24°C), combined with a humid environment. To keep humidity high, either a humidifier is necessary or the interior should be sprayed daily with dechlorinated water.

Tropical rain forest vivaria need to be relatively tall to house typical occupants such as spiders, frogs, snakes and lizards that are arboreal by nature. Careful designs incorporating suitable branches for climbing are important. A small waterfall with a bowl of water will help maintain humid conditions—units of this type are now available for use in vivarium surroundings. The floor covering can be moss and bark, together with logs. Coconut bark is sometimes preferred for a rain forest vivarium because it holds moisture effectively, although pine bark is another possibility. Lighting is important both for plant growth and the health of the occupants.

Temperate Woodland Vivaria

Temperate woodland vivaria are suitable for corn snakes, garter snakes, American box turtles and oak toads. It is important that the vivarium temperature should vary in a way that reflects changes in the wild. This temperature variation plays an important part in the life cycle of reptiles and amphibians. The temperature can be allowed to rise up to about 75°F (24°C), but there must be a cooler period during the winter, with temperatures dropping back to about 50°F (10°C), otherwise the occupants are unlikely to breed successfully. Occupants must feed well in the warmer periods because their appetite and resistance to disease declines with the temperature, and opportunistic infections can strike at this time.

▶ *A BALANCED VIVARIUM SETUP SUCH AS THIS IS SUITABLE FOR MANY FROGS, IN PARTICULAR FOR POISON DART FROGS.*

Housing will depend on the species concerned, with a moss enclosure and a suitable area of water being required by amphibians, while bark and wood chips are more appropriate for snakes. Easy access in and out of the water is important. For reptiles the woodland environment can be recreated using rockwork and clean, dry leaves, which also provide excellent hiding places.

Aquaterraria

Aquaterraria are suitable for mud turtles, map turtles, slider turtles and fire-bellied toads. This type of environment may or may not require heating, depending on the species concerned and the ambient temperature. Care needs to be taken where heating is used to ensure that the occupants will not be at any risk of burning themselves. They must also be able to move in and out of the water.

Plants such as *Elodea* and *Ceratophyllum* are ideal for growing in the water to allow the amphibians to rest at the surface. They can either be set in the substrate or allowed to float at the surface. A clear swimming area is preferred for turtles, however, but some species will spend longer on land than others, and this needs to be reflected in the design of their enclosure.

Filtration is needed to maintain suitable water conditions. An undergravel filter is adequate for amphibians, but a power filter will be needed for turtles. A bare floor to the aquatic area rather than a gravel covering will also make this section easier to keep clean. A light for basking purposes is essential for reptiles, and a fluorescent bulb for viewing purposes should be incorporated into the hood.

SETTING UP A BALANCED VIVARIUM

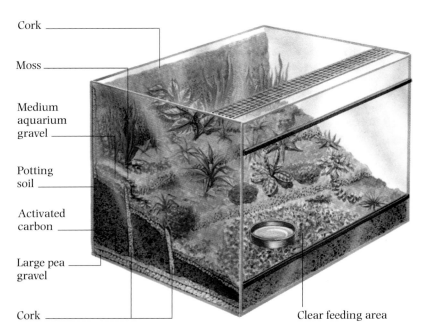

Cork

Moss

Medium aquarium gravel

Potting soil

Activated carbon

Large pea gravel

Cork

Clear feeding area

sheltered spot, out of the direction of the prevailing wind. Secure ventilation is important to keep the interior from getting too hot on sunny days. Hides and water should be provided; in the case of amphibians a small pond may be needed.

A movable run rather than a permanent enclosure could be provided for tortoises. It can be used as outdoor accommodation for the reptiles when the weather is good, and for keeping them confined indoors on inclement days. They will be able to benefit from the sun's rays and browse on fresh food, but they will not become chilled, which could cause them to develop a respiratory infection. There will also be less risk of any parasite problems, since the tortoises will be roaming more widely, and a buildup of worm eggs is less likely. Moving the run around also allows the vegetation to recover.

Aquaria

Totally aquatic aquaria are suitable for mata-mata turtles, axolotls, fire-bellied newts, dwarf clawed frogs, *Xenopus* frogs and Surinam toads, which rarely (if ever) venture onto land. Some aquatic turtles and frogs—the latter in general having a very flattened body shape that reduces water resistance as they swim—will thrive better in a setup where there are simply floating plants at the water's surface. They are likely to uproot any growing in the substrate as they swim. A rock that provides a resting opportunity will normally be adequate.

Water should be reasonably shallow, especially in the case of turtles. Soft-shelled turtles (*Trionyx* species) use their elongated nose rather like a snorkel to breathe atmospheric air without breaking above the water's surface. These turtles will bury into the substrate and so cannot be kept in a bare-floored tank. A power filter or even an external filter will be needed. Certain other species, notably aquatic snakes, may benefit from the addition of blackwater extract to the aquarium water (as sold for fish). This lowers the pH of the water and mimics conditions in the wild, caused by leaves accumulating in the water and releasing tannins that give the water a dark color.

Outdoor Accommodation

One of the most important considerations when planning outdoor accommodation is to stop the animals from escaping. If they were to get out they might survive in the wild and represent a hazard to the native wildlife. A brick- or block-built enclosure is therefore vital, with a suitable guard over the roof area. In the case of animals such as tortoises that may dig down, be sure the walls have adequate foundations. The siting of the enclosure will be influenced by the area of the yard. It should ideally be exposed to the early- morning, rather than midday, sun and be in a

Greenhouse or Solarium Housing

Although greenhouses may appear to be an ideal place in which to house herptiles and invertebrates, there are a number of practical difficulties that may preclude it. The major problem is that the temperature—even in a well ventilated greenhouse—can rise to very high levels, making it potentially dangerous for many species.

Another consideration is that in the winter when it is colder, additional heating will be necessary, and unless the structure is extremely well insulated, this can become almost prohibitively expensive. Furthermore, especially if you have included a pond of any kind, the evaporation

▶ *IN AN OUTDOOR SITUATION TORTOISE ENCLOSURES SHOULD BE MOVED AROUND TO AVOID OVERCROPPING OF A LAWN.*

◀ *BUDGETT'S FROG (LEPIDOBATRACHUS LAEVIS) IS AN UNUSUAL ADDITION TO A TOTALLY AQUATIC VIVARIUM.*

▼ *A POND AND SEMIAQUATIC SETUP IS AN ELEGANT FEATURE IN A SOLARIUM OR GREENHOUSE AS LONG AS IT IS TOTALLY ESCAPE-PROOF.*

of water will result in very high humidity, which can lead to the development of mold on the structure of the greenhouse itself.

Solariums and greenhouses can be beneficial in providing temporary accommodation for young tortoises living on a tortoise table by allowing the animals to bask in the sun's rays through an open window (glass will block beneficial parts of the sun's rays); it is important to provide them with shelter as well, so they can cool off as required.

In a large greenhouse a pond can be used to accommodate turtles. Ensure there is a surrounding dry area over which a basking light is fixed for the larger species that spend more time on land than in the water. Ideally, the pond should be set up so that there is plumbing to allow it to be drained without difficulty. In the relatively brightly lit surroundings of a greenhouse algal growth can become a problem. There is a chance that turtles will breed in this environment if a suitable area for egg-laying is incorporated.

Equally, a greenhouse can be used for adult tortoises that cannot be allowed out to roam safely in the backyard because of poor weather. Large individuals of tropical species such as Red-foots (*Geochelone carbonaria*), which cannot be hibernated through the winter in temperate areas, can be housed in a greenhouse, but ensure there is sufficient heating in winter.

A greenhouse can provide an ideal means of housing a range of arboreal species, ranging from chameleons to tree frogs. It is critical that the structure is completely escape-proof—even the smallest gaps must be sealed. Feeding stations should be clearly visible among the decor so that you can make regular checks to ensure that all occupants are eating well.

FOOD AND FEEDING

The basic constituents of the reptile and invertebrate diet are identical: proteins, carbohydrates and fats, augmented by vitamins, minerals and trace elements. The actual food that these creatures consume is, of course, very varied. In the past, when relatively little was known about the nutritional needs of these groups, they were often given unsuitable foods, which could lead to ill health and even premature death. Today, however, there is an ever increasing range of prepared foods available, especially for popular species, which has eliminated these problems and made it easier to care for the animals.

Nevertheless, there are still many herptiles and invertebrates that require live foods as part of their daily diet. If a potential owner dislikes the idea of using feeder insects for this purpose, this will have a direct influence on the species that they may want to keep. Snakes can also be problematic for some would-be owners, since they are carnivorous by nature and tend to be offered diets based on dead rodents and poultry, although a few species can be maintained on fish and invertebrates.

GREEN FOOD

A wide range of cultivated plants and weeds can be used for feeding herbivorous species, although a few are much more fussy, notably walking sticks, which prefer to feed on bramble (*Rubus* species). Relatively few herptiles or invertebrates eat grass, although an exception is the terrestrial giant spiny stick insect *(Eurycantha calarata)*. To supplement other foods, dandelions *(Taraxacum officinale)* are invaluable, with both the leaves and flowers being suitable. Some plants need to be avoided, particularly those growing from bulbs. Although vegetarian species tend to display some ability to distinguish between nontoxic and toxic food sources, they can still be harmed if they are fed unsuitable foods.

Grow Your Own
It is important to ensure that as far as possible the food has not been exposed to pesticides of any type. Ideally, the best solution is to grow your own. Even if there is no access to a backyard, a bright windowsill can be perfectly adequate. The simplest means of growing dandelions is to dig up the long roots and cut them into pieces of about 1 inch (2.5 cm) long. Plant them in free-draining compost in a relatively deep pot. Leave a portion of the root protruding just above the soil surface, and this will ultimately develop the leaves. Keep moist, in a relatively sunny spot, and the leaves will be ready in a few weeks. By setting up a number of pots, a good supply of leaves can be guaranteed, but beware of accidentally spraying the leaves with window cleaning solutions or other household chemicals.

The other major advantage of growing green food for your animals is that it will be fresh, and its vitamin content will be at its highest. Store-bought green food, which has been in transit for some time, will be less satisfactory.

For walking sticks, entire bramble plants can be planted in the enclosure, enabling the animals to clamber up and feed. Once they have stripped the leaves, the pot can be replaced. Another option is to cut branches of bramble and place them in a narrow-necked container of water. Pack the top of the container with tin foil, so there will be no risk of the walking sticks falling down the neck and drowning. It is particularly important to plan ahead for the winter, because bramble leaves can be hard to find at this stage, and the stick insects will starve. The leaves may also be brown around the edges; these unwanted edges should be trimmed off.

A number of salad plants can also be grown indoors from seed. Red lettuce is better than green, which contains

*◄ TORTOISES ARE VEGETARIAN, AND THEIR FOOD SHOULD OCCASIONALLY BE
LACED WITH MINERAL AND VITAMIN SUPPLEMENTS.*

Foods that have been chilled in a refrigerator must be warmed to room temperature. Avoid using prepared supermarket salads, since they may have been washed with chlorine-based chemicals. Always wash any fresh greenstuff or fruit thoroughly, preferably using dechlorinated water. Shake the food dry afterward to remove surplus moisture or blot it with a clean paper towel. The advantage of leaving it slightly damp is that powdered vitamin and mineral supplements sprinkled on the leaves will stick readily to the surface. Such supplements are important to ensure that the herptile's intake of calcium and similar micronutrients is sufficient.

Supplements that can be added to drinking water are available, but their ingredients are not as comprehensive as those of powdered supplements. Also, reptiles must drink regularly to benefit from a product of this type. It is not a good idea to use both types of supplement together, because of the risk of overdosing.

FEEDER INSECTS

Many reptiles and invertebrates will feed to a greater or lesser extent on feeder insects in vivarium surroundings; they also tend to be a mainstay of amphibian diets. Catching suitable invertebrates in backyards has risks. They may have been exposed to pesticides, which are likely to be harmful to the occupants of a vivarium. A number of invertebrates carry parasites, which they can pass on to animals that feed on them, endangering their health. Other issues associated with wild-caught invertebrates

very little in the way of nutrients. With sequential sowings a constant supply of fresh greenstuff is guaranteed.

Bought Food

Organic fresh fruit and vegetables are best, and vegetables such as carrots should be peeled to remove the chemicals concentrated on the skin. Avoid using wilted greenstuff or shriveled vegetables, since they are likely to be low in nutrients and might cause digestive upsets, which can sometimes prove difficult to treat, especially in tortoises.

It does no harm to follow seasonal trends, but changes to the diets of vegetarian reptiles should be introduced gradually, so that the beneficial population of bacteria and protozoa that help break down the food in their gut can be adjusted accordingly. Sudden significant changes, particularly switching from a diet comprising mainly greenstuff to one of fruit, are likely to trigger serious digestive upsets. Offer new foods gradually, increasing the quantity over a number of days, rather than suddenly switching an animal to a different diet.

▶ *BEARDED DRAGON (POGONA VITTICEPS) EATING A LOCUST. THESE INSECTS ARE AVAILABLE FROM COMMERCIAL SOURCES.*

are the problem of being able to obtain them all year round and the time-consuming task of hunting for them.

Mealworms and Waxworms

A large commercial breeding sector has developed producing feeder insects that can be purchased either in-store or by mail order. Mealworms, the larval form of the Meal Beetle *(Tenebrio molitor),* are popular, especially the mini mealworms, which typically measure 0.5–0.75 inches (13–18 mm). Regular mealworms are usually about 1 inch (2.5 cm) long, while so-called giant mealworms can grow to almost double that size, but are only suitable for larger species such as the Bearded Dragon *(Pogona vitticeps).* Supergiant Mealworms *(Zophobas morio)* are even larger.

All mealworms have a hard body casing composed of chitin, which is relatively indigestible for herptiles. They only have soft bodies for a short period when they have shed their skin, at which time they are white. Mealworms form a white pupa before hatching out as dark-colored meal beetles.

Waxworms *(Galleria mellonella)* are the larval stage in the life cycle of the Wax Moth and are much more

▲ SUPERGIANT, OR KING, MEALWORMS (ZOPHOBAS MORIO) ARE SUITABLE FOR LARGER REPTILES SUCH AS THE BEARDED DRAGON (POGONA VITTICEPS).

▼ COMMERCIAL BREEDING OF LOCUSTS IN INDONESIA.

digestible. Waxworms are especially valued as a tonic food, helping improve the body condition of species that may have recently come out of hibernation or are recovering from illness. Waxworms are far less palatable once they have pupated, at which stage they form a darker casing around themselves before emerging as moths.

Crickets and Locusts

Crickets are among the most versatile of all feeder insects for herptiles. Several species are cultured commercially for this purpose. Black Crickets *(Gryllus bimaculatus)*, also known as Field Crickets, are usually recommended for more humid vivarium environments. The Brown, or House, Cricket *(Acheta domestica)*, originating from the United Kingdom, is another relatively hardy species; the Banded, or Tropical, House Cricket *(Gryllodes sigillatus)* is less hardy.

All these species are sold at various stages in their life cycle from hatchlings through to adults, the size required being determined by that of the creatures being fed. Young crickets are approximately 0.1 inch (2 mm) long, making them ideal for frogs that have recently metamorphosed. They can grow to a maximum size of about 1.25 inches (3 cm) in the case of Black Crickets, with adult Tropical Crickets unlikely to exceed 0.75 inches (2 cm). As with all foods for herptiles, choose a smaller size when purchasing crickets to avoid any risk of choking.

In some areas where their sale is permitted, various species of locusts are also available as feeder insects, although they are more costly. Locusts grow to a significantly larger size than crickets, attaining a length of about 2.75 inches (7 cm). Being relatively slow movers, they are easier for many lizards to catch. Unlike crickets, uneaten locusts are not likely to attack the vivarium occupants. Locusts may, however, cause damage in a planted vivarium, since they are vegetarian. The higher temperatures required by locusts also mean that should they escape they are not likely to live for long in the home, whereas crickets may survive.

Cockroaches

A number of the invertebrates kept in vivarium surroundings can also be used as feeder insects. Over recent years various cockroaches, or "roaches," as they are often known, have become valued for this purpose. Although these invertebrates generally have a bad reputation, many species are not likely to infest the home if they escape.

The Lobster Roach *(Nauphoeta cinerea)*, which occurs naturally in the Caribbean region, is ideal as a feeder insect partly because, unlike many of its relatives, it does not have a particularly thick protective body casing. These roaches are likely to grow only a little larger than adult crickets and are easy to breed. Although they can climb

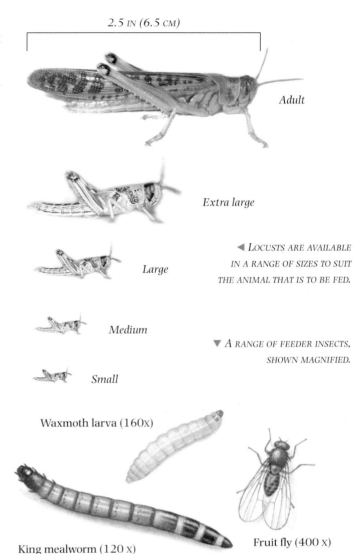

2.5 IN (6.5 CM)

Adult

Extra large

Large

◀ LOCUSTS ARE AVAILABLE IN A RANGE OF SIZES TO SUIT THE ANIMAL THAT IS TO BE FED.

Medium

▼ A RANGE OF FEEDER INSECTS, SHOWN MAGNIFIED.

Small

Waxmoth larva (160x)

King mealworm (120 x)

Fruit fly (400 x)

up the sides of a vivarium, which means they need to be kept in a covered enclosure, their wings are not functional, and so they cannot fly.

There are several other species of roach that do not climb; while this may be an advantage in terms of housing them, they are not useful as live food for arboreal species such as chameleons. Included here are the South American Orange-headed Roach *(Eublaberus prosticus)* and the Orange-spotted Roach *(Blaptica dubia)*, which are both attractive insects to keep and valuable feeder insects.

Orange-spotted Roaches are easily sexed at a glance, since only the males have wings. These roaches are more soft-bodied than either the Orange-headed or the Discoid Roach *(Blaberus discoidales)*, another New World species sometimes used for feeder purposes. The slower movements of Orange-spotted Roaches also make them more suitable for nervous reptiles. Kept in a warm environment at around 75°F (24°C), the females will be mature by about three months old. They will give birth to as many as 30 live young after a gestation period lasting roughly a month. Measuring approximately 0.1 inch (3 mm) at birth, the young will ultimately grow to about 1.5 inches (3.75 cm) when adult. This means they are suitable as food for a range of species as they mature.

Other Feeder Insects and Invertebrates

A number of other feeder insects are less readily available but can be obtained from special breeders. **Fruit flies** (*Drosophila* species) are an ideal and valuable food for small amphibians and tarantulas, although they are not permitted in all areas. These flies are purchased as a starter culture and will multiply rapidly. Banana skins are a traditional food for fruit flies, but there are also sugar-based foods that can be used very successfully for them. The so-called wingless strain of fruit fly is a favorite because it can be easily contained within the vivarium.

House flies (*Musca domestica*) are useful for certain lizards, particularly chameleons, as well as spiders, since they will move readily off the ground. The curled winged form is best, since it cannot fly but will clamber up decor.

Whiteworms (*Enchytraeus* species) are especially valuable for rearing young amphibians, but are only available in the form of starter cultures. To grow them on, use a small container, such as a clean, empty margarine tub, filled with a peat substitute substrate. Make several shallow holes in the substrate and divide the worms into small groups, placing a little bread moistened with milk on top of each group as a food source. Cover with the lid that has been punched with small holes for ventilation. Keep the container in a relatively warm spot, replacing the bread and milk regularly. After a month or so the worms can be dug up and separated from the substrate by tipping them into a saucer of dechlorinated water.

Earthworms (*Dendrobeana veneta*) are also available from certain live-food suppliers. They are ideal for larger amphibians such as various salamanders; they are also safe to use, whereas worms dug from the backyard can be hazardous. If using worms dug from the ground, they should never be offered immediately to the occupants of a vivarium. They should be kept in moist surroundings in a container packed with damp grass for a couple of days so that they can empty their intestinal tracts, which may contain harmful parasites or other microbes.

Redworms (*Eisenia foetida*) make a suitable alternative to Earthworms. They are often known under a variety of different names, including Tiger Worms and Trout Worms, since they are popular as fishing bait. They live close to the surface of the soil rather than burrowing into its depths, and are particularly favored by various amphibians.

Slugs and snails caught in backyard surroundings may have been exposed to toxic chemicals. At the very least,

▲ *LEFT: CULTURES FOR FRUIT FLIES (*DROSOPHILA *SPECIES).*
*RIGHT: EARTHWORMS (*DENDROBEANA VENETA*).*

therefore, they should be kept in a cool damp spot for a week or so before use to ensure as far as possible that they are healthy. Farmed snails are available from some live-food suppliers, and these should be quite safe.

Vitamin and Mineral Supplements

The nutritional value of feeder insects is less than ideal for many herptiles, particularly their calcium-to-phosphorus ratio. They have a relatively high level of phosphorus compared to calcium. As a result, reptiles are especially susceptible to calcium deficiency, with young, fast-growing individuals such as water dragons (*Physignathus* species), Bearded Dragons (*Pogona vittiveps*) and chameleons being particularly vulnerable.

While the use of supplements can compensate for this shortcoming, the lighting also needs to be correct in order to allow the calcium to be absorbed from the intestinal tract under the influence of vitamin D3 (see page 23). Supplements often also contain vitamin D3 to help avoid deficiency in this vitamin, which can result in calcium deficiency even if the animals receive an adequate dietary level of calcium.

The simplest way of improving the nutritional value of feeder insects is simply to sprinkle them with a vitamin and mineral supplement just before placing them in the vivarium. There are a range of products available for this purpose but, as always, choose one that has been formulated specially for use with reptiles.

It can be difficult to ensure that the powder sticks effectively to the feeder insects, especially with crickets; it is a good idea to place them in a plastic bag and add the powder, then shake it several times to create a fine dust. If you are using a special feeder to transfer the crickets to the animal's quarters, then add this supplement in the base.

▶ *FEEDER INSECTS ARE WIDELY AVAILABLE IN PET STORES AND OTHER*
OUTLETS AND ARE SOLD IN EASY-TO-HANDLE PLASTIC BOXES.

Hopefully, some of the supplement will stick to the crickets when they emerge from the feeder.

The diet given to feeder insects can have a significant impact on the nutritional value of the insect. For example, keeping mealworms in bran is counterproductive, since bran contains a chemical known as phytic acid. It blocks the uptake of calcium into the mealworm's body, worsening the phosphorus-to-calcium ratio in their bodies. The problem can be improved by keeping mealworms in chicken meal. Special foods are readily available for mealworms that are supplemented with key ingredients such as calcium. Herptiles and invertebrates will then benefit from the nutrition contained in the live-food's digestive tract. This method of supplementation is often called "gut loading."

Storing and Breeding Feeder Insects

Feeder insects are generally sold in ventilated plastic containers. As a rule, it is better to buy supplies fresh rather than keeping them for any length of time. This is particularly important in the case of waxworms, since they do not feed in the period leading up to pupation, and they lose weight at this stage. For mealworms either use special containers that are available or adapt a clean plastic container, such as an ice-cream carton, punching ventilation holes in the lid.

Crickets require much better ventilation than mealworms. Either use the special storage enclosures that are readily available or plexiglass containers made for other invertebrates and amphibians. Crickets can climb well, so it is imperative, especially with small sizes, that they are not able to escape through the perforations of the lid. A major advantage of using the commercially designed cages is that they can be used to dispense the crickets easily into the herptile's quarters, which is less easy with other systems. Some live foods, such as worms, can be left in the containers in which they were purchased. However, it is important to ensure that the lid is left on so that the substrate does not dry out.

Live foods must always be provided with water. For mealworms, their water requirement can be met by using pieces of apple, but be sure to replace them as they begin to shrivel up. Crickets and locusts are prone to drowning in open containers of water, so they are usually given special granules that allow them to obtain moisture. These granules can also be useful for other invertebrates that are likely to drown in open water.

All these commercially available live foods can be bred at home, but careful planning will be necessary to ensure your attempts at breeding them are successful. Mealworms are the easiest live foods to breed, but they have a relatively long life cycle. If mealworms are left to mature in a culture with food, the adult meal beetles will eventually lay eggs, and the young mealworms will hatch several months later. It is probably a good idea to see such foods as a supplementary food source, not least of all because cultures sometimes fail.

Dried Alternatives

Some people can be put off by handling live invertebrates, and it is possible to obtain dried alternatives. They are sold in cans, but often do not prove to be as palatable as live invertebrates. This applies in particular to amphibians, which are especially attracted by the movements of would-be prey. Turtles, on the other hand, can be persuaded to eat such foods readily from your hand, but it is important to remember that these may not represent a balanced source of nutrients, nor can they be gut-loaded like their live counterparts.

ANIMAL FOODS

Some herptiles naturally feed on aquatic prey such as fish. Many turtles and some snakes, such as garter snakes (*Thamnopis* species), will eat fish. Although fish can feature in the diets of these species in vivarium surroundings, it can create problems. Overreliance on fish as part of the diet can lead to the nutritional condition known as steatitis. From a practical standpoint, it is also very messy feeding fish to reptiles in the confines of a tank, since the water can rapidly become polluted, and the vivarium will smell very unpleasant. Separate feeding quarters may be recommended for turtles.

Raw meat has also been used in the past, particularly for turtles, but it carries a number of hazards. First, in any vertebrate the majority of the body's calcium is stored in the skeleton rather than the muscle, so feeding raw meat represents an unbalanced diet, which will lead to shell and bone abnormalities. Raw meat is also deficient in vitamin A, which is vital for healthy eyesight—relying on raw meat in the diet of turtles can lead to blindness. Furthermore, there is also a significant risk that they could acquire salmonella or E. coli bacteria from uncooked meat. As with fish, better alternatives are now available in the form of prepared foods.

▼ *CORN SNAKE (ELAPHE GUTTATA) EATING A DEAD MOUSE. DEAD ANIMAL FOODS SUCH AS MICE AND CHICKS ARE COMMERCIALLY AVAILABLE.*

Snake Food

Some turtles may eat some green food, but snakes feed entirely on animal protein. For many owners, this means purchasing dead **mice and rats** that are specially bred as food. These can be purchased in a frozen state, but they must be thoroughly thawed out before being offered to the reptile. Microwave ovens are not recommended for this purpose, because they may not thaw out the body cavity effectively. It is much better to allow the food to defrost in a refrigerator overnight, and allow it to warm up to room temperature before using it.

It is important to match the size of food closely to that of the snake. The smallest mice are one-day-old "pinkies," while the older, larger ones are known as fuzzies or fluffies. Both provide a less concentrated source of energy than adult mice. It is therefore important to offer mice to small snakes in sufficient quantites to meet their energy requirements—especially when they are growing—so they do not lose condition. Snakes feed naturally by striking at their prey and grabbing it with their teeth. All prey is usually swallowed head-first, because it is easier and less likely to get stuck in the esophagus. From the esophagus the food passes straight into the snake's stomach.

Dead day-old **chicks** produced as part of the poultry industry are also sold as snake food. These chicks can be acquired fresh or frozen, and they can also be offered to large lizards such as monitors. They should always originate from stock that is free from salmonella. Bulk frozen stock is usually packed in an insulated polystyrene box, sometimes with dry ice, to ensure that the food stays frozen. Transfer the frozen food into a freezer immediately. Any dry ice remaining in the packaging must not be touched with bare hands because it is so cold that it will burn; if left, it will safely vaporize.

For people who dislike the idea of offering chicks and rodents to reptiles, **snake sausages** are a good alternative—they are commercially available and provide a balanced diet. Snake sausages must not be confused with ordinary pork sausages, which are not recommended for snakes, although they look similar.

Feeding Snakes

There are a number of factors that will influence a snake's appetite, and this is true of other reptiles as well. For example, young growing snakes and those that are breeding will require more food than older, more sedentary individuals. Female breeding pythons, for example, will remain curled around their eggs after laying and will incubate them without the need to feed again until after the young have hatched. In the

▲ *SPECIALIZED FOODS ARE AVAILABLE NOT ONLY FOR THE MOST POPULAR HERPTILE SPECIES, BUT ALSO FOR DIFFERENT AGES.*

this is to weigh snakes regularly and adjust the amount of food offered accordingly.

DIETARY DEVELOPMENTS

Research over recent years has concentrated on the development of formulated diets, especially for the most popular reptiles and amphibians. Like prepared dog and cat foods, these are easy to store and should eliminate the risk of any nutritional deficiencies. There are now foods designed especially for individual species, such as Bearded Dragons (*Pogona vitticeps*) and Green Iguanas (*Iguana iguana*), as well as more general foods for groups of animals such as turtles. They are supplied in tubs—there may be a smaller grade intended for younger animals in addition to a larger size of pellet for older individuals. Although pellets predominate, foodsticks are available for turtles, and these can sometimes prove to be more palatable, in spite of their elongated shape.

It helps if the animals have been reared on this type of food, but in many cases it is not difficult to wean them across to a formulated food. The key is not to overfeed, because any excess will pollute the water. It is better to offer a small amount of food several times during the day, rather than one larger meal.

Assuming that the animals are feeding readily on a formulated diet, there is no need to use a supplement. This could even prove harmful over a period of time, because an excess of fat-soluble vitamins in the diet can cause illness, and calcium deposits may accumulate in the animals' arteries, affecting the blood flow.

Although formulated foods are generally very palatable, it may be necessary to moisten them slightly at first. Only treat a small amount in this way, because any leftovers will have to be discarded before turning moldy. In the case of vegetarian species such as tortoises, mix in the pellets with the animal's regular food; once the pellets are being eaten, gradually increase the amount being offered and simply pour them out of the container directly into the food dish.

For aquatic species such as turtles and newts, simply pour a small quantity of pellets onto the surface of the water. They should be snapped up relatively quickly, but in the case of turtles the palatability of formulated foods of this type does seem to differ markedly from variety to variety. If they refuse this type of food consistently, ask at your local pet store for an alternative that they may prefer. The shape of the food may be significant, and sometimes foodsticks seem to be more palatable than pellets. Also, it may be helpful to try dropping the food a short distance in front of the turtle's head rather than placing it next to its mouth. Giving the animal a better view of its food often encourages it to eat.

case of snakes from more temperate latitudes, their appetite will decline as the temperature drops shortly before they go into hibernation.

Sometimes snakes will refuse food—for example, when trying to switch an individual to a new type of food—in which case an odor-manipulating spray may help. Encouraging a snake to strike by moving the food a distance in front of its head, using special blunt-ended tongs that will not hurt its mouth, may be helpful. Try not to handle the food, or the snake will detect a human scent rather than that of its prey, and this is likely to make it less enthusiastic about eating. Never be tempted to offer live prey to a snake in a vivarium; this is illegal in many areas, and there are a number of cases where rodents have turned on snakes in the confines of a vivarium, inflicting serious injuries with their sharp teeth.

Snakes in vivaria expend less energy on hunting prey than their wild relatives. This effectively reduces their energy needs, so it is not uncommon for them to become overweight through overfeeding. This can ultimately be harmful, reducing their desire to breed and potentially shortening their life span. The simplest way of monitoring

GENERAL CARE

It is always a good idea to set up the vivarium in advance of obtaining the occupants. This will ensure that everything is working properly, particularly the all-important temperature control. Depending partly on which animals you want, a reasonable choice may be available at a local pet store, some of which specialize in species. Local pet stores are fine for the commonly kept herptiles, whose care requirements are the most straightforward, but for more specialized animals and rarer color varieties there are numerous breeders and suppliers who advertise their surplus stock in reptile magazines and on websites.

Ideally, it is better to see the animals before buying and to bring them straight back home. If this is impossible, they can be shipped, in which case special heat packs should be used to keep them warm in transit.

MAKING A CHOICE

The ease with which it is possible to recognize good health in herptiles and invertebrates varies depending on the creature concerned. A keen appetite is a useful indicator, but whereas reptiles such as tortoises will eat on a daily basis, spiders and snakes may display little, if any, interest in food if they have been fed recently or are preparing to shed their skins.

Choosing Healthy Animals

Overall body condition is often a better way of determining health. Avoid snakes and lizards that display evident signs of weight loss and appear too thin—this also often leads to sluggish behavior, particularly in the case of lizards. Usually these signs have a serious underlying cause, although in some cases it may be possible to nurse an animal back to health. This applies particularly in the case of wild-caught individuals, which are often badly afflicted by parasites. Suitable treatment can result in a rapid improvement in health, but initially this can be a worrying period. Specialized veterinary advice will be needed to establish the cause of the problem before any treatment can be given, and both will be costly.

With tortoises and turtles look for animals that are bright-eyed and lively. Any discharge from the nostrils, together with noisy breathing, are serious signs of ill health. If a tortoise is underweight, it will not be possible to tell by looking, since its body is masked by the shell.

▲ *REPTILES AND AMPHIBIANS ON DISPLAY IN A STORE. ALWAYS LOOK FOR CLEAN AND TIDY PREMISES, WHICH INDICATE THAT STOCK IS WELL CARED FOR.*

However, it is possible to measure and weigh the animal. If a chelonian is reluctant to open its eyes and if they also appear to be rather sunken in their sockets, this is generally an indicator of an underlying illness.

All aquatic species, from turtles to amphibians, can be at risk from fungal infections. Check for any superficial injury to the body that could become infected by opportunist fungi. These usually have a whitish appearance, creating a halo effect when the area is seen in the water. Treatment is often possible, certainly in the early stages, but again, recovery cannot be guaranteed. There may be another underlying condition that has lowered the animal's resistance to the fungal infection.

Be particularly wary of aquatic species that appear to have difficulty in swimming. Turtles that lurch over to one side, for example, are likely to be suffering from pneumonia, for which the prognosis is poor. Another common sign of ill health in turtles is lack of activity—look out for a turtle that hardly reacts when it is picked up, not moving its legs at all, or one that seeks to withdraw into its shell when it is not cold.

Lizards sometimes may be missing the terminal part of the tail. It may have been shed as a defensive mechanism, enabling the animal to escape from a predator. For this reason, lizards must be handled carefully. The loss of part of the tail appears quite painless, and there is no blood loss or subsequent risk of infection. The missing tip will grow again eventually, although it may often not reach the full length of the original. Sometimes the new tail can grow in a slightly unusual manner, for example, developing a short spur on the side. Such lizards are often described as "stub-tailed," and although they may not look as attractive as their full-tailed counterparts, this is not a cause for concern. Also, they usually cost less to buy in this condition.

Some herptiles and invertebrates can also regenerate missing or damaged limbs. Various amphibians, including newts, may lose toes, feet or even an entire leg as a result of shedding difficulties or fighting. These parts often regrow successfully, as long as they are not afflicted by fungus. In tarantulas and stick insects, among other species, regrowth occurs at their subsequent molt. Unfortunately, adult invertebrates that have finished shedding will be permanently handicapped following the loss of a limb.

Age Considerations

Age and life span can be important considerations when purchasing herptiles. Younger individuals are less costly than adult breeding animals, but it is often not possible to sex them successfully at this stage, nor is it a good idea to pair closely related stock together. Once they have reached adult size, however, it is not possible to determine how old they are, and so in some cases it is likely that they will be past their reproductive prime.

The typical life expectancy of snakes and larger lizards in the vivarium is between 10 and 15 years, which is significantly longer than in the wild. On the other hand, tortoises are well known for a life span that is similar to, and may frequently exceed, our own. Turtles generally live for a somewhat shorter period, averaging perhaps 30 years or so.

In the amphibian world bufonid toads are likely to live for up to 20 years, while many other species will live for over a decade. In the case of lizards and smaller amphibians, five years is likely to be the maximum life span.

Within the invertebrates there are some surprises relating to life spans, and there can also be marked differences between the sexes. Male tarantulas have an average life

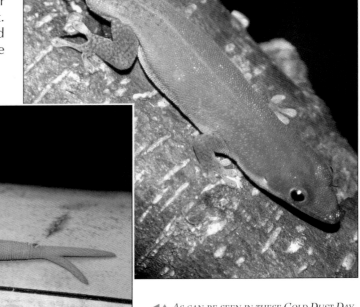

◄▲ *AS CAN BE SEEN IN THESE GOLD DUST DAY GECKOS (PHELSUMA LATICAUDA), BROKEN TAILS WILL REGROW AS A STUMP (ABOVE) OR EVEN AS A FORKED VERSION (LEFT).*

various parasites, usually linked with their diet. Their age will also be uncertain, and they may not settle in vivarium surroundings as well as captive-bred stock. Increasingly, their suppliers are setting up captive-breeding operations in countries of origin to supply the pet market, rather than relying on wild-caught stock. This ensures that the commercial benefits of the trade are kept in the region where the creatures occur, providing employment and contributing to the local economy, while at the same time ensuring that the creatures themselves are in better health.

Another method of rearing is known as ranching. The excess of eggs that many wild herptiles produce in order to allow for predation means that it is possible to take some of them and hatch them in captivity without any adverse effect on the overall population. Such animals are described as being captive-farmed (often abbreviated to C.F.), rather than captive-bred (C.B.).

◄ *YOUNG CHAMELEONS ARE REARED IN A COMMERCIAL ENTERPRISE IN INDONESIA.*

▼ *AN UNUSUAL ISLAND RACE OF DWARF BURMESE PYTHONS (PYTHON MOLURUS) IS BEING BRED TO ENTER THE VIVARIUM TRADE.*

expectancy of about five years, but their female counterparts may live for half a century.

These figures can have an impact on breeding. Young stock of longer-lived species, such as tortoises, will require five to 10 years before they attain sexual maturity. If you buy young stock, which is cheaper, but your ultimate goal is to breed tortoises, you will need to be patient and take into account the cost of housing and feeding the animals while waiting for them to reach maturity.

CAPTIVE-BRED VERSUS WILD-CAUGHT

While a significant percentage of herptiles available today are bred in collections, some are collected from the wild. International trade is tightly regulated under CITES, a treaty administered by the United Nations Environment Program (UNEP) and supported by more than 130 governments worldwide. CITES helps develop sustainable-use programs to prevent overexploitation of species brought into the trade. The trade itself brings benefits, since it creates a financial incentive to conserve the environment and thereby the species themselves.

There are some drawbacks to starting out with wild-caught reptiles, because they can be badly afflicted by

◀ *THE BEARDED DRAGON (POGONA VITTICEPS) HAS BECOME VERY POPULAR WITH REPTILE KEEPERS. A WIDE RANGE OF COLOR MORPHS IS NOW AVAILABLE, SOME OF WHICH ARE SHOWN HERE.*

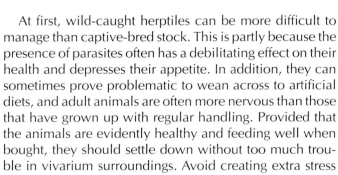

At first, wild-caught herptiles can be more difficult to manage than captive-bred stock. This is partly because the presence of parasites often has a debilitating effect on their health and depresses their appetite. In addition, they can sometimes prove problematic to wean across to artificial diets, and adult animals are often more nervous than those that have grown up with regular handling. Provided that the animals are evidently healthy and feeding well when bought, they should settle down without too much trouble in vivarium surroundings. Avoid creating extra stress

for the animals by ensuring that there is adequate cover for them, especially in the early stages.

Captive breeding by both hobbyists and professional breeders is increasing. One of the features of captive breeding is that it has allowed the development of new color variants, which are often more striking in appearance than the wild form. This is especially true of snakes, but also of some popular lizard species, such as the Leopard Gecko *(Eublepharis macularius)* and the Bearded Dragon *(Pogona vitticeps)*—(see page 52).

TRANSPORTATION HOME

Snakes, which are consummate escape artists, are carried in secure canvas bags, tied at the top. Chelonians may also be moved in this way, but the bag itself should be transferred to a cardboard box lined on the base with sheets of newspaper, which will soak up any urine—these animals are likely to empty their bladders when being moved.

The ventilated plastic boxes used for selling live foods are very useful as secure quarters when moving other invertebrates. They are also suitable for small lizards, including many species of geckos. If lined with moist paper towels or moss, they are equally useful for moving amphibians. It helps if the container is placed within a paper bag to create darker surroundings so the occupants will feel less exposed. The relatively few truly aquatic species, such as African clawed frogs, will need to be transported in the same way as tropical fish—in a plastic bag of water filled at the top with oxygen. This too should be placed inside another bag to keep it dark, in order to lessen the stress of the journey.

► *SNAKE BAGS ARE THE IDEAL WAY TO TRANSPORT SNAKES SAFELY.*

THE EARLY DAYS

New arrivals should be transferred to their quarters as soon as they arrive. Leave them to settle down quietly, and provide food and water. It is not unusual for tortoises in particular to charge around for a period after being confined on the journey home, but they will soon calm down and may then show some interest in food. Snakes, on the other hand, are unlikely to be interested in eating at first, and it may be a day or so before they regain their appetite. Walking sticks may even appear dead when unpacked, but if placed on the floor of their quarters they will soon stage a miraculous recovery, clambering back up a branch. Feigning death in this way is a natural defensive mechanism against predators.

First Feeding

Providing food similar to their usual diet has the benefit not only of encouraging them to eat but also reduces the likelihood of any digestive disturbance. This can be of particular concern in tortoises and other primarily vegetarian species, which rely on a beneficial population of microbes in their digestive system to assist them in breaking down their food. Sudden changes in diet, especially from fresh to pelleted food, for example, can shift this balance. It can cause a change in the gut flora, allowing harmful microbes to become established, which can endanger the reptile's health and even threaten its life. Wait for about two weeks to make changes to a new pet's diet. Then introduce new foods gradually, increasing the quantity on offer over the course of several weeks so that the digestive system can adapt accordingly.

A low-rimmed, heavyweight feeding bowl is recommended to aid overall hygiene by keeping the food and vivarium floor clean. The bowl should be washed regularly—but never in a sink used for human utensils because of the risk of spreading harmful bacteria such as salmonella. A separate bucket is best for this purpose, and disposable gloves should be used, just as when cleaning or handling the animals.

To encourage a feeding reflex in predatory herptiles, particularly snakes, simulate movement of the dead prey by gripping it with special feeding tongs. They should not be offered live vertebrate prey on welfare grounds; it may

even be illegal to do so in some areas. The feeding tongs should be blunt at the tips, to minimize the risk of causing injury to the snake. As a further precaution, they must also be protected with plastic covers. It is important to offer the food in such a way that the snake can strike at the head of the creature, avoiding any contact with the tongs. This is essential, because snakes always swallow their prey head-first so that the fur, feathers or scales will not stick in its throat. Once the snake has a firm grip on its prey, let go and withdraw the tongs from the vivarium.

For insectivorous lizards it is much better to use a special cricket feeder so that the insects cannot become a nuisance, irritating the vivarium occupants, but can emerge into their accommodation only in small numbers. This will encourage the lizards to hunt them as they would in the wild. It also prevents the crickets from drowning in the water container, which they are otherwise inclined to do. If it is possible to chill the crickets slightly beforehand, this will slow down their level of activity even more, making them easier for the vivarium occupants to catch.

Frequency of Feeding

The frequency of feeding differs among individuals and different species. Those that are primarily vegetarian will benefit from being offered food in limited amounts every day. This is because their food is high in fiber and low in energy, which means they must eat relatively large quantities to meet their nutritional needs. A tortoise outdoors can browse freely, but in a vivarium it is a good idea to provide food twice daily to ensure the food is fresh and not contaminated with bacteria. Walking sticks should have a constant supply of fresh food, arranged for most species in such a way that the stems will enable them to clamber around their quarters.

If you are using a formulated diet of any type, read and follow the instructions for use carefully. Bear in mind that moistened formula will deteriorate rapidly, so any that is left uneaten must be discarded within a day, before it has a chance to become moldy. In most cases offering too much food will simply result in it being wasted. However,

▶ *IN THE EARLY DAYS OF CAPTIVITY NEW ANIMALS MAY NEED TO BE HAND-FED, AS WITH THIS SKINK (EUMECES ALGERIENSIS).*

◀ *A DEEP FEEDING BOWL IS IMPORTANT TO PREVENT ANIMALS FROM UNNECESSARILY SPREADING FOOD AROUND A VIVARIUM.*

some species, such African monitor lizards (*Varanus* species), will eat to excess and can become seriously obese, which is likely to shorten their life expectancy significantly. In the wild they will eat heartily whenever food is plentiful, because they need to build up fat stores to see them through more arid periods when they estivate—becoming dormant in a similar way to some tortoises.

KEEPING VIVARIA CLEAN

A vivarium must be kept clean. Bacteria and fungi can multiply very rapidly in the confines of a vivarium, particularly under hot and humid conditions, threatening the health of the occupants. Spot cleaning of the substrate using an old spoon is therefore recommended, with more thorough cleaning being undertaken once a week or so, depending to a certain extent on the vivarium occupants. Those that are naturally messy, such as tortoises, are likely to need their quarters cleaned more regularly. Even if you are using a loose substrate, it can be helpful to line the tray with sheets of old newspaper. This will make it much easier to clean the floor area, since the substrate can be funneled into a bag or sack.

Aside from the presence of obvious dirt, water can deteriorate in quality and threaten the health of the vivarium occupants. Water bowls need to be washed out at least twice a week with a special safe disinfectant, intended for use with herptiles. Do not be tempted to use ordinary

household disinfectants because they could be fatal to the vivarium occupants. Follow the instructions for use carefully, and rinse off the disinfectant solution thoroughly afterward. When using a disinfectant within the vivarium itself, always clean the area scrupulously first—it will work more effectively as a result.

Semiaquatic Setups

Aquatic or semiaquatic herptiles will also need their water changed regularly, although filtration can help maintain the water quality for longer. Turtles are likely to prove to be very messy, particularly if they are fed on a diet of anything other than prepared pelletized foods. It is a good idea to have a separate tank to which the turtles can be transferred for feeding, particularly if items such as fish are offered. This type of food will otherwise pollute the water, giving it an unpleasant odor.

A feeding tank of this type requires no decor at all and simply needs to be filled to an appropriate depth with water at an equivalent temperature to that in their main quarters. The water should be poured away afterward down an external drain, so there is no risk of potentially harmful bacteria such as salmonella being introduced to a sink in which human food is prepared.

The frequency with which the main living area for the turtles needs to be stripped down depends on the animals' size and on the number of individuals sharing the same accommodation. Typically, it is likely to need cleaning

▼ *THE PLANTS IN A TROPICAL FOREST VIVARIUM SHOULD BE TRIMMED OCCASIONALLY TO MAINTAIN HEALTHY GROWTH AND ALLOW THE OCCUPANTS TO BE SEEN.*

once a week. Start by switching off and disconnecting the heaterstat and filter units as well as the lights. The simplest way to empty the tank is to use a siphon, of the type sold by fishkeeping stores. Failing this, a length of ordinary rubber tube will suffice as a siphon. However, you should never be tempted to suck the water through the tube to establish the flow, because it is all too easy to ingest dirty tank water accidentally.

Changing the water will make the tank cleaner, but it will not remove dirt from the gravel. A gravel cleaner may help and can be attached to a siphon. Alternatively, scoop out the gravel once the tank is empty and then wash it off, ideally using a strainer and allowing the water to flow down into a bucket.

If the power filter is not working effectively, it is probable that the core has become blocked by debris. The filter is easily stripped down, and the best way to proceed is to wash the filter material in a bucket of tank water. It will be less harmful than rinsing it in household water, which contains a chlorine-based chemical that is likely to kill off the beneficial bacteria in the filter material. At first the dirt from the filter core will turn the water cloudy, but before long it will become evident that the dirt has been removed from the foam cartridge, and the unit can then be reassembled.

Bear in mind that just because the water appears clean, this does not mean that the ammonia level has not risen significantly, seriously threatening the occupants' health. Water testing can be useful to determine ammonia levels, especially in the case of amphibians. Suitable testing kits are sold for fishkeeping purposes.

Aquatic Setups

For tanks housing aquatic amphibians, regular partial water changes should be adequate to maintain a healthy environment. Bail out or siphon off the water and replace it, not forgetting to use a water conditioner to neutralize the chlorine or chloramine in the freshwater before adding it to the tank. Check that the new water is at the same temperature as that in the tank.

Where water is being used in a waterfall this will also need changing regularly. In the case of misting units, avoid using household water in hardwater areas, because the dissolved salts are likely to be deposited over time, creating a whitish stain. More

significantly, these deposits may cause the unit to work less effectively by restricting its output.

In aquatic vivaria there is always a risk that signs of unwanted algal growth will start to become visible. There are many different types of algae, but most commonly they cause a greenish slime on the sides of the tank that can spread to the decor and can even develop on the shells of turtles. Excessive algal growth is often a sign that there is dissolved nitrate from the breakdown of waste in the tank and possibly that the lighting is being left on for too long each day.

It is possible to curb the algal growth directly by using a special cleaner, such as the devices that are sold primarily for fishkeeping purposes. They are available either in the form of a long-handled scraper or a magnetic cleaner, which works through the glass. If algal growth appears on the tank decor, the only solution is to scrub it off, while plants that are badly affected by algae may simply have to be discarded. In the longer term, adjustments to the lighting pattern should help prevent any significant recurrence. Typically, having the vivarium lights switched on for a maximum of eight to 10 hours per day should not result in marked algal overgrowth.

In amphibian tanks with an undergravel filter, clean the gravel every month or so when carrying out a partial water change, using a gravel cleaner. This removes the

▲ *IN AN AQUATIC SETUP THE WATER SHOULD BE PARTIALLY CHANGED PERIODICALLY TO MAINTAIN A HEALTHY ENVIRONMENT.*

bigger particles (known as mulm) that have accumulated. Large particles can decrease the effectiveness of this type of filter, since it relies on the flow of water through the gravel which acts as the filter bed.

Maintaining Plants

Over a period of time aquatic vegetation often starts to become rather leggy and will need to be pruned back. Beware that new plants added to a setup can introduce disease, so it is a good idea to dip them in a safe disinfectant solution and then rinse them off thoroughly before placing them in the vivarium.

In the case of terrestrial vivaria watch out for plants becoming moldy. This is often a sign of poor ventilation, which can also threaten the health of the occupants. Carefully chosen plants should not become too large for the vivarium, particularly if they are set in pots that will naturally help restrict their size. The shoots should be trimmed as necessary.

A backdrop made of cork bark is an ideal medium for training climbing plants, which can be fixed in place with staples. In this way they will ultimately spread across the area, creating a naturalistic impression.

BREEDING

The vast majority of herptiles and invertebrates reproduce sexually, with the transfer of sperm from male to female being a prerequisite. The process is not always the same as in mammals, however. In the case of newts, for example, the male produces a packet of sperm, known as a spermatophore, which the female collects in her hind legs and introduces to her body, fertilizing the eggs before she lays them. Most (but not all) amphibians return to water to breed—a few species have managed to free themselves to a great extent from this dependency simply by laying in moist surroundings on land.

Frogs and toads typically clasp each other in a mating embrace, known as an amplexus. The male usually grasps his partner behind her front legs, although fire-bellied toads (*Bombina* species) grip their partners around the hind quarters. Fertilization in these cases is external, with the male releasing his sperm over the eggs as they are laid—although inevitably some will remain unfertilized.

Snakes, lizards and tortoises reproduce by internal fertilization. In most cases mating occurs shortly before egg-laying. In a number of chelonian species, however, the female is able to retain viable sperm in her body for several years after a single mating, allowing her to produce fertile eggs throughout this period. This is obviously advantageous to slow-moving, solitary creatures that may roam over a wide area.

Some stick insects have dispensed with the need to mate: they reproduce by a process known as parthenogenesis, which results in females laying fertile eggs that are clones of their parent. This is true of the widely kept Indian Stick Insect *(Carausius morosus),* in which males are extremely scarce and often infertile. In some species both parthenogenetic and sexual reproduction can occur.

▲ *ASIAN LEAF FROGS (MEGOPHRYS NASUTA) IN AMPLEXUS.*

▶ *CHINESE BEAUTY RATSNAKE (ELAPHE TAENIURA FRISEI) INCUBATING EGGS.*

The hatching rate after mating is often higher than when the female effectively clones herself.

A number of reptiles prove to be remarkably devoted parents. Female crocodilians guard their chosen nest site and ultimately carry their offspring to water in their mouth, protecting the young from predators when they are at their most vulnerable. Female pythons wrap their body around the eggs and incubate them; regular muscular contractions assist in raising the temperature of the eggs.

As breeding success with many species has become far more common in vivarium surroundings, much more is known about the triggers that stimulate the onset of reproductive activity. Sexual maturity in reptiles and amphibians depends less on age than on size. Chelonians in particular will probably breed at an earlier age than would normally be the case in the wild, because they

often grow faster. Since females tend to be larger than males they mature more slowly, taking a year or so longer before they start breeding. The age at which herptiles start breeding is also a reflection of their life span—those that live only for a potentially short time mature earlier and experience a higher reproductive rate, which is why invertebrates may have hundreds of offspring.

Many frogs produce hundreds or even thousands of eggs because the hazardous nature of their life cycle means that only a tiny percentage survive through to adulthood in the wild.

SEXING

A number of general guidelines for identifying a true pair of herptiles are given here, but specific information can be found under the individual entries in the second part

◄ COMMON FLAT LIZARD (PLATYSAURUS INTERMEDIUS)—MATING PAIR, WITH THE MALE SHOWING DISTINCTIVE BREEDING COLORS.

of the book. The differences are often most apparent in lizards, with males of many species having obvious frills and crests. One of the most striking examples is Jackson's Chameleon *(Chamaeleo jacksonii)*, in which the male possesses three horns on his head, while the female has none. Following the discovery of this species, this extreme case of sexual dimorphism led scientists to believe that they were separate species.

Sexing Snakes and Lizards

Male lizards often tend to be slightly smaller in size than females and also more brightly colored in some cases, as in rock lizards, for example. A less evident but very important way of distinguishing the sexes, and one that is particularly useful in the case of smaller lizards such as geckos, often relates to the femoral pores. These small openings—named for the femur, or thigh bone—extend in rows down the upper part of each hind leg.

In order to be able to see whether femoral pores are present, indicating a male lizard, the easiest thing may be to transfer the lizard to a clear plastic box so it can be viewed from below. An empty live-food box is ideal, since it will have a lid to prevent the lizard from escaping. A similar approach works with newts and salamanders and enables you to examine their cloacal region without the risk of injuring their sensitive skin by holding them.

It is harder to sex most snakes visually, although in some species an obvious difference in tail length exists between the sexes. However, in both male lizards and snakes the copulatory organs known as hemipenes may be evident as a slight swelling just behind the base of the vent. The hemipenes are paired organs, which are everted during mating. The space present within each of these organs when they are inside the body can form a basis for sexing, because there is effectively a much larger gap in this region in males than in females.

Sexing probes can be used to measure this difference, although probing is not something to be undertaken without experience, since this technique can otherwise result in serious internal injuries. In the first instance it is important to use the correct size of sexing probe, which can be purchased from specialized suppliers. Probes are made either of stainless steel or a synthetic material and need to be coated with petroleum jelly or a similar lubricant before use.

The next step is to ensure that the snake or lizard is adequately restrained, to avoid any sudden movement. It is possible to count back the scales on the underside of the body from the vent. In the case of a female the probe will barely extend into the orifice for any distance, but with a male it will slide back much farther, typically as far as 10 scales back in the direction of the tail.

Sexing Turtles and Tortoises

As far as chelonians are concerned, the tail length can provide a guide to sexing. In males the tail may be longer, with the length from its base to the cloacal opening being longer than in females. This is a particularly useful way of distinguishing a number of aquatic chelonians.

The shape of the plastron can provide another clue, especially in the case of tortoises. The more domed shape of their shells means that there is often a more pronounced concave area on the male's plastron, which helps him balance more easily on the female's shell when mating.

Sexing Amphibians and Invertebrates

In the case of amphibians their gender is much easier to determine at the start of the breeding period. This is the time when the crests of male newts develop, and females swell with eggs. The cloacal area around the vent also changes in appearance at this stage, becoming much more swollen than usual in the male.

Male frogs and toads can also often be distinguished by physical changes as spawning time approaches. Their so-called nuptial pads, which are evident on the inside of the digits and which assist them in anchoring to the females when they are fertilizing the eggs, become much more evident. Many species become more vocal at the start of the breeding season, and you will notice the wrinkled appearance of the male's skin when it is resting. Males are also often smaller in size overall than females and have a more streamlined appearance.

Size can be important in distinguishing between the sexes in many invertebrates, notably tarantulas. Again, the males are not only generally smaller but also have swellings that look a little like miniature boxing gloves on their pedipalps, close to the mouth.

Although DNA sexing to distinguish true pairs has been very valuable in the avian field, it has not helped significantly with reptiles owing to technical difficulties. Only a relatively few species, such as the highly endangered Komodo Dragon (*Varanus komodoensis*), can be sexed in this way. On the other hand, it is possible to regulate the incubation temperature, thereby directly affecting the gender of the offspring. If you are purchasing from a reliable vendor, therefore, you can be certain of the sex of herptiles, even as hatchlings.

BREEDING TRIGGERS

There are a number of different triggers that stimulate the onset of breeding behavior, and these depend to some extent on the individual species. In the first place, the animals must be mature. Breeding animals need to be in good condition as well. As far as wild-caught stock is concerned, the presence of parasites can have a very debilitating effect, which may in turn be sufficient to ensure that

◄ SEXING TORTOISES. THE MALE (LEFT) DISPLAYS A LONGER TAIL THAN THE FEMALE (RIGHT).

◄ FEMALE HERMANN'S TORTOISE (TESTUDO HERMANNI) LAYING EGGS IN A SHALLOW HOLE.

they do not attempt to breed. If conditions appear to be ideal for breeding but nothing is happening or if the female persists in laying infertile eggs, it would be a good idea to have a vet check the animal in order to determine the cause of the problem.

Environmental Changes

Reproductive activity of many herptiles in the wild is stimulated by environmental changes, and these need to be replicated in the vivarium. Temperate species will undergo a period of hibernation over the winter, and are likely to start breeding again soon after they awaken as the temperature rises in the spring.

Species living closer to the tropics in more arid areas may be encouraged to breed if the relative humidity reading in their quarters is raised. Alternatively, you could even create a wet area for amphibians, mimicking a period of increased rainfall. This can be reinforced by a vivarium waterfall, incorporating a pump that circulates water on a closed system, combined with a misting unit. The result will be a sound like falling rain.

Dietary Changes

Dietary changes may stimulate breeding, in particular raising the protein level in the diet of omnivorous lizards. As the breeding season approaches, it is important to ensure that there is sufficient calcium in the diet of reptile

► FEMALE TARANTULA GUARDING HER SMALL BROOD OF SPIDERLINGS.

species that lay hard-shelled (calcified) eggs. Because calcium is a vital ingredient of eggshell, any deficiency can result in egg binding (see page 56).

It is not just calcium itself that is important, however—exposure to vitamin D3 in the form of sunlight or through appropriate vivarium lighting is crucial to ensure that the mineral can be absorbed into the body from the intestinal tract and utilized effectively.

Breeding Groups

In some cases it is advisable to avoid keeping herptiles in pairs for breeding purposes. Mating in the wild is usually a transitory phase, with males and females coming together and then going their separate ways. Within the confines of a vivarium, however, the female may not be able to escape from the male's attentions. In addition, since courtship can be quite ferocious, she may be left injured, or certainly feel sufficiently harassed that she will not feed properly and will start to lose condition.

As an example, male chelonians may snap at the legs of their prospective partner as a means of slowing them down. Then they may batter their shell and bite their skin when mating. The level of aggression differs among individual males, however, and also among species. Male Malaysian Box Turtles (Cuora amboinensis), for instance, have a reputation for aggressive behavior when mating.

Lizards too can prove aggressive and highly territorial at this stage, with males battling ferociously if confined together. Keeping more than one female in the company of a single male chelonian or lizard is therefore recommended, since it diverts the male's focus away from a single female. Even in the case of frogs, more females should be kept than males to avoid a female being persecuted. You need to watch for potential injuries incurred as a result of mating, and treat them as necessary.

Vivarium Changes

To encourage breeding, a number of adjustments to the vivarium—more dramatic in some cases than in others—may be needed. Amphibians generally return to water for spawning purposes and may spend the rest of the year in damp areas on land. In aquatic vivaria the inclusion of plants such as Canadian pondweed (*Elodea*) is recommended. The eggs may be randomly scattered among the vegetation or carefully hidden beneath the leaves, a behavior displayed by many female newts.

Salamanders too are likely to return to water at the start of the breeding period, although not all species lay eggs. Some females may retain the eggs in their body, producing either tadpoles or, in a few cases, miniature metamorphosed young.

Chelonians reproduce entirely by means of eggs, which they bury in the ground, so suitable facilities should be provided for this, including a damp area of substrate that must be at least 6 inches (15 cm) deep.

Most lizards also lay eggs, but they are not always buried. Many geckos hide them away, frequently sticking them inside a bamboo tube. Some snakes give birth to live young, whereas others reproduce by means of eggs.

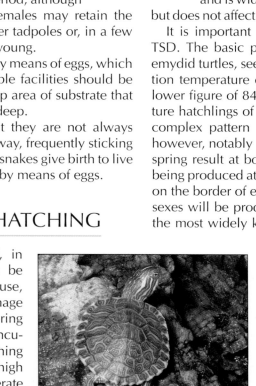

◄ *Frog spawn, showing fertile eggs (black) and infertile eggs (white).*

longer viable. You will probably even notice differences within the same clutch, since some eggs are likely to hatch significantly earlier than others.

Incubation Temperature

In many reptiles, including all crocodilians, the gender of the offspring is not genetically predetermined. Studies have shown that incubation temperature can be highly significant in determining the gender of the hatchlings. This is known as temperature sex determination (or TSD), and is widespread in chelonians and some lizards but does not affect any snakes, as far as is currently known.

It is important to understand the pattern involved in TSD. The basic pattern, which applies to tortoises and emydid turtles, sees females produced at a higher incubation temperature of up to 91.5°F (33°C) and males at a lower figure of 84°F (29°C). At an intermediate temperature hatchlings of both sexes can be anticipated. A more complex pattern has been identified in other families, however, notably mud turtles and side-necks. Female offspring result at both high and low extremes, with males being produced at intermediate temperatures. In this case, on the border of each temperature limit, offspring of both sexes will be produced. As far as lizards are concerned, the most widely kept and commonly bred example of a species displaying TSD is the Leopard Gecko (*Eublepharis macularius*), but the Moorish Gecko (*Tarentola mauritanica*) and various agamids also have this characteristic.

As a general guide, you will need to maintain a temperature of at least 84°F (29°C). Relative humidity is important in preventing the eggs from drying out, particularly those with parchment shells. To guard further against dessication, these eggs can be partially buried in damp vermiculite. You can tell by their appearance whether or not these eggs have

INCUBATION AND HATCHING

Once the eggs have been laid, in many cases they will need to be removed from the adults because, even if they do not eat or damage them, they may prey on the offspring after they have hatched. Special incubators are now available for hatching reptile eggs, and they achieve a high success rate. They are easy to operate and relatively inexpensive to buy. Unlike hens' eggs, it is critical that the those of reptiles are not turned regularly, otherwise this will have a fatal effect on the developing embryos.

There is no set incubation period for reptile eggs, and the hatching period can sometimes be protracted. Never be in too much of a hurry to discard eggs unless you are certain they are no

◄ *Young Map Turtles (Graptemys sp. and*
G. pseudogeographica pseudogeographica).
The temperature at which the eggs were
incubated will have determined their sex.

become dessicated. Handle them carefully, and when moving them do not tip them from the original position in which they were laid.

Vermiculite has the added advantage of being a relatively sterile substance, which will not encourage mold growth in the confines of the incubator. Even so, if there is obvious contamination of the shell with mold, this is not necessarily a sign that the egg will not hatch. Young reptiles seem to possess good defenses against potential infections of this type in the egg.

Hatching

Once the time for hatching nears, the reptile will cut its way out of the shell, using its so-called egg tooth, which is a sharp projection on the tip of the nose that disappears shortly afterward. Initially, the remains of the yolk sac that nourished the hatchling in the egg will be apparent, particularly in chelonians. This should soon dry up and be absorbed into the body, after which the young reptile will soon start feeding. Snakes will not feed for the first time until they have shed their skin.

Generally young reptiles must be kept warm at this stage because they are particularly susceptible to chilling. Aquatic species can be allowed into heated shallow water with easy access back onto land.

Amphibians eggs can succumb to fungus, but provided they are kept relatively warm, this will speed up the hatching process. It will soon be apparent within a few days which eggs are fertile, since they will contain the developing tadpoles, whereas infertile eggs will develop a whitish center.

Once the tadpoles hatch they will be inert at first, digesting the remains of their yolk sac and only starting to feed once they become free-swimming. It will probably be necessary to divide them into smaller batches as they grow, partly to maintain water quality and also to reduce the risk of cannibalism. Do not use a power filter in their quarters—it would be dangerous at this stage, although a gentle sponge filter should be safe.

The next critical phase will be when the the young emerge onto land, transformed into miniature amphibians—with just a trace of the tail remaining in the case of frogs and toads. Access to land should be facilitated by the inclusion of small stones around the edge of the water.

Small live foods will then be essential for rearing purposes, and their quarters will need to be kept moist by spraying, using dechlorinated water in a plant mister. Young amphibians are far more prone to dehydration than larger individuals. Carry on rearing them in small groups, or even individually in the case of highly cannibalistic species such as bullfrogs.

▼ *BURMESE PYTHONS (PYTHON MOLURUS) EMERGING FROM THEIR PARCHMENT-SHELLED EGGS.*

▲ *A GROUP OF CORN SNAKES (ELAPHE GUTTATA), SHOWING A NUMBER OF THE COLOR MORPHS THAT ARE AVAILABLE.*

COLOR MORPHS

The growing interest in color variants and the increased number available have led to a range of new words entering reptile-keeping terminology. The term "morph" is used to describe a new color or pattern of a type not normally encountered in any wild population of the species.

These changes occur because of alterations to the genes responsible for determining the animal's coloration. Since in many cases these changes would not benefit the species in the wild (because typically they make them more conspicuous), they do not spread rapidly through the population. They are therefore usually genetically recessive. This means that if you pair a color variant such as an albino Leopard Gecko with a normal-colored individual, all the offspring will appear to display normal coloring.

Yet the recessive albino gene has not disappeared entirely, for all the young will have one normal gene and one albino gene in their genetic makeup, or genotype, reflecting their parentage. Where breeders have carried out a pairing of this type they refer to the offspring as being "het" albinos, which is a shorthand way of saying they are heterozygous for the albino gene. The term "heterozygous" means that the genes are different, so the appearance, or "phenotype," of the Leopard Gecko in this case does not correspond to that of its genetic makeup, or "genotype."

This is important, because if you mate two "het" albinos, then on average one in four of the offspring should be albino themselves, because this color reemerges in the second generation. All genetic predictions are based on averages, however, so in some cases you may be lucky and have a higher percentage of albinos, while in other cases there may be none.

Beware though, because there is no way of distinguishing genuine "het" albinos from normal forms on the basis of their appearance, so you will have to trust the breeder. "Het" albinos are more expensive to purchase than "normals."

Apart from capitalizing on genetics, there is another way to influence the gecko's appearance—by selective breeding. Once a characteristic emerges, such as the tangerine morph, then breeders can use this as a basis to work on. By constantly choosing the individuals that have the best colors for breeding purposes, it can be possible to intensify the coloration. For example, early specimens of the tangerine morph were much paler than those being bred today.

There can also be variations among different bloodlines, which is why the original breeder's names are also sometimes added to the description of the color. Bell albinos, for instance, are characterized by the depth of coloration of their red eyes. In contrast, Rainwater (Las Vegas) albinos are often considered to have more pinkish suffusion on their bodies than either the Bell strain or the widely kept Tremper albinos.

HIBERNATION

Reptiles have developed a wide range of survival strategies according to the type of environment in which they occur. Species inhabiting temperate areas face a challenge over the winter months, because the environmental temperature is likely to drop too low for them to sustain an optimal level of activity. Difficulty in obtaining food is another trigger for hibernation. Once a reptile enters this physiological state, it becomes inactive, and its body temperature falls. The dramatically decreased level of activity means that the reptile's energy needs are also greatly reduced, and it can therefore survive without feeding in this state until warmer weather returns in the spring.

TORTOISES

Only certain species should be hibernated. Even then, it may not be essential or desirable in all cases, particularly with young or immature individuals. Animals that might hibernate in the wild will not die prematurely if they are kept awake over the winter in the vivarium. Only healthy individuals should be allowed to hibernate. You can assess whether a tortoise is in suitable condition to hibernate by weighing it and measuring its length in a straight line along the center of the carapace. These figures can be compared with the graph (below), which shows the optimal body condition for a tortoise of that size, below which it is dangerous to hibernate the reptile.

Only the Mediterranean Spur-thighed (*Testudo graeca*), Horsfield's *(Testudo horsfieldii)*, and Hermann's Tortoises *(Testudo hermanni)* should be hibernated. The temperature in their quarters should be allowed to fall back gradually first, which will allow any remaining food to pass through the digestive tract. Otherwise it would remain there over the winter and could decay, harming the gut tissue.

Never allow a tortoise to hibernate in straw or hay, which can harbor dangerous fungal spores; use shredded paper instead. Place the tortoise in a cardboard box with paper bedding around it, ensuring the sides of the box are tall enough so that the tortoise cannot climb out. If possible, fold the flaps in to create a dark environment, but make sure there is enough ventilation. Do not expect the tortoise to hibernate outdoors, where it could be attacked by foxes or rats. It needs to be kept secure, at a temperature of 39°F (4°C)—this figure is critical. Some breeders use specially adapted refrigerators for this purpose.

It is essential that the temperature does not go higher, because the reptile will then become active and utilize energy without feeding. It will also be at risk of dehydration. Nor do you want the temperature to fall much lower, or the animal could die of hypothermia. It is also important not to hibernate your tortoise for too long. A period from December through February should be sufficient. (See also page 55.)

OTHER SPECIES

For snakes from temperate areas, an annual fall-off in temperature is critical for encouraging breeding in the spring. In most cases, this will simply entail turning down the heating system in the vivarium rather than transferring the snakes to new accommodation. Make sure the reduction in temperature is carried out over several weeks and that it is increased again in a similar way in the spring, rather than suddenly going up or down. Do not provide the snake with food for two or three weeks before hibernation, which will be sufficient time to allow the gut to empty.

▶ *HIBERNATION GRAPH SHOWING THE IDEAL RELATIONSHIP BETWEEN CARAPACE (SHELL) LENGTH AND BODY WEIGHT OF A TORTOISE. OPTIMAL BODY CONDITION FOR HIBERNATION IS INDICATED (PINK EQUALS UPPER AND LOWER LIMITS; RED IS AVERAGE).*

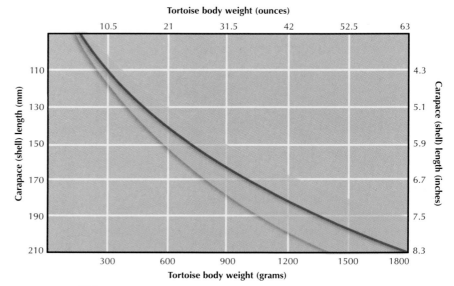

HEALTH CARE

Reptiles and amphibians rarely get ill, particularly once they are established in their quarters, provided that their environmental needs are adequately met. Problems are most likely to arise with newly acquired stock, simply because new arrivals will need time to adjust to an unfamiliar environment. When seeking to pair them up, therefore, do not immediately introduce the creatures together. Instead, keep the most recent acquistion separate for at least a couple of weeks, so you can be sure that it is eating well and is in apparently good health.

Particularly in the case of wild-caught reptiles, it is helpful to have their health status assessed by a veterinarian when you first acquire them. There are an increasing number of vets who have experience in working with this group of creatures, and it should not be too difficult to find one, especially if you live in an urban area.

PARASITES

One of the major problems that can afflict wild-caught reptiles is an overwhelming burden of internal parasites. These can have a very harmful effect on the reptile's overall state of health, resulting most demonstrably in a loss of appetite. This can then start a downward spiral—as the reptile loses weight and its condition deteriorates, it will be at greater risk of acquiring a potentially fatal bacterial or fungal infection.

Testing for such parasites requires a sample of droppings and is a relatively inexpensive procedure. There are now drugs available for deworming purposes that can be administered quite safely to reptiles and that are highly effective. After treatment the appetite of the reptile should improve markedly, as will its overall health.

External parasites are also a potential problem, but one that can usually be remedied more easily, since they tend to be conspicuous. This applies in particular to **ticks**, which swell up as they feed on the reptile's blood. The added danger with ticks, however, is that they are capable of transmitting blood infections if they have fed previously on a diseased animal.

Reptile ticks tend to be dark in color and they attach themselves to softer parts of the body where they can penetrate the skin most easily. In tortoises these parasites often congregate on the skin of the thigh area, but on snakes and lizards they are frequently present on the sides of the body. The tick anchors itself through the skin using its powerful mouthparts and swells in size as it starts to feed.

Although the initial temptation is to pull off the parasite, this action is not recommended because it is likely to detach the tick's body from its head, and the part left behind in the reptile's skin can create an infection. Although not an instant remedy, the safest way of removing the tick is to smother its body, especially its rear end, in petroleum jelly. This blocks its breathing pores, and it is forced to release its grip and drop off. There are devices for detaching ticks, often sold for dogs, but they may not always be reliable. Since the life cycle of a tick is complex and can involve more than one host species, it is fairly certain that these parasites will not breed in vivarium surroundings, so they are easy to eliminate.

Unfortunately, this is not the case with snake **mites**, which are tiny and barely visible to the naked eye. They tend to hide away, making it difficult to locate them. A secondhand vivarium should therefore always be treated for snake mites, just in case they are lurking—they are particularly good at concealing themselves in nooks and crannies and can remain alive for months, even in the absence of snakes. Eliminating them from the outset is much easier than having to do so later. Special sprays that can be used safely with reptiles are available and must be used strictly in accordance with the instructions. It will be necessary to treat both the snakes and their surroundings. Thorough cleaning of the vivarium is also vital when seeking to curb these parasites. They too will suck blood and can transmit other diseases, as well as causing irritation.

◀ *AGAMA LIZARD SUFFERING FROM BLOOD-FEEDING MITES* (HIRSTIELLA TROMBIIDIFORMES*).*

▶ *AN IGUANA RECEIVES TREATMENT AT A VETERINARY CLINIC THAT SPECIALIZES IN CARING FOR REPTILES.*

SIGNS OF ILLNESS

The most obvious signs of illness in reptiles are dullness and loss of appetite. Should these symptoms appear, check first that the surroundings are heated to a temperature suitable for the species concerned and that there is adequate full-spectrum lighting (which acts as an appetite stimulant) before deciding your pet is unwell.

In the case of colorful species, a darkening of the skin is another indication that all is not well. Dehydration can be the cause, so give a tortoise or lizard a shallow bath of warm water, to which a vitamin and mineral supplement has been added.

HIBERNATION CONCERNS

When a tortoise wakes up after a period of hibernation, its eyes may be slightly sticky and require bathing. Warm, shallow baths given daily are the way to correct the accompanying dehydration that is likely to arise during hibernation. In addition to this treatment offer pieces of tomato, over which a vitamin and mineral mix can be sprinkled. A healthy tortoise should then regain its appetite fully within two weeks of emerging from hibernation.

If it is still showing little or no interest in food by this stage, however, seek veterinary advice. The most likely cause is so-called "mouth rot," which will be manifested

by cheesy-looking areas on the tongue, combined with halitosis. Seek treatment immediately to reduce the risk of the infection spreading farther down the digestive tract, where it will be much harder to treat successfully. Snakes can also suffer from this problem.

DIETARY DEFICIENCIES

Nutritional problems used to be quite common. In the past young turtles, for example, were at risk from swollen eyes, reflecting a deficiency in vitamin A, and also soft shells, caused by an imbalance in the level of calcium in the diet or in the ratio of calcium to phosphorus, or a lack of vitamin D3. Thankfully, however, the introduction of well-balanced formulated foods has meant that such problems are rare today and are totally preventable.

There are times, however, when it may be necessary to increase the calcium level in the diet, particularly for lizards such as geckos prior to egg-laying. The body's demand for calcium is raised at this stage, because this mineral is a key component of the eggshell. A calcium deficiency (or a shortage of vitamin D3, which regulates calcium stores in the body) is likely to cause a condition in the female lizard known as **egg-binding**. Because the shells fail to form fully, she is unable to lay her eggs effectively, and they remain trapped in her body, creating an obstruction. Always be alert to the risk of this problem when a female is about to lay, particularly if she has already laid recently. She is likely to become unsteady on her hind feet and may even appear paralyzed. Seek veterinary advice without delay. An injection to induce egg-laying or, in extreme cases, surgery will be necessary to save her life.

▲ GREEN ANOLE (ANOLIS CAROLINENSIS) SHEDDING ITS SKIN. IF VIVARIUM CONDITIONS ARE TOO DRY, SHEDDING MAY BE INCOMPLETE.

directed by a vet. Several treatments are often needed over the course of several days. Handle the patient carefully. Cleaning of the main tank is also recommended to reduce the level of fungal organisms present.

AMPHIBIAN HEALTH CONCERNS

As in the case of reptiles, many amphibian health problems can be traced back to environmental problems. Rough handling is a major cause of so-called **red leg**. This occurs when bacteria invade the skin through a minor injury, creating an infection that usually causes reddening in the vicinity of the hind legs. Treatment can be difficult, although antibiotics may help. **Fungal disease** is also a potential problem. It can strike at the site of an injury, such as the foot of a newt that has been bitten by a companion in the tank. Such injuries can easily happen during feeding, which is why it is better to try to offer food to members of a pair separately, in different parts of the tank.

A fungal infection often has an area resembling a halo or piece of cotton batting surrounding it. The most effective treatment is an antifungal cream applied to the affected area while the amphibian is out of the water, as

SHEDDING DIFFICULTIES

Various members of the three main groups of animals covered in this book can occasionally encounter difficulty in shedding their skin. This often indicates that the vivarium surroundings are too dry. Raising the relative humidity may help, but problems with shedding are also not uncommon if the creature has recently been ill. Veterinary help will be needed. The risk with many geckos is that traces of old skin will compress around the base of their large toe pads, cutting off the blood flow and causing the loss of digits, making it difficult for the lizard to climb in the future.

Snakes normally shed quite cleanly, losing their color and appetite temporarily beforehand. However, there is a particular risk in snakes, namely that the skin over the eyes, known as the spectacles, may remain in place. This will have to be carefully removed by a vet. The situation is not as critical in newts, simply because if they lose a toe as the result of a shedding problem, it will probably regrow.

Shedding difficulties in tarantulas can be much more critical, resulting in the spider being unable to escape easily from its previous body casing. Transferring it to a very humid environment can solve the problem.

SKIN SWELLINGS

Occasionally, swellings of various types crop up on the surface of the body, and these may turn out to be **tumors**. These growths are particularly common in *Lacerta* lizards and are triggered by a viral infection; although unsightly, they do not grow very large but tend to form clusters on different parts of the body. In males they are common on the head, but they are most likely to be seen around the vents of female lizards because the males sniff this part of the female's body during courtship, transferring the infection. Treatment is rarely successful; although the tumors can be removed, they will usually regrow because the virus itself has not been eliminated from the lizard's body.

Tortoises may develop swellings on the sides of the neck. They may look like tumors but they are often simply local infections, called **abscesses**, which will have to be removed by surgery.

◀ A TORTOISE SUFFERING FROM AN ABSCESS ON THE NECK.

area without any significant blood loss. The discarded part of the tail often undergoes muscular contractions after it has been shed, as a way of distracting the would-be predator away from the rest of the lizard, which has scampered off. There is usually nothing to be concerned about if you acquire a so-called stub-tailed individual that is missing part of its tail. It will regrow to a limited extent over the course of a few months, but it is unlikely to attain its full length again.

BURNS

Sadly, burns are not uncommon in vivarium surroundings and they can have serious consequences for the animal concerned. Arboreal snakes that curl up next to the heat source are particularly at risk. A safety shield should be installed to prevent direct contact from the outset. Any burns must receive prompt veterinary care to minimize the severity of the injury. Similarly, heaterstats in aquatic vivaria should always be fitted with a specially designed protective cover to keep the occupants away from direct contact with the heat source.

TAIL LOSS

The ability to lose its tail is a normal defensive reaction in many lizards. The lizard's body is equipped to shed this

DIGESTIVE PROBLEMS

A range of potentially harmful microbes can be present in a herptile's gut. Seek veterinary advice if a pet's droppings alter significantly in appearance, particularly if the animal appears off-color and lethargic. Tests can then be carried out to establish the precise cause, ensuring the most appropriate treatment can be given. Always protect yourself from the slight risk of acquiring a zoonotic infection such as salmonellosis by using disposable gloves to clean out the vivarium and by disposing of soiled bedding carefully, since not all reptiles may display symptoms of infection. Use a vivarium disinfectant regularly, too, and always wash your hands thoroughly after attending to a pet's needs.

◀ GOLD-DUST DAY GECKO (PHELSUMA LATICAUDA) WITH BROKEN TAIL. THE WOUND WILL HEAL BUT WILL LEAVE A DEFORMED STUMP.

REPTILES

▲ *GREEN TREE PYTHON (MORELIA VIRIDIS)*

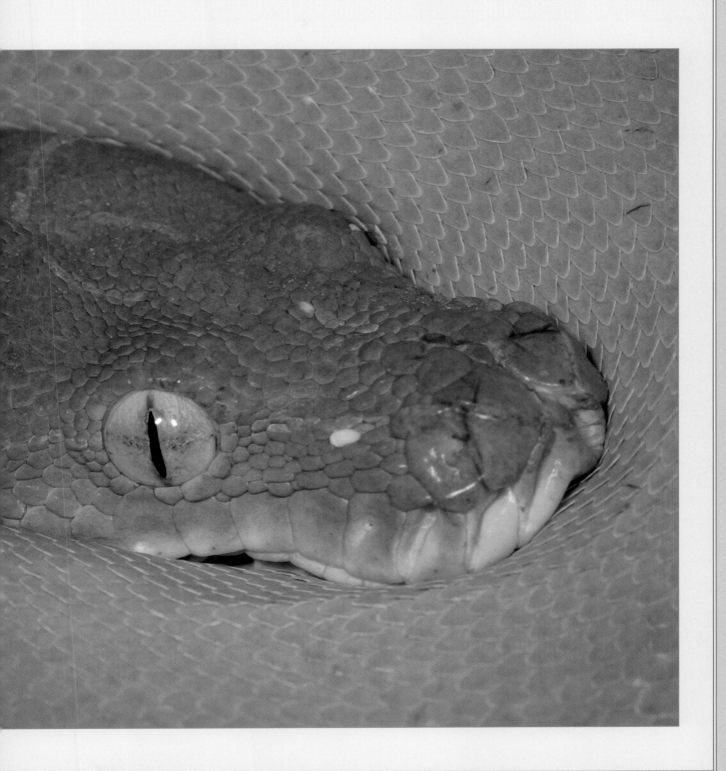

SNAKES
ORDER SQUAMATA (part)

▲ *RARE COLOR FORM OF RETICULATED PYTHON (PYTHON RETICULATUS).*

Snakes are classified within the reptilian order Squamata, along with lizards. There are about 2,900 different species recognized worldwide, although there are no snakes present on various islands, including New Zealand. By far the largest family is the Colubridae, which consists of about 1,800 species—the rest are divided among a further 17 families.

Snakes first evolved about 100 million years ago, long after the chelonians and crocodilians. The most primitive members of the group are relatively small in size. Theirs is a rather wormlike existence, concealing themselves below ground. In spite of the absence of limbs, however, most snakes have become adept at moving on the surface of the soil. A number of species can climb well and they are able to swim, too, as seen in sea snakes.

Perhaps surprisingly, the lack of limbs is not a distinguishing feature of snakes—among their closest relatives, there are lizards such as the Slow Worm (*Anguis fragilis*) and worm lizards (amphisbaenians) that also have this characteristic. Snakes do, however, lack eyelids and, unlike lizards, cannot blink. The arrangement of their jaws is also distinctive, being sufficiently flexible to allow them to catch and swallow large prey. All snakes are predatory in their feeding habits, with more specialized members of the group hunting prey such as invertebrates or fish.

Certain species of snakes, such as rattlesnakes (*Crotalus* species), possess venom. This is frequently used to overpower prey but can also be used in a defensive way, causing serious or even fatal injuries to humans. Venomous snakes make up only a tiny percentage of the world's species, however, and their highly specialized requirements place them outside the scope of this book.

BOAS AND PYTHONS
Family Boidae (subfamilies Boinae, Pythoninae)

This family includes the largest snakes in the world, such as the Green Anaconda *(Eunectes murinus)* and the Reticulated Python *(Python reticulatus)*. Whereas pythons (Pythoninae) are absent from the Americas, boas (Boinae) are found in both the Old and the New Worlds. There is a fundamental distinction in the breeding habits of these two groups of snakes—while boas produce live young, pythons lay eggs, and python females display a remarkable degree of parental care. They incubate the eggs themselves, coiling their bodies around the clutch. Here they remain, regularly twitching their bodies. These muscular contractions are thought to generate heat, which helps warm the eggs. Only after hatching will a female python seek to feed again, taking no further interest in her young once they have hatched.

Both boas and pythons are popular vivarium subjects, although their large size means they are less suitable as pets—especially for novices or young owners—than some of the smaller species of snakes that can be handled more easily. There is an ever-increasing range of color morphs of both boas and pythons available, some of which currently fetch very high prices. These new colors and patterns have led to increasing interest in this group of snakes over recent years.

MADAGASCAR GROUND BOA

Boa (Acrantophis) madagascariensis   Family Boidae (Boinae)

These particular boas have an iridescent cast over them. There is an indistinct dark streak running down the center of the back, with prominent dark oval blotches on the upper sides of the body, and duller brownish markings below.

DISTRIBUTION: *Southern Madagascar.*

SIZE: *Up to 15 ft (4.5 m), but usually much smaller.*

ACCOMMODATION: *As with other members of this group of snakes, it is important to provide a box in its quarters where the snake can hide away. A typical temperature range of between 77°F (25°C) and 86°F (30°C) will be suitable for them.*

BEHAVIOR: *Found in more arid, less wooded surroundings than Dumeril's Boa (Boa dumerili) and is essentially terrestrial.*

DIET: *Generally prefers rodents to birds.*

▼ MADAGASCAR GROUND BOA (BOA MADAGASCARIENSIS)

BREEDING: *Cooling in winter stimulates breeding behavior. Up to six young boas are born about 250 days following mating. They are likely to be at least 22 in (56 cm) long at birth.*

BOA CONSTRICTOR

Boa constrictor   Family Boidae (Boinae)

The appearance of these popular constrictors is highly variable, the most distinctive being the red-tailed form found in the Guianas. Boas from more southerly areas of the species' range are relatively dark in color.

DISTRIBUTION: *Ranges widely through South America. Also found in Central America and on various Caribbean islands.*

SIZE: *Typically 8–13 ft (2.4–4 m).*

ACCOMMODATION: *Arboreal by nature, these snakes need a vivarium that allows them to climb easily on branches. They must also have a water bowl in which they can immerse themselves. A temperature up to 86°F (30°C) is required, especially for young Boa Constrictors. Cooling adults to about 72°F (22°C) for a month or more encourages breeding.*

BEHAVIOR: *Males boas will use the cloacal spurs to rub the female as part of their courtship, prior to mating.*

DIET: *Prefers mammalian prey but will also take chicks.*

BREEDING: *Females give birth to anywhere from eight to 40 live young, about 35 weeks after mating. Newly born boas typically measure up to 20 in (51 cm) and can be reared on pinkies at first.*

▼ BOA CONSTRICTOR (BOA CONSTRICTOR) VARIATIONS: 1 BELIZE; 2 HOG ISLAND; 3 HONDURAS; 4 MEXICO.

DUMERIL'S BOA

Boa dumerili   Family Boidae (Boinae)

These boas are a pale brown and beige color overall, with darker brown blotches that may have a reddish hue associated with them. The patterning is such that blotches often predominate on the sides of the body, forming bars across the back. The head tends to be more of a grayish shade, with streaking evident here. Dumeril's Boas are not as commonly kept as some other boas by hobbyists, but they are now being bred in greater numbers.

DISTRIBUTION: *Northern part of the island of Madagascar, often in forested areas.*

SIZE: *Up to 11 ft (3.4 m), but usually smaller.*

ACCOMMODATION: *Temperature up to 86°F (30°C), dropping back over the winter to about 77°F (25°C). The vivarium door should be fitted with a lock, as for all snakes, since these reptiles can be adept at escaping from their quarters.*

BEHAVIOR: *Tends to spend much of its time on the ground.*

DIET: *Rodents and chicks.*

BREEDING: *Cooling triggers mating, with the young being born up to 10 months later. About eight youngsters can be expected, averaging about 17 in (43 cm) in length.*

SOLOMON ISLAND BOA
(PACIFIC BOA; VIPER BOA)

Candoia carinata   Family Boidae (Boinae)

The most distinctive feature of these boas is the presence of a wavy line running down the back, resembling that of a viper, although these boas are not venomous. Their body coloration is very variable, ranging from cream through gray to brick red.

DISTRIBUTION: *Various islands through the Pacific, including New Guinea, the Solomons and New Hebrides.*

SIZE: *About 4 ft (1.2 m).*

ACCOMMODATION: *Include securely placed branches, which allow this snake to climb and rest off the ground; they should be heavy enough to support its weight.*

BEHAVIOR: *Hunts lizards and frogs as well as small mammals in the wild.*

DIET: *Mice are favored.*

BREEDING: *Litter sizes can be large—up to 64 individuals—but stillbirths are common too, especially in big litters. Pinkies can be used for rearing purposes.*

▲ EMERALD TREE BOA (CORALLUS CANINUS)

EMERALD TREE BOA

Corallus caninus   Family Boidae (Boinae)

These very attractive boas have green upper parts, with variable white streaking running down the midline of the back, which creates a highly individual patterning. They are surprisingly similar in appearance to the Green Tree Python *(Morelia viridis)*, which is found in Asia.

DISTRIBUTION: *Amazon Basin in northern South America, extending from the Guianas to Brazil, Bolivia and Peru.*

SIZE: *Up to 8 ft (2.4 m).*

ACCOMMODATION: *This boa needs an arboreal setup, including a securely held branch for climbing. The environment needs to be warm, with a basking area where the temperature is up to 80°F (27°C). Make sure the heat source is adequately screened so the snake cannot burn itself.*

BEHAVIOR: *Spends all the time off the ground, even drinking there by catching rainwater in its coiled body as it rests curled around a branch. Offer tepid water in a similar way.*

DIET: *Usually prefers rodents, but will take chicks.*

BREEDING: *Raising the relative humidity level by spraying often encourages mating. Gestation lasts six to seven months. The young are red, orange or brown in color, although they still display white markings on the body.*

RAINBOW BOA

Epicrates cenchria   Family Boidae (Boinae)

The Rainbow Boa is another species that varies widely in appearance through its range, with as many as 10 distinctive subspecies recognized. Its background color can vary from a pale yellowish brown to a coppery bronze shade, with black markings. There is an iridescent hue apparent over the body, and the scales appear smooth. The Brazilian race *(E. c. cenchria)* tends to be the most sought after in the hobby.

DISTRIBUTION: *Extends from Costa Rica down to northeastern Argentina and Paraguay.*

SIZE: *Up to 6 ft (1.8 m).*

ACCOMMODATION: *These boas will climb, and this should be reflected in their housing, with well-supported branches provided. They must also be able to bathe in a suitable container of water.*

▲ *RAINBOW BOA (EPICRATES CENCHRIA)*

▲ *KENYAN SAND BOA (GONGYLOPHIS COLUBRINUS LOVERIDGEI)*

BEHAVIOR: *It is not uncommon for young females particularly to have stillborn young, so avoid any unnecessary stress or handling.*

DIET: *Rodents preferred to birds.*

BREEDING: *Cooling from the typical vivarium temperature down to around 68°F (20°C) for a month or so has proved to trigger mating. The young, which are relatively large and can number more than 20, will be born just over six months later.*

KENYAN SAND BOA

Gongylophis colubrinus   Family Boidae

Kenyan Sand Boas are variable in coloration, but they tend to be yellowish with darker markings. Several races are recognized. Sand boas have an overall cylindrical shape and a short tail.

SYNONYM: *Eryx colubrinus.*

DISTRIBUTION: *Ranges through northern and eastern parts of Africa. Also present in the Arabian Peninsula.*

SIZE: *Up to 26 in (65 cm).*

ACCOMMODATION: *A thick layer of sandy substrate, about 8 in (20 cm) deep, is useful for this species, which will often burrow out of sight. Check that the water bowl is securely supported, however, so it cannot collapse onto the snake as it burrows. Provide water, but the vivarium should not have a high humidity. The temperature reading at ground level should be up to 86°F (30°C) during the day, with a thermal gradient across the vivarium; the temperature should be allowed to drop back at night.*

BEHAVIOR: *These snakes are naturally adept at ambushing prey from beneath the sand and will readily emerge when fed in vivarium surroundings.*

DIET: *Usually favors rodents.*

BREEDING: *Winter cooling to 68°F (20°C) for several weeks triggers mating. Up to 17 young, averaging 6 in (15 cm) in length, born between four and six months later.*

INDIAN SAND BOA
(JOHN'S SAND BOA)

Eryx johnii   Family Boidae (Boinae)

Like various other sand boas, these snakes tend to be a yellowish brown shade which helps them blend in with their background when they are not buried beneath the surface. This particular species is distinguished by its very short tail.

DISTRIBUTION: *Southern central Asia, extending from Iran eastward to western Bengal in India.*

SIZE: *Up to 39 in (99 cm).*

ACCOMMODATION: *Since these snakes do not climb, they do not require tall vivaria, but as with all members of this genus, they must be able to burrow into the substrate.*

BEHAVIOR: *Indian Sand Boas can be active at any stage during the day or night and soon learn to emerge when offered food.*

DIET: *Rodents preferred.*

BREEDING: *Can be housed in pairs. Mating is likely to be triggered by a falloff in vivarium temperature. The young should be mature by about two years of age.*

RUSSIAN SAND BOA
(DESERT SAND BOA)

Eryx miliaris   Family Boidae (Boinae)

Dark brownish banding extending over the top of the body, with blotches on the sides, help identify this species. The background

▲ INDIAN SAND BOA (ERYX JOHNII)

color is often grayish. The eyes are small, reflecting the snake's subterranean habitat.

DISTRIBUTION: *Ranges from central Asia east to Mongolia.*

SIZE: *12–18 in (30–45 cm).*

ACCOMMODATION: *A setup as recommended for the Kenyan Sand Boa (Gongylophis colubrinus) is required. The temperature should be lowered at night, reflecting what happens naturally in the snake's desert environment.*

BEHAVIOR: *Its cylindrical shape helps it burrow effectively.*

DIET: *Rodents, although will eat chicks.*

BREEDING: *Similar to the Kenyan Sand Boa, although these Asiatic sand boas are less commonly available. Young are born during the northern summer months.*

TARTAR SAND BOA

Eryx tataricus   Family Boidae (Boinae)

Three distinctive subspecies of this particular sand boa are recognized, and their coloration varies accordingly. Their patterns can be more conspicuous than those of related species and consist generally of a series of black markings on a dull brownish background.

DISTRIBUTION: *Extends from the eastern side of the Caspian Sea to western China.*

SIZE: *24–42 in (80–110 cm).*

ACCOMMODATION: *The needs of this sand boa are the same as that of the Kenyan Sand Boa* (Gongylophis colubrinus) *and other related species.*

BEHAVIOR: *Overall these sand boas tend to be most active around dusk, when they hunt not only rodents and birds but also lizards in the wild.*

DIET: *Rodents of suitable size preferred.*

BREEDING: *Similar requirements to those of related species.*

ROSY BOA

Charina (Lichanura) trivirgata   Family Boidae (Boinae)

A relatively small species, the Rosy Boa is attractively patterned, although its coloration is variable, depending partly on the subspecies. There are typically three dark bands running along the length of the body, separated by pale stripes that can vary from tan to a rosy red shade.

DISTRIBUTION: *Southwestern North America, in southern California and southwestern Arizona, ranging south into Mexico.*

SIZE: *Up to 40 in (100 cm).*

ACCOMMODATION: *A leaf-litter substrate is often appreciated by these snakes. Heating should be to at least 77° F (25° C) but can drop back slightly over the winter period. Provide a branch for climbing.*

BEHAVIOR: *Rosy boas are nocturnal and mainly terrestrial by nature. This snake may curl into a tight ball, keeping its head hidden, when it senses it is about to be handled.*

DIET: *Will feed on both rodents and chicks.*

BREEDING: *Between six and 10 young are born after a period of 18 weeks following mating. They measure about 12 in (30 cm) long at this stage.*

MADAGASCAR TREE BOA

Boa mandrita   Family Boidae (Boinae)

This species is slightly variable in appearance. The variations reflect geographical differences, with those from northern areas of the island being yellowish rather than green. Darker patterning is evident on this background coloration.

SYNONYM: *Sanzinia madagascariensis.*

DISTRIBUTION: *Rain forest areas in Madagascar, off Africa's southeastern coast.*

SIZE: *Up to 8 ft (2.4 m).*

ACCOMMODATION: *Requires a vivarium that allows it to climb easily, resting on branches. The vivarium should be kept relatively humid and warm, mimicking a rain forest environment.*

BEHAVIOR: *These snakes may hunt both on the ground and among branches. They often seem to develop fixed food preferences.*

DIET: *Generally favor avian prey over rodents.*

BREEDING: *Litters average about eight young, but they may have to be force-fed if they refuse food after shedding for the first time. Young mice are usually provided as a first food.*

◀ *TARTAR SAND BOA* (ERYX TATARICUS)

CHILDREN'S PYTHON

Antaresia childreni   Family Boidae (Pythoninae)

These pythons have distinctive purplish brown markings present along the back. Their body color is brown, becoming lighter on the flanks.

SYNONYM: *Liasis childreni.*

DISTRIBUTION: *Throughout northern Australia.*

SIZE: *2–5 ft (0.6–1.5 m); occasionally up to 6 ft (1.8 m).*

ACCOMMODATION: *Children's Pythons can climb, so their vivarium should be designed accordingly. It also needs to be kept warm, from 77–86°F (25–30°C). There is no need to spray their quarters, but a water bowl must be provided.*

BEHAVIOR: *In common with other pythons, females brood the eggs by curling around them. Hatching takes about two months.*

DIET: *Prefer rodents, but will eat birds.*

BREEDING: *Drop the vivarium temperature to as low as 59°F (15°C) to trigger breeding. The clutch, consisting of about 10 eggs, can be anticipated about five months later.*

CALABAR PYTHON

Charina (Calabaria) reinhardtii   Family Boidae (Pythoninae)

The rounded, conical head shape of this python reveals that it is a burrowing species. Its overall coloration is brownish black, with irregular lighter speckling over the body.

DISTRIBUTION: *Tropical areas of western and central parts of Africa.*

SIZE: *Up to 3.5 ft (1.1 m).*

ACCOMMODATION: *A vivarium for Calabar Pythons should have a relatively deep forest-type substrate into which they can burrow, with a covering of leaf litter. The surroundings need to be relatively humid and warm— between 77 and 86°F (25 and 30°C).*

BEHAVIOR: *If threatened, this snake will keep its tail raised, while hiding its head among the coils of its body to try to protect itself.*

DIET: *Rodents, particularly mice.*

BREEDING: *Calabar Pythons are not especially prolific. Females will lay two to four eggs in April/May, which they may incubate, although the eggs can be incubated artificially if necessary. The young should hatch after about six or seven weeks. Successful breeding and hatching are rare.*

◄ ROSY BOA (CHARINA TRIVIRGATA), VARIATIONS: *1 WHITEWATER; 2 MEXICAN; 3 SAN FELIPE; 4 SASLOWI.*

WHITE-LIPPED PYTHON
(D'ALBERTI'S PYTHON)

Leiopython albertisii   Family Boidae (Pythoninae)

As its name suggests, this species has a prominent white or creamy area around the mouth, extending down to the throat. Its body coloration varies among individuals, from an attractive reddish brown through to a grayish shade. The head is often darker, and the body is iridescent. Gray individuals tend to be more common in southern parts of its range.

DISTRIBUTION: *Occurs on New Guinea and adjacent smaller islands in the Torres Strait. Also present in Australia.*

SIZE: *Up to 10 ft (3 m).*

ACCOMMODATION: *The vivarium should have a relatively deep substrate with a covering of leaf litter and be tall enough to allow the pythons to climb around. The temperature should be kept at about 86°F (30°C).*

BEHAVIOR: *Rather aggressive by nature. Hunt a wide variety of prey, including lizards in the wild.*

DIET: *Can be fed both rodents and birds.*

BREEDING: *Mating is followed by egg-laying about two months later, with a typical clutch comprising about a dozen eggs. The young should hatch after a similar interval and measure about 12 in (30 cm) at this stage.*

CARPET PYTHON
(DIAMOND PYTHON)

Morelia spilota (spilotes)   Family Boidae (Pythoninae)

Carpet Pythons are very variable in color. Their underlying color is brownish, broken by black markings. The southern Australian population *(Morelia spilota spilota)* has distinctive diamond-

▼ WHITE-LIPPED PYTHON (LEIOPYTHON ALBERTISII)

shaped patterning on the upper side of its body, which is olive black in color.

SYNONYM: *Python spilotes.*

DISTRIBUTION: *Present in New Guinea and through much of Australia, except for the extreme west and the southeastern corner.*

SIZE: *Up to 13 ft (4 m), but more typically may reach only half this length.*

ACCOMMODATION: *A vivarium providing facilities for climbing is necessary, along with a suitable box where the snake can hide. A typical temperature between 77 and 86°F (25 and 30°C) will be suitable, falling back slightly for several weeks to encourage mating.*

BEHAVIOR: *A highly adaptable species, the Carpet Python can be found in terrain ranging from rain forest to desert areas. Tends to become active at dusk.*

DIET: *Rodents.*

BREEDING: *Clutches are often large, numbering over 50 eggs on occasion, although a clutch of about 20 is more common. The female will incubate them for 10 weeks or so, after which time the young pythons emerge. They are relatively large, measuring 16 in (41 cm) or more.*

GREEN TREE PYTHON

Morelia viridis   Family Boidae (Pythoninae)

One of the most beautifully colored of all pythons, this snake is most likely to be confused with the Emerald Tree Boa *(Corallus caninus)*. Adults are green with a white or yellow broken stripe running down the back. Very occasionally, sky blue individuals with no yellow pigment crop up. Young vary in color from yellow to reddish brown.

DISTRIBUTION: *The Aru Islands and New Guinea, east to the Solomon Islands and south to Australia's Cape York Peninsula.*

SIZE: *Up to 6 ft (1.8 m).*

ACCOMMODATION: *Arboreal by nature, so housing has to be planned accordingly, with branches and plants for cover. In terms of temperature and relative humidity a typical rain forest environment is needed.*

BEHAVIOR: *Green Tree Pythons have a relatively large head and particularly fearsome front teeth. This helps them grab birds more effectively.*

DIET: *Birds and rodents.*

BREEDING: *Clutch size can be up to 25, with incubation lasting about eight weeks at a temperature of 86°F (30°C). The young obtain adult coloring once they are about a year old.*

▶ FORMS OF GREEN TREE PYTHON (MORELIA VIRIDIS): *1 YOUNG REDDISH; 2 YOUNG YELLOW; 3 ADULT GREEN; 4 ADULT KAFIAU ISLAND YELLOW; 5 ADULT PARTLY RETAINING YELLOW COLORATION.*

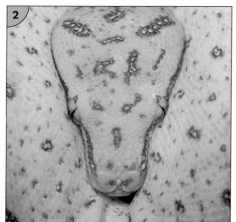

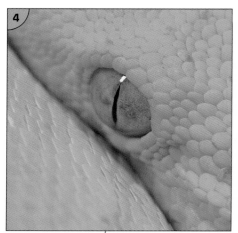

BLOOD PYTHON

Python curtus   Family Boidae (Pythoninae)

Highly variable blotched patterning is characteristic of this species, but it is their underlying pinkish red coloration that explains their common name. Individuals with the brightest coloration reputedly originate from Sumatra.

DISTRIBUTION: *Found in Malaysia and on the islands of Sumatra and Borneo.*

SIZE: *Up to 9 ft (2.7 m).*

ACCOMMODATION: *This is not an easy species to maintain successfully. High humidity in its quarters is essential, as well as adequate bathing facilities, since blood pythons are invariably found close to water. They also need to be kept at a temperature between 86 and 90°F (30 and 32°C).*

◄ *MALAYSIAN BLOOD PYTHON (PYTHON CURTUS BRONGERSMAI)—TWO VARIANTS.*

BEHAVIOR: *These snakes are nocturnal hunters and should be fed at night.*

DIET: *Rodents. Individuals that are reluctant to eat can have their appetite rekindled by allowing them to bathe.*

BREEDING: *Clutches of 10 to 15 eggs are laid, but females often refuse to brood them. They need to be incubated at 90°F (32°C), and the young usually hatch within about three months.*

BURMESE PYTHON

Python molurus   Family Boidae (Pythoninae)

It is the dark-phase Burmese Python (*Python molurus bivittatus*) that is commonly kept, while the lighter colored nominate race from India and Sri Lanka is rare. Dark brown blotches with black borders, broken by cream coloration and signs of a spearlike marking on the head, typify these snakes. Color morphs now exist as well.

DISTRIBUTION: *Extends across Indochina through the Malay Peninsula and to southern China.*

SIZE: *Females can reach up to 16.5 ft (5 m), but males are smaller.*

ACCOMMODATION: *The large size that these snakes attain makes the housing of adults expensive, and the space required needs to be considered carefully, particularly since the young grow fast. Accommodation for these pythons must also include climbing and bathing opportunities.*

▼ BURMESE PYTHON (PYTHON MOLURUS). LEFT: YELLOW FORM WITH NORMAL FORM BEHIND; RIGHT: ALBINO FORM.

▲ BALL PYTHON (PYTHON REGIUS): 1 NORMAL;
2 HIGH CONTRAST; 3 PASTEL.

BEHAVIOR: *Captive-bred snakes will normally reach maturity in just three years, by which time the physical differences between the sexes will be apparent.*

DIET: *Should receive a varied diet of birds and rodents.*

BREEDING: *Mating takes place in the winter, when the temperature in their quarters is lowered slightly. Clutches may consist of as many as 55 eggs, which females usually incubate reliably. Hatching generally occurs within 11 weeks.*

BALL PYTHON
(ROYAL PYTHON)

Python regius   Family Boidae (Pythoninae)

The popularity of these pythons has grown dramatically over recent years thanks to the emergence of numerous color morphs in domestic strains. Their natural patterning is a deep brownish shade. Tan blotching, usually with lighter edging, is apparent on the body.

DISTRIBUTION: *Western and central parts of Africa.*

SIZE: *Typically up to 4 ft (1.2 m).*

ACCOMMODATION: *Their smaller size makes these pythons more manageable than some species. The vivarium should incorporate climbing and bathing facilities as well as hiding places. Ball Pythons are nocturnal snakes.*

BEHAVIOR: *They are known as Ball Pythons because of the way that young snakes in particular will curl up into a ball if they feel threatened.*

DIET: *Rodents. Tempt reluctant feeders to eat with dead gerbils. Odor transference may help wean them onto mice—wipe the body of a mouse with that of a gerbil before offering it to the snake. This problem is less common today, however, now that most Ball Pythons are captive-bred.*

BREEDING: *About six eggs are laid. The hatching period is variable but generally lasts up to three months.*

RETICULATED PYTHON

Python reticulatus   Family Boidae (Pythoninae)

Not only is this the largest of all pythons and one of the biggest snakes in the world, it also has a rather aggressive temperament, making it hard to handle as well as to accommodate. It is recognizable by its yellowish body color and black markings, which are combined with a relatively thin body shape.

DISTRIBUTION: *Tropical areas of Indochina, eastward to the Philippines and south through Indonesia.*

SIZE: *Can reach 32 ft (10 m), but averages 16–20 ft (5–6 m).*

ACCOMMODATION: *A large enclosure is required, with the opportunity for the snake to submerge itself in a heated pool. Branches for climbing must be fixed securely.*

▲ ▶ *RETICULATED PYTHON (PYTHON RETICULATUS). ABOVE: T+ ALBINO;*
RIGHT: VERY RARE ALL-WHITE INDIVIDUAL.

BEHAVIOR: *Handle young regularly so they should remain tractable as they grow larger. Always take care, however, since they can be dangerous.*

DIET: *Rodents and birds. Large pythons may eat whole chickens and rabbits.*

BREEDING: *Typically 30 to 50 eggs may be laid, about four to five months after mating. Hatching takes about eight weeks, with the young pythons already being about 30 in (76 cm) at this stage.*

AFRICAN ROCK PYTHON

Python sebae   Family Boidae (Pythoninae)

The African Rock Python is similar to the Burmese Python *(Python molurus)* but lacks the arrowhead marking on the head. Dark blotches are evident on the body, and the underside is paler. This is one of the less popular larger snakes.

DISTRIBUTION: *Occurs widely across Africa, south of the Sahara.*

SIZE: *Can reach 20 ft (6 m).*

ACCOMMODATION: *A suitably spacious enclosure with a rocky area in which the snakes can hide is essential for these large pythons. A water container must also be provided. The temperature in the enclosure should be in the range of 77–86°F (25–30°C), and a basking spot is needed.*

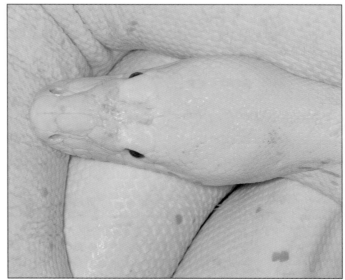

BEHAVIOR: *Tends to be more aggressive than its Asian relative, but hatchlings that are handled regularly may be better tempered as adults.*

DIET: *Rodents and poultry.*

BREEDING: *Clutch size may consist of up to 60 eggs, with hatching occurring after about 15 weeks. Hatchlings are rarely less than 18 in (45 cm) in length.*

COLUBRID SNAKES
Family Colubridae

The family Colubridae is not just by far the largest group of snakes, it is also the most diverse and has a worldwide distribution. Colubrid snakes range from small species that are no more than 8 inches (20 cm) in length up to the largest members of the family, which can reach 13 feet (4 m) long. Members of the group display a wide range of lifestyles—some are aquatic, while others may burrow underground. Although the majority are not venomous, there are a few, such as the Mangrove Snake (*Boiga dendrophila*), which can inflict a bite of this type and whose ownership is subject to legal control in a number of countries as a result.

TRANS-PECOS RATSNAKE

Bogertophis subocularis   Family Colubridae

Striking yellowish tan or cream coloring helps distinguish this species, with the so-called blond form being the palest. There are a series of darker H-shaped markings on the body, although the head is free from markings.

SYNONYM: *Elaphe subocularis.*

DISTRIBUTION: *Big Bend and Trans-Pecos area of Texas and southern New Mexico, extending southward into northern central parts of Mexico.*

SIZE: *Up to 6.5 ft (2 m).*

ACCOMMODATION: *An arid setup is needed, mimicking the area of the Chihuahuan Desert where this species occurs. Keep warm during the summer—up to 86°F (30°C)—but cool down the enclosure to as low as 59°F (15°C) in winter.*

BEHAVIOR: *The large eyes of this snake are indicative of its crepuscular lifestyle—it is most active at dusk, often hiding away underground during the day.*

DIET: *Mice.*

BREEDING: *Up to nine eggs may be laid about seven weeks after mating. Hatching may take up to four months, with the young being able to take pinkies as a first food. The young measure about 11–13 in (28–33 cm) and their markings are lighter versions of the adult coloration.*

▲ *CHARCOAL CORN SNAKE (ELAPHE GUTTATA)—MORE VARIATIONS OVERLEAF.*

▲ *MOTLEY ALBINO CORN SNAKE (ELAPHE GUTTATA)—MORE VARIATIONS OVERLEAF.*

CORN SNAKE

Elaphe guttata   Family Colubridae

Highly recommended for beginners, the Corn Snake is now bred in about 1,000 or more different color forms. It also has a natural variance in appearance through its range, with the blotched patterning of the nominate race being much more colorful than the brownish gray Great Plains form (*Elaphe guttata emoryi*).

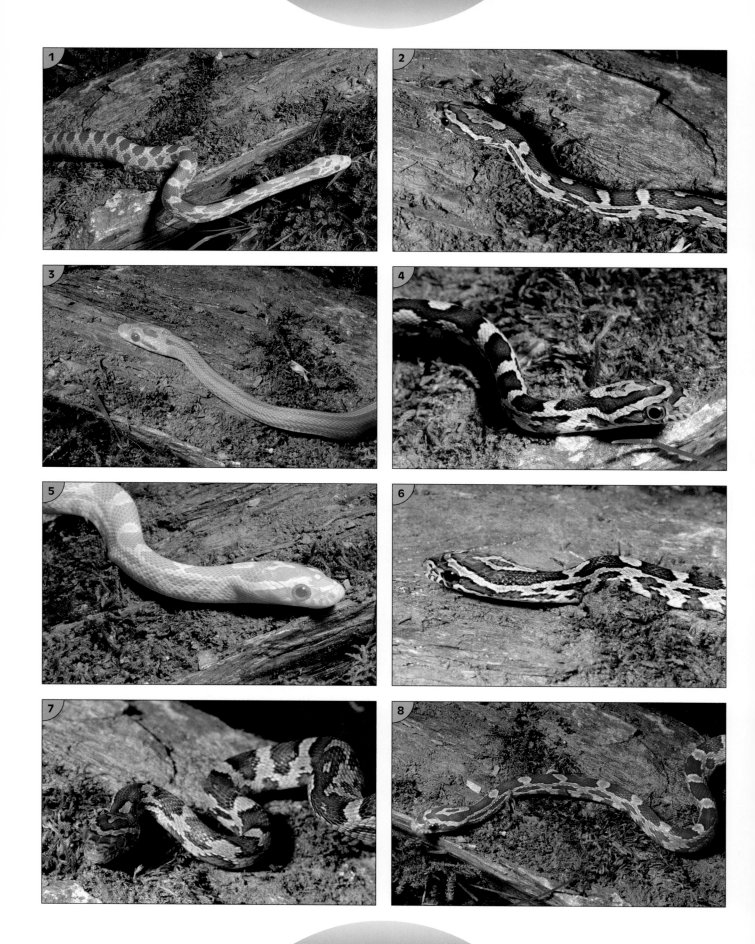

DISTRIBUTION: *Southeastern United States, from southern New Jersey to Florida and through the Gulf Coast area into Mexico. Some western populations, in eastern Utah, for example, are isolated.*

SIZE: *Up to 6 ft (1.8 m) but normally shorter.*

ACCOMMODATION: *Vivarium design should incorporate the opportunity for climbing and a retreat in which the snake can hide. Allow the temperature to reach up to 86°F (30°C), dropping back at night. A winter cooling period is also recommended.*

BEHAVIOR: *Emerges at dusk to hunt, often in the vicinity of buildings; may prey on bats.*

DIET: *Rodents.*

BREEDING: *Mates in early spring. Clutches consist of as many as 20 eggs, hatching after a period of about eight weeks. The young snakes will measure 10 in (25 cm) or more at this stage and may be mature within 18 months.*

AMERICAN RATSNAKE

Elaphe obsoleta   Family Colubridae

Five races of this particular ratsnake are recognized. The most distinctive is possibly the Yellow Ratsnake (*Elaphe obsoleta quadrivittata*), whose yellowish color is broken by four dark lines running the length of the body. The Texas Ratsnake (*E. o. lindheimeri*) is black with yellowish markings. Darker variants include the Gray Ratsnake (*E.o. spiloides*) and the Florida Ratsnake (*E. o. rossalleni*).

DISTRIBUTION: *Ranges widely over eastern North America from Ontario, southwestern Minnesota, and southern Michigan to Florida and western Texas, and south into Mexico.*

SIZE: *Varies from approximately 3–8 ft (0.9–2.4 m).*

ACCOMMODATION: *Similar to the Corn Snake (Elaphe guttata).*

BEHAVIOR: *In northern areas,these ratsnakes may retreat into underground burrows with rattlesnakes during the winter months, which may afford them some protection from predators.*

DIET: *Rodents.*

BREEDING: *Mating occurs either in fall or spring. As many as 30 eggs may be laid, and they are often concealed in leaf litter. Hatching will take at least two months.*

◀ *CORN SNAKE (ELAPHE GUTTATA), COLOR VARIATIONS: 1 BLOOD RED ALBINO; 2 AZTEC; 3 STRIPED ALBINO; 4 CARAMEL; 5 SNOW; 6 BLACK AND WHITE; 7 OKATEE; 8 HYPOMELANISTIC.*

▶ *AMERICAN RATSNAKE (ELAPHE OBSOLETA ROSSALLENI)*

EUROPEAN RATSNAKE
(FOUR-LINED RATSNAKE)

Elaphe quatuorlineata   Family Colubridae

Only the nominate western race possesses the characteristic longitudinal stripes running down the body. The eastern race (*Elaphe quatuorlineata sauromates*) has a blotched appearance. The European Ratsnake is one of the largest of all ratsnakes.

DISTRIBUTION: *Southeastern parts of Europe, northward to the southwest region of the former USSR and southward to Italy, including Sicily.*

SIZE: *6 ft (1.8 m).*

ACCOMMODATION: *Relatively cool surroundings are required by this species. Up to 77°F (25°C) should be adequate in summer, falling back as low as 50°F (10°C) in winter.*

BEHAVIOR: *A winter cooling period is essential, mimicking temperature changes in the wild that lead to mating in the spring.*

DIET: *Mice.*

BREEDING: *Clutches can be small, consisting of just six eggs. They can hatch in about a month, at which stage they measure about 12 in (30 cm). Young of both races are similar, being spotted in appearance at first.*

CHINESE BEAUTY RATSNAKE

Elaphe taeniura   Family Colubridae

Ratsnakes have a wide distribution, but those from Asia are less commonly kept and bred than those from the New World. Chinese Beauty Ratsnakes are characterized by a relatively elongated, triangular-shaped head. The underlying background color is yellowish brown, with a range of blackish blotches, some of which may have paler centers, on the body. These fade toward the tail, where they are replaced by a prominent stripe down the center of the back. The underside of the body is pale yellow.

▲ PRAIRIE KING SNAKE (LAMPROPELTIS CALLIGASTER)

DISTRIBUTION: *Ranges eastward from Assam in northeastern India to northern China and through Indonesia.*

SIZE: *To just over 8 ft (2.4 m).*

ACCOMMODATION: *As for the American Ratsnake* (Elaphe obsoleta). *A winter cooling period for adult snakes is advisable to encourage successful breeding.*

BEHAVIOR: *An adaptable species, encountered in a number of different environments through its range.*

DIET: *Rodents primarily.*

BREEDING: *Mating occurs early in the year, and clutches consist of less than a dozen eggs, which hatch about three months later.*

FOX SNAKES

Elaphe vulpina and *Elaphe gloydi*   Family Colubridae

These snakes display large, dark, chestnut brown blotched areas on the body, with their underlying coloration being a paler shade of brown. Those of the western nominate species *(Elaphe vulpina)* have more blotches, which are smaller in size than those of the eastern species *(E. gloydi)*.

DISTRIBUTION: *From the Great Lakes region of Canada southward into northern-central parts of the United States. Reaches eastern Nebraska and south as far as northwestern Indiana and eastern Missouri.*

SIZE: *Up to 6 ft (1.8 m).*

ACCOMMODATION: *Its northerly distribution means this species should be kept relatively cool, between 68 and 77°F (20 and 25°C). It will hibernate over the winter in cool surroundings, at a reduced temperature of 50°F (10°C).*

BEHAVIOR: *Can vibrate its tail, rather like a rattlesnake. Often found in damp areas.*

DIET: *Rodents.*

BREEDING: *After mating in the spring, typically about a dozen eggs may be laid as a single clutch, hatching after a period of about eight weeks.*

GRAY-BANDED KING SNAKE

Lampropeltis alterna   Family Colubridae

This species can be identified by a striking combination of gray bands separated by reddish orange crossbanding with black edging, although the patterning is highly individual. The scales of the Gray-banded King Snake appear very smooth.

SYNONYM: *Lampropeltis mexicana alterna.*

DISTRIBUTION: *The Big Bend region of southern Texas, extending south into northern Mexico.*

SIZE: *Up to 4 ft (1.2 m).*

ACCOMMODATION: *Plenty of retreats are important in a vivarium for this terrestrial snake, which naturally inhabits fairly arid surroundings. Winter cooling is necessary—down to 59°F (15°C)—for successful breeding.*

BEHAVIOR: *Unfortunately, this species is shy by nature, and usually only hunts at night. Lizards form the main item in its diet in the wild, but it will also prey on smaller snakes.*

DIET: *Will take mice.*

BREEDING: *Mating occurs in spring, with a clutch consisting of up to nine eggs. Hatching subsequently takes up to 11 weeks, with the young snakes being about 10 in (25 cm) long.*

PRAIRIE KING SNAKE (MOLE SNAKE)

Lampropeltis calligaster   Family Colubridae

This is another species with highly variable patterning. Prairie King Snakes vary from brownish to a tan color with reddish blotches evident over the top of the body. The patterning tends to become less distinctive in older individuals.

DISTRIBUTION: *Ranges in the United States from central Maryland south to northern Florida and extends westward to eastern Texas and southeastern Nebraska.*

SIZE: *Up to about 4.5 ft (1.4 m).*

ACCOMMODATION: *Keep at approximately 77°F (25°C) in summer, but drop the temperature back over the winter period for a couple of months. Include a suitable retreat in the vivarium.*

BEHAVIOR: *Hides away in underground burrows of other species or even buries itself under the surface of the soil, which explains why the yellow-bellied subspecies* Lampropeltis calligaster rhombomaculata *is called the Mole Snake.*

DIET: *Mice.*

BREEDING: *Up to 17 eggs form the clutch and are buried in the soil. Hatching typically occurs about seven weeks later. They should be mature by their second year.*

COMMON KING SNAKE

Lampropeltis getula (getulus)   Family Colubridae

Identification of this snake is complicated, since approximately seven different races are recognized. California King Snakes *(Lampropeltis getula californiae)* rank among the most colorful of the species, with pale yellow or whitish banding alternating with blackish banding. Florida King Snakes *(L .g. floridana)* may show light blotches, while the Mexican black form *(L. g. nigriutus)* is

completely black once adult, even on the underside of the body. Color morphs are also now widely kept.

DISTRIBUTION: *Represented widely across North and Central America.*

SIZE: *Up to 4 ft (1.2 m).*

ACCOMMODATION: *As for the Prairie King Snake* (Lampropeltis calligaster).

BEHAVIOR: *These are predatory snakes and should not be housed with smaller individuals, because they may prey on them. Keep a watch at feeding time to ensure they do not fight over food.*

DIET: *Mice.*

BREEDING: *Mating takes place in the spring. Typical clutches consist of about 10 eggs, with hatching occurring seven to 10 weeks later.*

▲ COMMON KING SNAKE (LAMPROPELTIS GETULA)

▼ FLORIDA KING SNAKE (LAMPROPELTIS GETULA FLORIDANA)

▲ *Subspecies and varieties of Milk Snake* (Lampropeltis triangulum):
1 Sinaloan (L. t. sinaloae); *2* Central Plains (L. t. gentilis); *3* Honduran
(L. t. hondurensis); *4* Pueblan Apricot (L. t. campbelli); *5* Honduran
Tangerine (L. t. hondurensis).

MEXICAN KING SNAKE

Lampropeltis mexicana   Family Colubridae

There are three recognized subspecies of this attractive tricolored king snake, although their coloration differs widely among individuals, even of the same race. The Durango Mountain King Snake (*Lampropeltis mexicana greeri*) tends to be mainly grayish, with relatively narrow black-edged red bands. The situation is typically reversed in Nuevo Leon's King Snake (*L. m. thayeri*), which is largely red. The nominate race, the San Luis Potosí King Snake, tends to be intermediate in appearance.

DISTRIBUTION: *Occurs in the mountains of northern Mexico.*

SIZE: *Up to 3.5 ft (1.1 m).*

ACCOMMODATION: *As for other king snakes, allow the wintertime temperature to drop to 59°F (15°C) or even slightly lower, to condition them for breeding in the spring.*

BEHAVIOR: *A highly predatory species that may prey on its own kind.*

DIET: *Mice.*

BREEDING: *The nominate race tends to be most prolific, laying up to 15 eggs in a clutch. The other two lay on average five to six eggs. Hatching usually takes place between two and three months later.*

MILK SNAKE

Lampropeltis triangulum   Family Colubridae

There is much variation in the appearance of the Milk Snake throughout its wide distribution, and numerous subspecies are recognized as a result. One of the larger and most colorful is the Honduran Milk Snake (*Lampropeltis triangulum hondurensis*).

DISTRIBUTION: *Extends widely through North America south through Central America into northern parts of South America.*

SIZE: *Up to 5 ft (1.8 m), depending on the subspecies.*

ACCOMMODATION: *The temperature range required for Milk Snakes depends partly on their natural area of distribution. Those from Central America, which are more commonly kept than those found in South America, should be kept at a temperature up to 86°F (30°C).*

BEHAVIOR: *North American races are relatively small, creating difficulties in rearing the young if they cannot manage pinkies on hatching.*

DIET: *Mice.*

BREEDING: *Varies to some extent, based on the origins of an individual. Try to keep subspecies pure whenever possible. Expect six to seven eggs, which should hatch between eight and 11 weeks later.*

CALIFORNIAN MOUNTAIN KING SNAKE

Lampropeltis zonata   Family Colubridae

This is a very attractive and distinctive king snake thanks to its broad red bands, which are edged with narrower bands of black and are also separated by intervening creamy white bands.

DISTRIBUTION: *Occurs in the mountainous areas of California, Baja California and Oregon.*

SIZE: *Up to nearly 3.5 ft (1.1 m).*

ACCOMMODATION: *Requires a good selection of hiding places in its quarters, being shy by nature. You must allow the vivarium temperature to fall back over the winter if breeding is to be successful.*

BEHAVIOR: *Lizards form the major item in the diet of these snakes in the wild.*

DIET: *Will take mice, but may have to be weaned onto them by rubbing them gently again the body of a skink, to transfer the lizard's scent.*

BREEDING: *Expect clutches of three to eight eggs. The incubation period lasts roughly between eight and 10 weeks.*

▼ DURANGO MOUNTAIN KING SNAKE (LAMPROPELTIS MEXICANA GREERI)

MEXICAN PARROT SNAKE

Leptophis ahaetulla   Family Colubridae

These brightly colored snakes vary in appearance through their range, and about a dozen different subspecies have been identified. They are variable shades of green, resembling those of many parrots, which explains their common name. Their appearance may have a yellowish hue, particularly on the underside of the body, while bright bluish green coloration is often apparent on the head.

DISTRIBUTION: *A wide-ranging species that, in spite of its name, ranges from Mexico as far south as Argentina in South America.*

SIZE: *Up to about 4 ft (1.2 m).*

ACCOMMODATION: *Requires a warm vivarium, heated to 86°F (30°C), with leaves and hiding places on the floor. It inhabits quite dry surroundings in the wild rather than tropical rain forest but, as always, provide a water bowl. Parrot snakes do not climb and will not require a tall vivarium.*

BEHAVIOR: *These snakes are active during the day, adding to their interest as vivarium subjects, although they are not commonly kept.*

DIET: *Mice.*

BREEDING: *Not well documented, but a typical clutch size can vary from five to 15 eggs.*

ROUGH GREEN SNAKE

Opheodrys aestivus   Family Colubridae

This attractively colored snake is bright green with yellow underparts. The pupils are also yellow. Its body is slender and

tapers along its length. The scales on the body are keeled, which serves to distinguish this species from its close relative, the Smooth Green Snake *(Opheodrys vernalis)*.

DISTRIBUTION: *Southeastern United States, from southern New Jersey west to eastern Kansas and Texas, extending south into eastern Mexico.*

SIZE: *Up to about 3.5 ft (1.1 m).*

ACCOMMODATION: *Since this is an arboreal species, there must be a good choice of branches in the vivarium for climbing. The temperature should be in the range of 77–86°F (25–30°C), with a spacious water container in which the snake can bathe.*

BEHAVIOR: *These snakes can swim well, dropping down from a branch into water below to escape danger if threatened. They inhabit areas close to water.*

DIET: *Will take a variety of invertebrates, especially crickets. Ensure they are gut-loaded or dusted if necessary with a vitamin and mineral powder beforehand.*

BREEDING: *May mate both during the fall and in the spring. Females lay up to a dozen eggs, with the hatching period sometimes being as short as five weeks, although it may continue in the wild for three months. The young measure about 7 in (18 cm) at this stage.*

PACIFIC GOPHER SNAKE
(BULL SNAKE)

Pituophis catenifer   Family Colubridae

The taxonomy of gopher snakes is confused, with what were previously classified as subspecies now tending to be grouped as species in their own right. In the case of the Pacific Gopher Snake the body is dark with yellowish stripes extending along its length. There are clearly spaced dark blotches in the vicinity of the head, with some gray areas on the sides of the body. Some individuals display more blotches than stripes overall, and there is also a striped albino form.

DISTRIBUTION: *Extends from western Oregon southward through western and central parts of California as far south as Santa Barbara county.*

SIZE: *Can reach just over 8 ft (2.4 m).*

ACCOMMODATION: *A typical vivarium needs to be heated to between 77 and 86°C (25 and 30°C) during the summer, dropping back to approximately 59°F (15°C) for a couple of months in the winter.*

BEHAVIOR: *Gopher snakes rank as being among the largest species in North America and are versatile hunters, seeking their prey on the ground.*

DIET: *Rodents and birds.*

BREEDING: *After mating in the spring a female is likely to lay within a couple of months. A typical clutch may consist of about seven eggs, which hatch about nine weeks later, depending on the temperature.*

▲ ROUGH GREEN SNAKE (OPHEODRYS AESTIVUS)

NORTHERN PINE SNAKE

Pituophis melanoleucus   Family Colubridae

The Northern Pine Snake is another member of the gopher snake group that is relatively variable in coloration. The ground color of these snakes can range from white or yellow to gray. There are generally black blotches present on the body, often becoming more brownish in color toward the tail.

DISTRIBUTION: *Parts of the eastern United States, extending from southern New Jersey down through parts of Virginia, Kentucky, Tennessee and the Carolinas. Present also in northern areas of Alabama and Georgia.*

SIZE: *Can grow to about 8 ft (2.4 m).*

ACCOMMODATION: *As for the Pacific Gopher Snake (Pituophis catenifer).*

BEHAVIOR: *Opportunistic hunters, these snakes are linked with areas of pine woodland. They will rear up and hiss if threatened.*

DIET: *Rodents.*

BREEDING: *Eggs are concealed in burrows or beneath fallen branches. Hatching data as for the Pacific Gopher Snake.*

DEKAY'S SNAKE
(BROWN SNAKE)

Storeria dekayi   Family Colubridae

Eight different subspecies of this small snake are recognized. They are relatively plain, and their body color varies from gray to shades of brown, depending on the race. There is a pale stripe down the back, with a row of faint spots on either side.

DISTRIBUTION: *Ranges very widely from southern Quebec in Canada down though most of central and eastern parts of the United States into Mexico, occurring as far south as Honduras in Central America.*

SIZE: *Up to about 21 in (53 cm).*

ACCOMMODATION: *Should incorporate a moist area of substrate, a water bowl and suitable retreats. The temperature should ideally match the area where the subspecies is found—cooler for snakes originating in northern parts of the species' range and warmer for those found farther south.*

BEHAVIOR: *Active during the day, Dekay's Snake tends to favor damp areas where its prey is likely to be most readily available.*

DIET: *Hunts slugs, earthworms and snails.*

BREEDING: *Normally gives birth to 5–15 young, which are born in the summer through to early fall. They average about 4 in (10 cm).*

PLAINS GARTER SNAKE

Thamnophis radix Family Colubridae

An attractive and easily managed group of snakes, garter and ribbon snakes are so called because of their relatively slender shape. The Plains Garter Snake has a bright orange stripe running down the center of its back, with parallel bluish green stripes on each side.

DISTRIBUTION: *Central part of North America, extending from southern Alberta southward to New Mexico and east to Indiana. Some isolated populations also exist, for example, in southwestern Illinois.*

SIZE: *Reaches just 28 in (71 cm).*

ACCOMMODATION: *Keep moderately warm—up to 77° F (25° C)—allowing the temperature to drop down to about 59° F (15° C) for a couple of months over the winter. Bathing facilities are essential, since these snakes inhabit damp areas. Sphagnum moss is useful as a floor covering and should*

▲ COMMON GARTER SNAKE (THAMNOPHIS SIRTALIS)

be sprayed regularly using dechlorinated water. Must be cooled over the winter if breeding is to be successful.

BEHAVIOR: *Active during the day, often hunting amphibians; also seen to bask regularly.*

DIET: *Earthworms and, if available, formulated food, both of which are preferable to fish.*

BREEDING: *Litter size is very variable, with a single litter consisting of anywhere from half a dozen to 60 offspring. They measure about 6 in (15 cm) at birth. The young are born during the summer.*

COMMON GARTER SNAKE

Thamnophis sirtalis Family Colubridae

The extensive range of this species means that it has been split into a number of distinctive races and is very variable in appearance. The striped patterning tends to be cream in color, with the body itself being significantly darker. These snakes are ideal for beginners, since they are relatively easy to maintain.

DISTRIBUTION: *Occurs extensively through southern Canada and much of the United States, except for the central region. Has the largest range of any North American snake.*

SIZE: *From 18 in (46 cm) up to 52 in (1.3 m).*

ACCOMMODATION: *Common Garter Snakes occur in damp areas but should not be kept on a sodden substrate. Provide an accessible water bowl and plenty of retreats in their quarters.*

BEHAVIOR: *Garter snakes generally hibernate together in groups, and mating occurs after they awake in spring.*

DIET: *Earthworms and, if available, formulated food, both of which are preferable to fish.*

BREEDING: *Provide an area of sphagnum moss where the female can produce her litter. Ensure the vivarium is completely escape-proof.*

▲ PLAINS GARTER SNAKE (THAMNOPHIS RADIX)

LIZARDS
ORDER SQUAMATA (part)

▲ PEACOCK GECKO (PHELSUMA QUADRIOCELLATA)

There are more than 4,500 different species of lizards in the world today, and they make up the largest surviving group of reptiles. Their distribution is extensive, and there are few areas of the world other than Antarctica where members of this group are not present. Perhaps unsurprisingly, they reach their greatest diversity within the tropics. Some species are at home scampering over sand dunes in the baking heat of the desert, whereas others are able to survive the bitter cold of winters within the Arctic Circle.

Members of the group vary widely in size from species that are just a few inches long up to the impressive Komodo Dragon *(Varanus komodoensis),* which can grow to over 9 feet (3 m) long. These gigantic monitor lizards are restricted to just a few Indonesian islands, where they are strictly protected.

Other related species can protect themselves by biting and lashing out with their powerful tails. Smaller lizards have evolved a more passive approach to the threat posed by would-be predators. If seized, they shed part of their tail. In theory this allows them to escape, minus a portion of the tail, which will regrow in due course. There are only two venomous lizards in the world—the Gila Monster *(Heloderma suspectum)* from the southwestern United States and Mexico, and the Beaded Lizard *(H. horridum),* which occurs in Mexico and Guatemala.

Lizards in general rank as the most agile of reptiles, being able to run, climb and swim. Some have skin flaps extending along the sides of the body, enabling them to glide safely down from tall trees. Walking up vertical surfaces also presents no difficulties for many geckos.

Lifestyles differ widely, ranging from burrowing species that live underground through to chameleons that can clamber very safely along slender branches. The reproductive habits of lizards are also diverse because, although most members of the group lay eggs, some of which may have parchmentlike rather than hard shells, others give birth to live young.

GECKOS
Family Gekkonidae

The family Gekkonidae contains some 900 species with a worldwide distribution. A surprising number of them are present on remote islands. One obvious characteristic of some species is their remarkable ability to run directly up and down vertical surfaces. This results from the adhesive properties of the microscopic hairlike projections on their toes, which give the lizards increased traction when climbing on surfaces off the ground. Other more terrestrial species lack this feature.

Unlike some other lizards, geckos do not grow to a large size. Accommodating them in vivarium surroundings is therefore relatively straightforward, although their natural agility means that catching them can be difficult. They do not usually become especially tame but they are ideal occupants for an attractive themed vivarium.

Breeding in these surroundings is often feasible. All gecko species reproduce by means of eggs, which are often are stuck in place or buried, and need to be handled very carefully if taken elsewhere for incubation. In contrast to those of some lizards, the eggs of geckos are hard-shelled rather than having a parchmentlike covering.

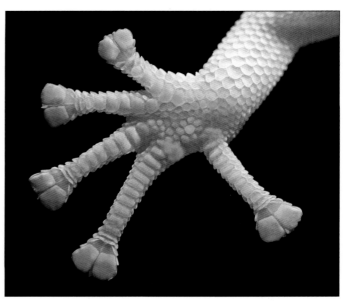

▶ *A GECKO FOOT, CLEARLY SHOWING THE FLATTENED, ENLARGED TOE PADS AND BODY SCALES.*

▲ *MALAYSIAN CAT GECKO (AELUROSCALABOTES FELINUS)*

MALAYSIAN CAT GECKO

Aeluroscalabotes felinus   Family Gekkonidae

These geckos are an attractive golden brown with some striping on the back. The females are significantly larger than the males. Malaysian Cat Geckos should be housed separately because they can be aggressive by nature.

DISTRIBUTION: *Through the Malaysian Peninsula and also on Borneo.*

SIZE: *6 in (15 cm).*

ACCOMMODATION: *Keep in a setup of the rain forest type, with a temperature range between 77 and 82°F (25 and 28°C) and high humidity. Regular spraying is essential. Provide climbing opportunities in the vivarium, adding artificial vines and also plants for this purpose. The presence of a fluorescent tube mimicking daylight will help both the geckos and the plants.*

BEHAVIOR: *This is an unusual gecko because, despite lacking enlarged toes, it climbs rather than being terrestrial in its habits.*

DIET: *Provide a range of suitable invertebrates, such as gut-loaded crickets.*

BREEDING: *Females lay clutches consisting of two eggs. Currently, successful breeding is not commonly achieved for these geckos.*

SPIDER GECKO

Agamura persicus   Family Gekkonidae

These geckos are predominantly silvery gray in color, which helps them merge in with their background. They are so called because of their thin legs, which resemble those of a spider. The tail is relatively short. Females are significantly larger than the males when adult.

DISTRIBUTION: *Southwestern Asia; present in Afghanistan, Iran and Pakistan.*

SIZE: *4 in (10 cm).*

ACCOMMODATION: *Dwelling in arid countries in the wild, this species requires a dry, sandy substrate in the vivarium, with rockwork that provides hiding places. Allow the temperature to rise to 86°F (30°C) during the daytime, and create a thermal gradient across the vivarium. Allow the temperature to fall back at night.*

BEHAVIOR: *This terrestrial species can be persuaded to emerge from its retreats during the daytime if fed; it can also be active at night.*

DIET: *Small invertebrates, such as gut-loaded crickets.*

BREEDING: *Cool conditions for four weeks or so should act as a breeding trigger, with egg-laying likely about a month later. Females lay clutches of two eggs in succession.*

WESTERN BANDED GECKO

Coleonyx variegatus   Family Gekkonidae

A broken pattern of bands across the body helps identify this species. The body markings, which extend to the tail, consist of brownish and yellowish bands, and there is a narrow pale stripe

▲ SPIDER GECKO (AGAMURA PERSICUS)

above the eyes. The head is spotted on its upper surface, and individuals are variable in their appearance.

DISTRIBUTION: *Extends through southwestern parts of the United States from southern California and parts of Nevada, Arizona and Utah to Baja California and northern Mexico.*

SIZE: *Up to 6 in (15 cm).*

ACCOMMODATION: *Requires an arid-country setup, similar to that of the Spider Gecko (Agamura persicus). A heat spot should be available for basking purposes and a number of retreats provided as hiding places.*

BEHAVIOR: *The slitlike pupils of this gecko indicates it is primarily nocturnal in its habits.*

DIET: *A range of invertebrates, including gut-loaded crickets of suitable size.*

BREEDING: *Can lay up to three clutches in a year, each consisting of two eggs. Hatching takes about six weeks. The markings of the young are more pronounced than those of the adults.*

▼ WESTERN BANDED GECKO (COLEONYX VARIEGATUS)

▲ LEOPARD GECKOS (EUBLEPHARIS MACULARIUS)—
COLOR FORMS: *1 TYPICAL JUVENILE; 2 TANGERINE; 3 CARROT-TAIL HYPO; 4 HYPO PASTEL; 5 ALBINO; 6 SNOW.*

LEOPARD GECKO

Eublepharis macularius   Family Gekkonidae

Only adults of the species display the spotted patterning that is characteristic of Leopard Geckos—the youngsters have a striped appearance. A profusion of different color morphs of this species has developed over recent years, including individuals with tangerine orange or white coloring. Leopard Geckos in general are easy to keep and make an ideal introduction to this group of lizards.

DISTRIBUTION: *Southern-central parts of Asia, extending from Iraq to northwestern India.*

SIZE: *Up to 8 in (20 cm); males are larger than females.*

ACCOMMODATION: *A sandy vivarium with hiding places and a basking spot will be required. The hottest part of the vivarium can be allowed to reach 82° F (28° C) during the day, dropping back at night to about 72° F (22° C). Natural lights that mimic sunlight are recommended together with a damp area, which is especially important for egg-laying.*

BEHAVIOR: *Males can be rather aggressive toward each other, and it is better to keep them apart. Trios consisting of a male and two females can prove compatible, however.*

DIET: *A variety of suitable invertebrates, treated with a special vitamin and mineral powder.*

▲ TOKAY GECKO (GEKKO GECKO)

BREEDING: *Females lay as many as five clutches of two eggs during the year. The eggs hatch after about two months at 80° F (27° C), but the incubation temperature will affect the gender of the hatchlings. To trigger breeding in adults, provide a cooler "winter" period for several weeks, with the temperature dropping to at least 59° F (15° C).*

TOKAY GECKO

Gekko gecko   Family Gekkonidae

The Tokay Gecko is one of the largest of the geckos. It is also very colorful, being grayish blue with orange spots on the body. Some color variants have emerged over recent years, notably a leucistic (yellow) form, but they have not become especially popular. The slit pupils reveal that these geckos are primarily nocturnal, and they use their broad toe pads to support their body weight.

DISTRIBUTION: *Southeast Asia.*

SIZE: *Up to 14 in (36 cm).*

ACCOMMODATION: *A largely arboreal species, which needs to be housed in a large vivarium that provides stout branches and retreats off the ground. The surroundings should be humid and warm—between 77 and 86° F (25 and 30° C)—and regular spraying with warm dechlorinated water is necessary. This will also provide the gecko with an opportunity to drink.*

BEHAVIOR: *The Tokay Gecko is a particularly vocal species and is named for the sound of its call. It is a surprisingly aggressive species and is not averse to biting, especially when handled. For this reason, males should not be housed together.*

DIET: *Eats larger invertebrates, and may even take pinkies too.*

BREEDING: *Should be housed only in pairs. Females lay clutches of two eggs, with the hatching period varying widely from 100 to 200 days.*

HELMETED GECKO

Geckonia chazaliae   Family Gekkonidae

The most evident feature of this species is the shape of its head, which creates the impression of a helmet. Overall, the gecko is a light shade of grayish brown, and its tail length corresponds to that of its body. The legs of the Helmeted Gecko are long and relatively thin.

DISTRIBUTION: *Found in northwestern parts of Africa, from Senegal to Morocco.*

SIZE: *4 in (10 cm).*

ACCOMMODATION: *The Helmeted Gecko originates from an arid part of the world, so it requires a dry, sandy substrate, with rockwork to provide retreats. The temperature should be allowed to reach 86° F (30° C) during the day, dropping back at night. A small container of water should always be available, as for other species.*

▼ HELMETED GECKO (GECKONIA CHAZALIAE)

▲ ▶ AFRICAN FAT-TAILED GECKO (HEMITHECONYX CAUDICINCTUS)—COLOR FORMS: *1* SPECKLED; *2* BROWN-BANDED; *3* TANGERINE; *4* FAWN.

BEHAVIOR: *The Helmeted Gecko is a terrestrial species that becomes most active at night. It can be extremely vocal at times, especially when handled.*

DIET: *This gecko will prey on a range of small invertebrates, including gut-loaded crickets.*

BREEDING: *Within about two weeks of mating, a clutch of two eggs can be anticipated. They will be buried in the sand. The eggs are fragile and can be easily damaged if dug up. The young will be mature about nine months later.*

AFRICAN FAT-TAILED GECKO

Hemitheconyx caudicinctus   Family Gekkonidae

As their name suggests, these geckos have broad stumpy tails. The body coloration is brownish red. A series of broad bands alternating light and dark run down the body from head to tail, separated by narrow white edging. These geckos do not have expanded toe pads.

DISTRIBUTION: *Relatively dry areas in western Africa, from Senegal to northern Cameroon.*

SIZE: *8 in (20 cm).*

ACCOMMODATION: *A hot, relatively dry vivarium is needed for these geckos, with cork bark or rockwork provided as retreats in which the lizards can hide away. African Fat-tailed Geckos thrive under similar conditions to those preferred by the Leopard Gecko (Eublepharis macularius).*

BEHAVIOR: *In spite of their placid appearance, these lizards can inflict a painful bite if handled carelessly.*

DIET: *A range of invertebrates should be offered, either gut-loaded or sprinkled with a special supplement.*

BREEDING: *Usually breed quite readily, with females laying clutches of two eggs. Hatching takes 60 to 75 days at 85°F (29°C).*

MARBLED VELVET GECKO

Oedura marmorata   Family Gekkonidae

Velvet geckos are so called because of the smooth appearance of the body. The markings of older Marbled Velvet Geckos appear less clearly defined, whereas young individuals display a series of striking bluish gray and yellow bands on the body. The tail of all members of the species is short and tapers along its length, and the head is angular in shape. The tips of the toes are enlarged.

DISTRIBUTION: *Northern and central parts of Australia.*

SIZE: *Up to 7 in (18 cm).*

ACCOMMODATION: *A reasonably dry setup will suit these geckos, since they tend to spend much of their time on the ground, although they can climb as well.*

BEHAVIOR: *Marbled Velvet Geckos usually hide away under rocks or branches during the day, emerging at dusk, at which time they will start to hunt.*

DIET: *Invertebrates of suitable size. Do not house Marbled Velvet Geckos with smaller lizards, which they may eat.*

BREEDING: *Two soft-shelled eggs form a typical clutch. Hatching at 86°F (30°C) takes about two months. Their free-breeding nature means that, although Australian in origin, these geckos are widely available elsewhere in the world.*

BIBRON'S GECKO

Pachydactylus bibronii　　　　　　Family Gekkonidae

The body of this gecko has white and brown spots, arranged roughly in bands. In common with other members of the genus, the toes are stocky in shape, which has led to these lizards becoming known collectively as thick-toed geckos.

DISTRIBUTION: *Widely distributed through southern Africa, north to Angola in the west and Tanzania in the east.*

SIZE: *8 in (20 cm).*

ACCOMMODATION: *A sandy floor will be needed in the vivarium, with suitable decor to provide retreats and possible breeding sites. A temperature of about 77°F (25°C) is recommended, falling back slightly at night.*

BEHAVIOR: *These geckos are relatively social by nature and can be kept in colonies, but newcomers are likely to be bullied.*

DIET: *Will feed on a range of invertebrates.*

BREEDING: *Eggs are laid in pairs out of sight, such as in the crevices of rocks or on the underside of cork bark. Hatching will take about two months at 80°F (27°C). Females may lay up to six clutches in succession.*

COMORO ISLANDS DAY GECKO

Phelsuma comorensis　　　　　　Family Gekkonidae

The back of the Comoro Islands Day Gecko is green with brownish blotches, and there are pale sky blue and pale red patches on its head. A blackish stripe runs down each side of the body. The underparts are pale, creating what appears to be another white stripe beneath.

DISTRIBUTION: *Restricted to Grande Comoro in the Comoro Islands, off Africa's southeastern coast.*

SIZE: *5 in (13 cm).*

ACCOMMODATION: *An arboreal vivarium is necessary, with a daytime temperature of 78–86°F (26–30°C) being recommended, dropping back at night. A nighttime spray to increase the humidity is recommended.*

BEHAVIOR: *Do not attempt to keep males together, since they are aggressive and territorial by nature.*

DIET: *A range of invertebrates that climb, with gut-loaded crickets being a useful staple.*

BREEDING: *Supply hollow bamboo tubes for egg-laying. The female will enter a tube and glue a pair of eggs to the inside. The tube can then be removed. Hatching is likely within seven weeks at a temperature of 28°F (32°C).*

GOLD-DUST DAY GECKO

Phelsuma laticauda　　　　　　Family Gekkonidae

Day geckos are characterized in part by their individual color patterns. Red markings vary in particular. In addition to the blue and red markings on the head, there is a sprinkling of spots resembling gold dust present on the neck and upper back. Green coloration predominates elsewhere.

DISTRIBUTION: *Northern Madagascar and nearby Nosy Be as well as the Comoro Islands.*

SIZE: *Up to 5 in (13 cm) depending on the subspecies.*

ACCOMMODATION: *A warm humid environment will suit these geckos well, with the temperature ranging between 77 and 82°F (25 and 28°C). Branches should be supplied for climbing, and plants can also be included. Regular spraying will help maintain the humidity.*

BEHAVIOR: *The rounded pupil of these geckos confirms that, like other* Phelsuma *species, they are active during the day rather than at night.*

DIET: *A range of suitable live foods. A feeding station can be provided off the ground.*

BREEDING: *Two eggs are normally laid in a clutch but not glued in place. Hatching is likely to take just over six weeks.*

LINED DAY GECKO

Phelsuma lineata　　　　　　Family Gekkonidae

A number of races of this day gecko have been identified. The basic coloration consists of dark green upper parts with brownish markings—either forming a blotch or broken into spots—evident on the back, in front of the hind legs, and becoming finer down the tail. There are red and blue markings on the face.

▶ *MADAGASCAR GIANT DAY GECKO (PHELSUMA MADAGASCARIENSIS)*

◀ *GOLD-DUST DAY GECKO (PHELSUMA LATICAUDA)*

DISTRIBUTION: *Restricted to the island of Madagascar.*

SIZE: *May be up to 6 in (15 cm) long, depending on the subspecies.*

ACCOMMODATION: *A setup similar to that of the Gold-dust Day Gecko (Phelsuma laticauda) is required. Spray regularly, so the gecko can drink. Tall plants, especially mother-in-law's tongue (Sansevieria), can be included in the enclosure, providing vertical surfaces on which the gecko can climb.*

BEHAVIOR: *Since the species is active during the day, a fluorescent tube that mimics the wavelengths of daylight is recommended to prevent metabolic problems.*

DIET: *Gut-loaded crickets and other invertebrates. In addition, provide a small container of honey water, which day geckos often like to drink.*

BREEDING: *As for the the Gold-dust Day Gecko.*

MADAGASCAR GIANT DAY GECKO

Phelsuma madagascariensis Family Gekkonidae

The Madagascar Giant Day Gecko, as its name suggests, is the largest of the 25 species of day geckos. Occurring in several races, its basic color scheme is identical. It is green on the upper parts, with variable red markings here. These marks are much more prominent in some cases than others.

DISTRIBUTION: *Occurs on Madagascar, off Africa's southeastern coast.*

SIZE: *Can reach up to 12 in (30 cm) depending on the subspecies.*

ACCOMMODATION: *These geckos should be kept in sexed pairs. A typical day gecko vivarium is required, but correspondingly larger in size. Humidity is important, especially when the lizards are shedding, to avoid loss of the enlarged toe pads.*

BEHAVIOR: *Their coloration enables these and other day geckos to remain hidden among vegetation, but they can scamper away fast if threatened.*

DIET: *A range of invertebrates of suitable size, preferably gut-loaded.*

BREEDING: *Hatching takes longer than in related species, lasting up to 11 weeks in some cases. The young will not thrive unless they are kept in humid surroundings, and they must be exposed to suitable daylight tubes.*

PEACOCK DAY GECKO
(FOUR-SPOT DAY GECKO)

Phelsuma quadriocellata Family Gekkonidae

The presence of dark spots in the axillary region behind the front legs helps identify this species, although in subspecies *Phelsuma quadriocellata bimaculata* the spots are less apparent. There is a second pair of spots on each side of the body, in front of the hind limbs. The body coloration is otherwise mainly green with reddish markings, particularly down the back.

DISTRIBUTION: *Coastal region of the island of Madagascar.*

SIZE: *About 3.5 in (9 cm) to nearly 5 in (13 cm) depending on subspecies.*

ACCOMMODATION: *A setup similar to that of other species of day geckos, but take particular care to ensure there are no gaps through which these relatively small geckos might escape.*

BEHAVIOR: *These day geckos can become quite bold.*

DIET: *Invertebrates of suitable size and a little honey water. The water container should be washed and replenished daily. This is also a substitute for drinking water. Females will eat a little grated cuttlebone (as more commonly sold for budgerigars) to supplement their intake of calcium.*

BREEDING: *Hatching is ikely to take just over six weeks. The neck area of females often swells prior to egg-laying as a result of calcium deposits, which are used in the formation of the eggshells.*

FLYING GECKO

Ptychozoon kuhli   Family Gekkonidae

These geckos are grayish brown, with heavy webbing between the toes. Skin folds extend along the sides of the body, and there is a scalloped frill on the edges of the tail. The flat body shape and the flaps and frills help these geckos remain disguised when resting on tree bark. Although they do not "fly" as such, the webbed feet and tail frill enable the lizards to glide for short distances.

DISTRIBUTION: *Southeast Asia; present on the Malaysian Peninsula and offshore islands, including Sumatra, Java and Borneo.*

▲ GARGOYLE GECKO (RHACODACTYLUS AURICULATUS)

SIZE: *8 in (20 cm).*

ACCOMMODATION: *A tall vivarium with vertical branches at both ends will encourage the geckos to glide between the branches. Reasonably humid conditions and a temperature of 77–86°F (25–30°C) are required.*

BEHAVIOR: *These amazing geckos use skin folds on the sides of the body to glide from one vertical branch to another.*

DIET: *A range of invertebrates, such as gut-loaded crickets.*

BREEDING: *Keep in pairs. Prior to breeding, males develop swellings at the base of the tail. Clutches of two eggs are laid every six weeks or so by the female. The incubation period lasts about 14 weeks.*

▼ FLYING GECKO (PTYCHOZOON KUHLI)

GARGOYLE GECKO

Rhacodactylus auriculatus   Family Gekkonidae

The overall color of the Gargoyle Gecko is brownish, and there are distinct small swellings on the head. The tail is very short and has a sticky underside, which helps the lizard anchor itself onto the bark of trees.

DISTRIBUTION: *New Caledonia in the Pacific, east of New Guinea.*

SIZE: *8 in (20 cm).*

ACCOMMODATION: *An arboreal enclosure is required, incorporating cork bark and branches. The temperature can range from 82°F (28°C) in the day to about 72°F (22°C) at night. The relative humidity should be low.*

BEHAVIOR: *These geckos can be noisy. They emerge from their hiding places behind bark at night and sometimes remain out through the early morning.*

DIET: *Gargoyle Geckos are primarily frugivorous, eating* Freycinetia *fruits in the wild. Bananas can be used as a substitute, dusted with a vitamin and mineral powder. Other fruits, such as apricots, can also be offered. Gargoyle Geckos may also eat some invertebrates and, unlike many geckos, they can be persuaded to feed from the hand.*

BREEDING: *Unlike its close relative from the same part of the world—the Rough-snouted Giant Gecko* (Rhacodactylus trachyrhynchus)—*this species is an egg-layer. Hatching takes up to two months at an incubation temperature of 79°F (26°C). It will take up to eight months before young males can be sexed by the swollen area around their vent.*

DESERT GECKO

Stenodactylus petrii   Family Gekkonidae

The Desert Gecko is a small species. Its body markings consist of pale blotches on a darker background. The tail may show more definite banding, and it narrows along its length to a blunt tip.

The underside is pale, while the slender toes end in small claws. The eyes are large in relation to the size of the body.

DISTRIBUTION: *North Africa and the Middle East, from Algeria to Israel.*

SIZE: *4 in (10 cm).*

ACCOMMODATION: *A sandy substrate with some rocks present will be required by these small terrestrial lizards. They should be kept at a temperature of 86°F (30°C) during the daytime, falling back to 68°F (20°C) at night.*

BEHAVIOR: *The Desert Gecko is a nocturnal species that emerges under cover of darkness. A night light in the vivarium is therefore recommended, to aid viewing.*

DIET: *Small invertebrates, such as gut-loaded crickets, should be offered toward nightfall, when these geckos are most likely to be hunting for food.*

BREEDING: *Lowering the vivarium temperature over the winter should serve as a trigger for breeding. Females bury their eggs, which are very fragile, in the substrate. At a temperature of 86°F (30°C) hatching takes just over two months. Ensure the young geckos do not suffer from dehydration, since this can be fatal.*

MOORISH GECKO

Tarentola mauritanica   Family Gekkonidae

Adults of the Moorish Gecko are predominantly grayish in color, whereas the young are likely to show traces of darker barring, which disappears as they grow older. A series of distinctive large scales can be seen on the back, and the head is very broad. The toes are enlarged.

DISTRIBUTION: *Occurs widely through the Mediterranean area and on the Canary Islands.*

SIZE: *6 in (15 cm).*

▼ *MOORISH GECKO (TARENTOLA MAURITANICA)*

ACCOMMODATION: *A relatively warm environment, with basking spots reaching 82°F (28°C) suits these lizards well. They also require a natural fluorescent light to help them synthesize vitamin D3.*

BEHAVIOR: *Cooling over the winter period to a temperature as low as 50°F (10°C) is recommended, to mimic the temperature changes the geckos are likely to be exposed to in the wild.*

DIET: *A range of invertebrates, including crickets and waxworms, which are a valuable conditioning food.*

BREEDING: *Males are territorial and need to be kept separate from each other. A calcium supplement is recommended, since the eggs are hard-shelled. They should be kept on a dry substrate and will hatch up to 10 weeks later at about 80°F (27°C).*

GIANT FROG-EYED GECKO
(WONDER GECKO)

Teratoscincus scincus   Family Gekkonidae

This gecko's coloration is typically a pale sandy yellow, with irregular brownish stripes running down the body in the direction of the tail. The eyes are very prominent, resembling those of many frogs and explaining the species' common name. They may help the gecko's night vision. Giant Frog-eyed Geckos need to be handled very carefully because their skin is easily damaged.

DISTRIBUTION: *Asia, ranging from Iran to western China.*

SIZE: *8 in (20 cm).*

ACCOMMODATION: *It is essential to provide a suitable sandy substrate into which these geckos can burrow, and the lower reach of the tank should be damp. This can be accomplished by extending a tube to this area, out of sight. The hottest part of the vivarium should be 86°F (30°C), with this figure dropping back at night.*

OTHER GECKOS

Striped Gecko (*Gekko vittatus*)

Range: An island species, occurring from Java east via New Guinea to Oceania.

Size: 8 in (20 cm).

Habitat: Wooded areas.

Yellow-headed Gecko (*Gonatodes albogularis*)

Range: Northern South America. Introduced to various Caribbean islands and Florida.

Size: 4 in (10 cm).

Habitat: Varied habitat, often in the vicinity of buildings.

Web-footed Gecko (*Palmatogecko rangei*)

Range: Namibia, southwest Africa.

Size: Up to 5 in (13 cm).

Habitat: Desert.

▲ GIANT LEAF-TAILED GECKO (UROPLATUS FIMBRIATUS)

BEHAVIOR: *These geckos have a particularly characteristic defensive pose that causes them to look like an angry cat—they arch their back and rub their tail scales together to create a rattling sound.*

DIET: *Various invertebrates should be provided, such as waxworms, gut-loaded mealworms and crickets .*

BREEDING: *Relatively low humidity is required for the eggs to hatch successfully. The young emerge after a period of eight to 12 weeks. Use a calcium supplement to minimize the risk of egg-binding, since females will lay repeatedly once they start breeding.*

GIANT LEAF-TAILED GECKO

Uroplatus fimbriatus   Family Gekkonidae

The basic color of the Giant Leaf-tailed Gecko is brownish, and the body is marked with a spotted pattern. The most distinctive characteristic, however, is the tail. Not only is it fairly short, but it is significantly flattened in shape. Their toes are well equipped with lamellae (thin plates) on the underside to enable them to climb well.

DISTRIBUTION: *Madagascar, off Africa's southeastern coast.*

SIZE: *10 in (25 cm).*

ACCOMMODATION: *These geckos require a humid warm environment, typically around 77–82°F (25–28°C), dropping back slightly at night. Trunks for climbing purposes should be provided.*

BEHAVIOR: *These geckos are nocturnal by nature and it is not unusual for them to remain inactive on a tree trunk, head directed downward, for hours at a time. When on the move, they also tend to be slower than other geckos.*

DIET: *Invertebrates that climb are favored by these geckos, since they can pick them off the branches.*

BREEDING: *It is possible to see the eggs in the female's body just prior to laying. Once laid, they will be concealed on the floor of the vivarium. At an incubation temperature of 78°F (25°C), expect the young to emerge after an interval of two to three months.*

CHAMELEONS

Family Chamaeleonidae

amous for their ability to change color as a means of communication, chameleons (Chamaeleonidae) are among the best-known lizards. However, this physiological response is apparent, albeit in a less dramatic way, in other families too.

The fabled hunting skills of chameleons, whose long sticky tongues can be shot out of the mouth to seize quarry in the blink of an eye, are also well known. Their strange appearance has attracted hobbyists to them, but in the past chameleons have proved difficult to keep and breed successfully in vivaria. Even today, some species still represent a challenge.

SOUTHERN DWARF CHAMELEON

Bradypodion ventrale   Family Chamaeleonidae

The natural coloration of these small chameleons varies from brown to gray, with lighter mottling. When males are excited, however, they become transformed, turning a darker shade of bluish black.

DISTRIBUTION: *Coastal areas of southern Africa, including the eastern Cape; there is also an isolated population in Namibia.*

SIZE: *Up to about 6 in (15 cm).*

ACCOMMODATION: *An arboreal setup with plenty of cover provided by the leaves of real or artificial plants (or a combination of the two) is recommended. Spray the plants, since the chameleons are most likely to drink from droplets here. A temperature around 75°F (24°C), dropping back slightly at night, should be adequate. A full-spectrum fluorescent bulb should also be incorporated.*

BEHAVIOR: *These chameleons will hide away beneath leaves or even seek refuge on the ground if they feel threatened.*

DIET: *A variety of small invertebrates.*

BREEDING: *Females of this species give birth to live offspring. A typical litter size ranges from 10 to 20 young. Two broods may be born over the course of a year.*

OTHER CHAMELEONS

Fischer's Chameleon (Two-horned Chameleon) (*Bradypodion fischeri*)

Range: East Africa, in Kenya and Tanzania.

Size: 8–15 in (20–38 cm) depending on the subspecies.

Habitat: Montane forest.

▲ FISCHER'S CHAMELEON (BRADYPODION FISCHERI)

Armored Stub-tailed Chameleon (*Brookesia perarmata*)

Range: Western Madagascar, off Africa's southeastern coast.

Size: 5 in (13 cm).

Habitat: Tropical forest.

▲ ARMORED STUB-TAILED CHAMELEON (BROOKESIA PERARMATA)

Lobed Chameleon (*Chamaeleo dilepis*)

Range: Much of Africa south of the Sahara.

Size: 12 in (30 cm).

Habitat: Savanna.

Mountain Chameleon (*Chamaeleo montium*)

Range: West Africa, in the Cameroons.

Size: 14 in (35 cm).

Habitat: Montane forest.

LEAF CHAMELEON

Rampholeon brevicaudata   Family Chamaeleonidae

The group of small leaf chameleons in the genus *Brookesia* are protected to some extent by spines, especially on the head. Nodules are present elsewhere on the body. In this species, however, there are no horns on the upper jaw or above the eyes. The tail is very short.

DISTRIBUTION: *East Africa, occurring in upland areas of savanna.*

SIZE: *About 4 in (10 cm).*

ACCOMMODATION: *Surroundings should be kept humid, along with areas where they can bask. Be sure to shield any heat source for these and other chameleons, so they cannot burn themselves.*

BEHAVIOR: *The color-changing abilities of the Leaf Chameleon are limited, although it can vary the depth of its brown coloration.*

DIET: *Small invertebrates such as gut-loaded crickets should be provided.*

BREEDING: *Relatively small clutches numbering up to 10 eggs can be anticipated. These are buried in the substrate about six weeks after mating. Hatching will take up to seven weeks at 78°F (25°C). Small live foods such as aphids and fruit flies have proved useful for rearing purposes, as have hatchling crickets.*

▲▼ *VEILED CHAMELEON (CHAMAELEO CALYPTRATUS)—MALE (ABOVE) AND FEMALE (BELOW).*

VEILED CHAMELEON
(YEMEN CHAMELEON)

Chamaeleo calyptratus Family Chamaeleonidae

The Veiled Chameleon has proved to be one of the easiest of all chameleons to keep and breed in vivarium surroundings. As they mature, males develop a particularly tall helmet on their heads, which can be 2 inches (5 cm) high. The general body color is green with some white flecking.

DISTRIBUTION: *Occurs in the Middle East, being found in both Yemen and Saudi Arabia.*

SIZE: *Can grow to 12–20 in (30–50 cm).*

ACCOMMODATION: *A spacious, well-ventilated enclosure will be required, equipped with full-spectrum fluorescent bulbs. The temperature should be warm, up to 90°F (32°C) during the daytime, dropping as low as 64°F (18°C) at night.*

BEHAVIOR: *Females that are not ready to mate signal this fact to a male by transforming their coloration to dark green and black, although some lighter flecks are still apparent on their body.*

▼ JACKSON'S CHAMELEON (CHAMAELEO JACKSONII)—MALE.

DIET: *Although it feeds on invertebrates, the Veiled Chameleon displays an unusual fondness for fruit such as dates and for dandelion flowers, both of which can be lightly sprinkled with a vitamin and mineral powder.*

BREEDING: *Females of this egg-laying species can be surprisingly prolific, laying anywhere from 25 to 90 eggs, which they bury in a deep container of moist sand. Hatching is likely to take up to six months.*

JACKSON'S CHAMELEON
(THREE-HORNED CHAMELEON)

Chamaeleo jacksonii (jacksoni) Family Chamaeleonidae

Although males may become bright green when excited, a gray-green color is more commonly seen in this species. Males have three pronounced forward-pointing horns, the thickest of which is on the snout, with the other two being above the eyes. These horns are present in the females of some races, but they are much shorter.

DISTRIBUTION: *East Africa. Occurs in the forests of Kenya and Tanzania, often at altitudes above 10,000 ft (3,000 m).*

SIZE: *Up to 14 in (35 cm).*

ACCOMMODATION: *As with most other chameleons, this species requires a large area of arboreal vegetation in which to roam. Special light mesh*

▲ MELLER'S CHAMELEON (CHAMAELEO MELLERI)

enclosures are available from specialized stores and are a much better housing option than traditional vivaria for most of these lizards.

BEHAVIOR: *These chameleons are exposed to a very wide daily temperature shift. Heat the enclosure to 95°F (35°C) under a heat lamp and establish a thermal gradient. Allow the temperature to drop to 50°F (10°C) at night.*

DIET: *Invertebrates of various types, particularly crickets of suitable size.*

BREEDING: *Up to 40 live young will be born about six months after mating takes place.*

MELLER'S CHAMELEON

Chamaeleo melleri   Family Chamaeleonidae

A serrated dorsal crest running down the center of the back is characteristic of this large species. There are also neck folds on each side of the body. The basic coloration is green, with both black and yellowish areas on the body, although males can become much more brightly colored when displaying.

DISTRIBUTION: *In the montane forests of East Africa.*

SIZE: *Up to 24 in (60 cm).*

ACCOMMODATION: *A similar enclosure to that recommended for Jackson's Chameleon (Chamaeleo jacksonii) is required. Heat sources can be suspended over the enclosure, along with lighting as necessary.*

BEHAVIOR: *Meller's Chameleons move in the typical chameleon way, in a slow deliberate manner, with the long prehensile tail helping ensure they do not fall off a branch.*

DIET: *A variety of invertebrates of suitable size should be provided.*

BREEDING: *Females of this species lay eggs, often more than 40 in a single clutch. Once the young hatch, they require suitably small live food. They should grow rapidly on a varied diet and may be mature by a year old.*

PANTHER CHAMELEON

Furcifer pardalis   Family Chamaeleonidae

The coloration of Panther Chameleons can be particularly striking. Males are vibrantly colored with different color patterns depending on their geographic location. For example, those from the island of Nosy Be are bright blue. Females are less variable in appearance, being dull shades of green or brown.

DISTRIBUTION: *Northern parts of Madagascar and small islands such as Nosy Be just off Madagascar's north coast.*

SIZE: *From 12–20 in (30–50 cm); males are typically much larger.*

ACCOMMODATION: *These chameleons need plenty of space, because persistent quarreling if they are confined together means that they will be stressed, which will have a detrimental effect on their health. Warm and humid surroundings are required, with ventilation also being important.*

BEHAVIOR: *Aggressive by nature, like most chameleons. Males especially must not be kept together.*

DIET: *Invertebrates of various types.*

BREEDING: *Females which are not ready to mate adopt an aggressive stance with their mouths open. When mating occurs, they become more colorful for a time. Up to about 40 eggs may be laid, hatching anytime from six months to a year later. Young males can soon be recognized by their gray coloration.*

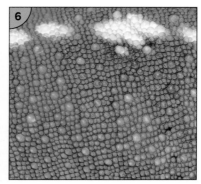

▲ *PANTHER CHAMELEON (FURCIFER PARDALIS)—COLOR VARIATIONS AND RACES: 1 BROWN MALE; 2 JUVENILE; 3, 5 AMBANJA; 4 NOSY BE; 6, 7 AMBILOBE.*

TEGUS AND MONITORS
Families Teiidae and Varanidae

While tegus (family Teiidae) are a New World group, monitors (family Varanidae) are widely distributed across Africa, extending through much of Asia and south to Australia. What links them together is that, although young hatchlings look very cute, these lizards will generally grow rapidly to a large size. This makes them not only potentially difficult to accommodate but dangerous to handle. Their powerful tails can inflict a painful blow, and their sharp teeth and claws are capable of causing serious injuries.

CHILEAN DWARF TEGU
(SPOTTED MONITOR LIZARD)

Callopistes maculatus   Family Teiidae

Members of this genus are known collectively as monitor tegus thanks to their superficial similarity with monitors, although they belong to completely different families. In spite of being known as the Chilean Dwarf Tegu, this species grows to a large size. It is brownish in color with darker spots often highlighted by white borders.

DISTRIBUTION: *Occurs in northern and central parts of Chile.*

SIZE: *Up to 39 in (100 cm).*

▼ CHILEAN DWARF TEGU (CALLOPISTES MACULATUS)

▲ COMMON TEGU (TUPINAMBIS TEGUIXIN)

ACCOMMODATION: *A fairly arid enclosure lined with sand and rocks should be provided. It needs to be heated with a heat lamp to create a localized temperature as high as 95°F (35°C) for basking purposes.*

BEHAVIOR: *In common with some African monitors, these lizards estivate in southern areas. They rely on fat supplies stored in their tail to sustain them over this period.*

DIET: *A variety of large invertebrates and pinkies should be provided, although these tegus tend to favor smaller lizards in the wild.*

BREEDING: *The aggressive tendencies of Chilean Dwarf Tegus means that this is unlikely to be achieved in the confines of a typical vivarium.*

COMMON TEGU

Tupinambis teguixin   Family Teiidae

The Common Tegu is black with yellowish spotted bands across its body, these bands becoming more definite in appearance along the tail. It bears a resemblance to the Nile Monitor *(Varanus niloticus)*.

DISTRIBUTION: *Found widely through central and eastern parts of South America.*

SIZE: *Can reach 4.6 ft (1.4 m).*

ACCOMMODATION: *A large vivarium will be required, with a good covering of substrate that will allow these tegus to dig. A burrow should be carefully sited here as well, providing an underground retreat. An area that allows them to climb is also important, along with a large container of water in which a tegu can immerse itself.*

BEHAVIOR: *Like monitors, tegus can be gluttonous in their feeding habits. If necessary, they should be slimmed down to prevent them becoming obese. If they do become overweight, their expected life span of 10 or more years will be shortened.*

DIET: *Meat-based foods such as dead day-old chicks. Also eats eggs and may even take some flowers and fruit.*

BREEDING: *Unlikely to be achieved without difficulty, partly because of the space required. Normally seeks out a termite nest for egg-laying in the wild, digging in with its sharp claws. Up to eight eggs are laid. The termites repair the damage, and the young tegus break out once they hatch.*

SAVANNA MONITOR
(BOSC'S MONITOR)

Varanus exanthematicus   Family Varanidae

A number of subspecies are recognized through the wide range of this species. One of the most distinctive is the white-throated form *(Varanus exanthematicus albigularis)*, which is sometimes considered to be a distinct species. Savanna Monitors are grayish brown overall with paler markings on the body.

DISTRIBUTION: *Much of Africa south of the Sahara, apart from rain forest areas.*

SIZE: *Up to 3–3.5 ft (0.9–1.1 m).*

ACCOMMODATION: *A large enclosure will soon be required for a young Savanna Monitor. The temperature should be raised to 95°F (35°C) so that the lizard can warm itself here. Some rockwork should also be added, and check that the door is firmly closed. A pond area that allows the monitor to bathe and which can be easily cleaned will also be necessary.*

BEHAVIOR: *These lizards are usually highly territorial, so to prevent fighting, avoid keeping males together.*

▶ *SAVANNA MONITOR (VARANUS EXANTHEMATICUS)*

DIET: *A true carnivore, so offer a wide range of dead day-old chicks, pink mice and similar items. Proprietary foods supplemented with vitamins and minerals may also be available.*

BREEDING: *It may be up to two months after mating before the female lays her eggs. She is likely to lose her appetite toward the end of this period. This is quite normal. Clutches are hidden away, and may comprise more than 60 eggs.*

NILE MONITOR

Varanus niloticus   Family Varanidae

The attractive and individual yellow and black markings of these monitors are most evident in young hatchlings but, unfortunately, they tend to fade as the lizards grow older. There may be slight variations in the arrangement of the banding on the body depending on the subspecies concerned.

DISTRIBUTION: *Found throughout much of Africa, although absent from the northwest of the continent.*

SIZE: *6.6 ft (2 m).*

ACCOMMODATION: *These potentially huge lizards are capable of swimming and climbing well. Suitable facilities must be provided in their enclosure, making them hard to accommodate in the home.*

BEHAVIOR: *Nile Monitors are unpredictable. While handling from an early age may make them more tractable, there are often times when one of these lizards will react aggressively. Always wear gloves and protect your arms and other vulnerable areas of the body, because they can inflict very painful scratches with their claws if they struggle, quite apart from biting.*

DIET: *A wide range of meat-based foods should be provided.*

BREEDING: *Even true pairs may fight, making breeding attempts fraught. Introduce them on neutral territory and separate them after mating. Eggs may take over 30 weeks to hatch. A slightly higher incubation temperature of about 90°F (32°C) will favor development of female offspring.*

AGAMIDS
Family Agamidae

The agamids (family Agamidae) are a diverse group of lizards in terms of lifestyle and appearance. They vary in size as well, ranging from less than 12 inches (30 cm) to more than 3 feet (0.9 m) long. A number are agile climbers, and some can swim well, whereas others have opted for a subterranean lifestyle. Their diversity in many ways parallels that seen in the iguanids, but what sets them apart is their distribution. Agamids are represented on all continents of the Old World, while iguanids occur only in the New World. Agamids include the so-called dragons, such as the widely kept Bearded Dragon (*Pogona vitticeps*) and the Asian Water Dragon (*Physignathus cocincinus*).

RED-HEADED AGAMA
(RAINBOW LIZARD)

Agama agama   Family Agamidae

Although Red-headed Agamas are mainly reddish brown when resting, their coloration can be highly variable. Males can become especially colorful, at times displaying blue and yellow markings. They have a small crest evident at the nape of the neck and a long tail. The toes are also long, helping these lizards climb well if necessary.

DISTRIBUTION: *Occurs in central and western parts of Africa.*

SIZE: *16 in (40 cm).*

ACCOMMODATION: *The active nature of these agamids means that they need a large vivarium. The floor area is significant, since they are largely terrestrial by nature. A hot basking area of 95°F (35°C) or so should be incorporated, along with full-spectrum lighting. The relative humidity should be low.*

BEHAVIOR: *Coloration is influenced by the environmental temperature and the lizard's own mood. Males are aggressive and need to be housed apart from each other.*

DIET: *Various invertebrates and pinkies.*

BREEDING: *Females will lay clutches of 10 eggs or more. Incubation lasts six to eight weeks at a temperature of 86°F (30°C).*

BEARDED TOAD-HEADED AGAMA

Phrynocephalus mystaceus   Family Agamidae

The spines at the corner of this agamid's mouth help explain its common name—if the lizard senses danger, it can erect the spines, giving it a "beard." The head itself is large, while the toes are long and slender. Grayish brown coloration predominates.

DISTRIBUTION: *Central parts of Asia. Present in northern parts of Iran and Afghanistan.*

SIZE: *10 in (25 cm).*

ACCOMMODATION: *Requires a hot, arid vivarium with a localized basking temperature up to about 95°F (35°C). Allow the temperature to drop at night to 77°F (25°C) or even slightly lower. Because these lizards are active during the day under intense sunlight, full-spectrum lighting which meets their ultraviolet requirement is essential to their well-being. The vivarium can have a sandy substrate, with rocks added as retreats. Regular localized spraying is necessary to provide droplets which the lizards will drink.*

BEHAVIOR: *Toad-headed agamas often dig into the ground to create burrows into which they can retreat when the sun is at its hottest.*

DIET: *Invertebrates of various types—spiders are often favored if available.*

BREEDING: *Not easily achieved. One to six eggs are likely to be laid in a clutch.*

◀ RED-HEADED AGAMA (AGAMA AGAMA)

ASIAN WATER DRAGON

Physignathus cocincinus   Family Agamidae

Adults of this species are predominantly green in color and have a distinctive serrated crest running down the center of the back, from the neck to the tip of the tail. There are paler markings in the vicinity of the throat. The young lack the crest, and often display dark banding on the body.

DISTRIBUTION: *Throughout Southeast Asia and islands to the south.*

SIZE: *Up to 32 in (80 cm).*

ACCOMMODATION: *Needs to be large with an extensive area of water since these lizards are semiaquatic by nature. Branches that extend out over the water, allowing the lizards to plunge in, are necessary for climbing. A temperature of about 82°F (28°C) is required. The water heater should be protected with a special casing. Full-spectrum lighting is also essential to guard against bone deformities, which will otherwise soon become evident, particularly in young Asian Water Dragons.*

BEHAVIOR: *These lizards are largely arboreal and will dive into water as a way of escaping danger. Adults especially can be nervous and, compared*

▲ ASIAN WATER DRAGON (PHYSIGNATHUS COCINCINUS)

with youngsters, are hard to tame successfully.

DIET: *Invertebrates, a little dog or cat food, and some soft fruit.*

BREEDING: *Females lay up to a dozen eggs per clutch, with incubation lasting about 12 weeks.*

RANKIN'S DRAGON

Pogona brevis   Family Agamidae

The naturally placid nature of members of this genus has helped ensure their popularity as pets in the home. They are smaller than the Bearded Dragon (*Pogona vitticeps*) and not yet available in a range of color variants, although the appearance of individuals can differ widely. They are basically a dirty sandy brown shade, with paler markings often evident on their back.

SYNONYM: *Pogona henrylawsonii.*

DISTRIBUTION: *Central and western parts of Queensland, Australia.*

◄ BEARDED DRAGON (POGONA VITTICEPS)—SEE PAGE 41 FOR COLOR VARIANTS.

DISTRIBUTION: *Eastern parts of Australia, away from the coast.*

SIZE: *20 in (50 cm).*

ACCOMMODATION: *An arid style of vivarium is required by these lizards, with a basking area of at least 95°F (35°C), reflecting their natural habitat. Full-spectrum lighting is essential, since young bearded dragons can suffer from skeletal problems caused by a lack of vitamin D.*

BEHAVIOR: *These lizards inflate their beard only when under threat, at which time they will try to intimidate their opponent with this display.*

DIET: *Specially formulated diets are now widely available for these insectivorous lizards.*

BREEDING: *Males can be identified by the presence of pores on the hind legs, extending over the femoral area. They also undertake a bobbing display with their head. The female may lay up to 30 eggs about a month after mating. The eggs will be buried in suitable a container of sand, and hatch after about 12 weeks.*

DAB LIZARD

Uromastyx acanthinurus   Family Agamidae

A number of these lizards are available and are sometimes simply offered under the generic name of *Uromastyx*. This species is the most colorful, displaying sporadic colorful areas on the body ranging from reddish orange via yellow to lime green.

DISTRIBUTION: *Northern Africa, from Senegal eastward to Egypt.*

SIZE: *24 in (60 cm).*

ACCOMMODATION: *Originating from arid areas, Dab Lizards will burrow into the substrate. They will therefore use earthenware pipes concealed in the substrate, provided the entrance is left open. The temperature should be 95°F (35°C) in the hottest part of the vivarium and should be allowed to drop at night to 68°F (20°C). Full-spectrum lighting is essential.*

BEHAVIOR: *The cute appearance of Dab Lizards conceals a rather aggressive side to their nature. Males should not be housed together.*

DIET: *Primarily herbivorous, eating items such as dandelions (flowers and leaves) as well as vegetables, including cabbage, when other foods are in short supply. Offer a good range, though, and sprinkle them with a vitamin and mineral supplement. Dab Lizards may be persuaded to take specially formulated herbivorous foods and will also eat invertebrates occasionally. Females will seek out invertebrates when coming into breeding condition, looking for an extra source of protein.*

BREEDING: *Up to 25 eggs may be laid in a container of moist sand. Hatching takes 85 to 100 days at a temperature of 86°F (30°C).*

SIZE: *13 in (33 cm).*

ACCOMMODATION: *Accommodation as recommended for the Asian Water Dragon (Physignathus cocincinus) is required, with a basking area where the temperature is at least 95°F (35°C). Cooling down to 68°F (20°C) for a couple of months will help stimulate breeding in the spring.*

BEHAVIOR: *Avoid keeping males of the species together because they are territorial by nature, and bullying is likely. A male can be housed with several females, however, without serious disputes breaking out.*

DIET: *Proprietary foods are recommended, the use of which will help avoid any nutritional deficiencies.*

BREEDING: *Details are similar to those for the Asian Water Dragon. Basking opportunities are very important for young Rankin's Dragons to guard against skeletal problems arising from vitamin D deficiencies.*

BEARDED DRAGON

Pogona vitticeps   Family Agamidae

The Bearded Dragon has become the most popular pet lizard in the world, being easily tamed and handled as it is, especially if obtained as a hatchling. The basic color is brownish, and the famous beard is formed by spiny projections around the sides of the head and down onto the throat. Reddish and yellow variants have become increasingly common over recent years thanks to selective breeding.

SKINKS

Family Scincidae

More than 1,200 different species of skinks (family Scincidae) are found worldwide. The vast majority of them are terrestrial in their habits, and some live a subterranean existence, burrowing underground. The legs in most cases are short, and the body is relatively elongated. The cylindrical shape of the body gives them a rather serpentine appearance. They are easy to cater to in vivarium surroundings, and some species can become remarkably tame, although they may bite if they are handled carelessly.

MONKEY-TAILED SKINK

Corucia zebrata   Family Scincidae

Pale whitish brown coloration is characteristic of this species. The tail is long and prehensile, helping anchor the skink onto a branch when it is resting, just as in the case of some monkeys. Their legs are powerful too and are equipped with strong claws which enable them to dig into the bark, providing a good grip as they clamber around.

DISTRIBUTION: *Solomon Islands in the Pacific, to the east of New Guinea.*

SIZE: *Up to 26 in (65 cm).*

ACCOMMODATION: *These arboreal skinks often retreat during the daytime into tree hollows. Their housing should be planned accordingly, with retreats of this type available and fixed securely in place. A tall mesh enclosure rather than a standard vivarium is preferable, since it affords more space. Heating and lighting should be provided above, out of reach.*

BEHAVIOR: *It is quite normal for these skinks to eat their own droppings—this may help them obtain more nutritional benefit from their food on a second passage through the digestive tract.*

DIET: *Largely plant matter, including fruit such as apples and vegetation such as dandelion leaves. Can also be offered chopped hard-boiled eggs occasionally.*

BREEDING: *Females give birth to just a single youngster after a period of about eight months following mating. The young skink remains with its mother for some time, and she may even carry her offspring around on her back. This maternal care may provide some protection against snakes in the wild.*

▲ MONKEY-TAILED SKINK (CORUCIA ZEBRATA)

FIVE-LINED SKINK

Eumeces fasciatus   Family Scincidae

Young Five-lined Skinks are so different in appearance from adults that it was initially thought they belonged to a separate species. They are dark in color, with yellow or white stripes running down their body and a bright blue tail at this stage. As they mature, however, the stripes disappear, and their body becomes a brownish color.

DISTRIBUTION: *Canada and the eastern United States, from southern New England, Wisconsin, Ontario and Kansas to northern Florida and Texas.*

SIZE: *9 in (22 cm).*

ACCOMMODATION: *A woodland setup is recommended, with a covering of leaves on the surface and small branches to provide additional cover. Keep relatively humid. Temperature should be from 77–86°F (25–30°C).*

BEHAVIOR: *Active during the day. These skinks should be cooled down to about 59°F (15°C) over the winter, to encourage breeding.*

DIET: *Invertebrates of suitable size, and pinkies in the case of larger individuals.*

BREEDING: *Males have reddish suffusion on the head. Clutches comprise four to 15 eggs, which are buried in the substrate. Hatching is likely to take four to six weeks.*

STRIPED SKINK

Mabuya striata   Family Scincidae

Sexing is straightforward in this species, because the iridescent males are much more brightly colored than the females. They are bronze with black and white spots on the body and an orange tail. Young of both sexes and females have a blue tail.

DISTRIBUTION: *Southern and eastern parts of Africa.*

SIZE: *8 in (20 cm).*

ACCOMMODATION: *The vivarium should have a sandy base and some rockwork. The temperature should be 77–82°F (25–28°C), dropping back slightly at night. Full-spectrum lighting should be included.*

OTHER SKINKS

Emerald Tree Skink (*Lamprolepis smaragdina/Dasia smaragdina*)

Range: Islands from New Guinea north to the Philippines.

Size: 10 in (25 cm).

Habitat: Rain forest.

Cunningham's Skink (*Egernia cunninghami*)

Range: Southern parts of Australia.

Size: 14 in (36 cm).

Habitat: Rocky terrain.

Rainbow Rock Skink (**Blue-tailed Skink**) (*Mabuya quinquetaeniata*)

Range: Occurs widely through eastern Africa.

Size: 10 in (25 cm).

Habitat: Adaptable, often occurring in savanna.

African Fire Skink (*Riopa fernandi*)

Range: Western Africa, south to Angola.

Size: 14 in (36 cm).

Habitat: Moist forest.

BEHAVIOR: *Hides away out of sight beneath vegetation. Suitable retreats are therefore important in vivarium surroundings to ensure these skinks feel secure. They will then settle down more quickly and are less likely to injure themselves.*

DIET: *Invertebrates of various types.*

BREEDING: *This species bears live young, with four offspring forming a typical brood. They should be moved to separate rearing accommodation.*

BERBER SKINK
(DOTTED SKINK)

Novoeumeces schneideri   Family Scincidae

The upper area of the body is a rusty shade of brown. A series of white spots edged with black and some broader orange bands alternate down the length of the body. The underside is a pale yellowish shade.

◄ *Five-lined Skink* (*Eumeces fasciatus*)—*juvenile*.

SYNONYM: *Eumeces schneideri.*

DISTRIBUTION: *Northwestern Africa.*

SIZE: *16 in (40 cm).*

ACCOMMODATION: *Originating from an arid area, these skinks require a sandy substrate into which they can burrow, as well as rockwork for retreats. The temperature should be about 86°F (30°C), giving them an opportunity to bask during the day, but dropping back slightly at night. A full-spectrum fluorescent bulb is also required.*

BEHAVIOR: *These skinks can be aggressive toward each other, even in the case of females. Try to divide the vivarium up into distinct areas using rockwork and other decor, since this should reduce the risk of conflict.*

DIET: *Invertebrates and finely diced soft fruit, which can be sprinkled with a vitamin and mineral supplement.*

BREEDING: *An egg-laying species. The female Berber Skink produces clutches averaging between five and 10 eggs, although it is not easy to persuade these lizards to breed in vivarium surroundings.*

BLUE-TONGUED SKINK

Tiliqua scincoides   Family Scincidae

The most distinctive feature of these skinks is the bright blue tongue, as their name suggests. Their body coloration can vary from grayish to brown, with as many as 10 darker bands being apparent across the body. Dark stripes also run along the sides of the head, passing through each eye.

DISTRIBUTION: *Occurs in northern and eastern parts of Australia.*

SIZE: *18 in (45 cm).*

ACCOMMODATION: *These skinks will burrow into the substrate. Any rocks must therefore be adequately buried on the floor of the vivarium so that they cannot be undermined. The temperature should be 86°F (30°C) during the day. Short lengths of drainpipe of suitable dimension can be provided as retreats.*

BEHAVIOR: *Be sure to provide a large bowl of water because these skinks like to bathe.*

DIET: *Omnivorous by nature. Will eat invertebrates, fruit, vegetables and can also be given a little dog food.*

BREEDING: *About 100 days after mating, as many as a dozen youngsters may be born. At this stage they will already be about 6 in (15 cm) long, and will be mature by two years of age.*

◄ *African Fire Skinks* (*Riopa fernandi*)—*mating pair.*

IGUANIDS

Family Iguanidae

In its broadest sense the family Iguanidae contains 11 subfamilies, but in recent years these have been raised to family level, an arrangement that is accepted to various degrees. In the following entries these new families are indicated in parentheses.

Iguanids are diverse in terms of their size, appearance and lifestyle, and a number of them make interesting vivarium occupants. This is partly a reflection of the fact that they are active during the day rather than at night. It is also possible to breed a number of species successfully in vivarium surroundings. Furthermore, if you dislike the prospect of having to feed invertebrates, then there are several herbivorous species to choose from, although they tend to be relatively large in size.

GREEN ANOLE
(AMERICAN CHAMELEON)

Anolis carolinensis   Family Iguanidae (Polychrotidae)

These attractive lizards are straightforward to keep, and their size makes them easy to accommodate. They tend to be greenish in color, but this can vary dramatically depending on their mood. If stressed for any reason, they are likely to become transformed to a dark brown shade. This explains their rather misleading alternative name—they are not related to true chameleons.

DISTRIBUTION: *Throughout the southern United States from southern Virginia to Texas. Also present on Caribbean islands, including the Bahamas.*

SIZE: *9 in (22 cm).*

ACCOMMODATION: *Arboreal by nature, Green Anoles require plenty of branches in their quarters for climbing. Plants can also be incorporated here, and full-spectrum lighting will help ensure the health of the lizards as well as the plants. A temperature of 79°F (26°C) is recommended during the day, dropping back to 72°F (22°C) at night.*

BEHAVIOR: *These anoles can easily suffer from dehydration, so spray their quarters daily. Allowing them to bathe in a shallow container of warm water, with a vitamin and mineral supplement added, can help correct this problem.*

DIET: *Invertebrates of suitable size, such as gut-loaded crickets.*

BREEDING: *Males inflate the pink-colored fold of skin under the chin, known as a dewlap, when displaying. Single eggs will be laid repeatedly by the female and buried in the substrate. Hatching is likely to take eight to 12 weeks at a temperature of 84°F (29°C).*

PLUMED BASILISK
(DOUBLE-CRESTED BASILISK)

Basiliscus plumifrons   Family Iguanidae (Corytophanidae)

The Plumed Basilisk is predominantly green in color with faint bluish white spots on the body. At the back of the head and extending down the neck is a tall helmet, which may measure 2.5 inches (6 cm) in height. A crest runs down the back, and another is present along the tail. The toes are long and slender.

DISTRIBUTION: *Central America, occurring from Guatemala to Costa Rica.*

SIZE: *Up to 28 in (70 cm).*

ACCOMMODATION: *A spacious vivarium of the rain forest type is required. Branches for climbing and an extensive area of water are essential. The water needs to be heated to about 77°F (25°C), while the vivarium should have a hot spot of closer to 90°F (32°C). Do not allow the nighttime temperature to fall significantly. Full-spectrum lighting is necessary.*

BEHAVIOR: *Basilisks are able to run across the surface of water if threatened, using their long toes. They can also swim and dive very effectively.*

◀ GREEN ANOLE (ANOLIS CAROLINENSIS)

▲ PLUMED BASILISK (BASILISCUS PLUMIFRONS)

DIET: *Can be fed on invertebrates and may even eat a little fruit laced with a vitamin and mineral powder. Will also eat some fish, so foods formulated for garter snakes may be given.*

BREEDING: *Males are aggressive and should be housed separately. Females may lay up to 20 eggs in a clutch, which hatch after 70 to 150 days.*

COLLARED LIZARD

Crotaphytus collaris   Family Iguanidae (Crotaphytidae)

A black collar around the back of the neck helps identify this lizard. The males are the more colorful sex, having yellowish markings on their backs and pale greenish blue underparts. White spotting is also evident over the back. Females in contrast tend to be sandy brown in color.

DISTRIBUTION: *From Utah and Colorado in the west, down via Texas and Arizona into Mexico.*

SIZE: *14 in (36 cm).*

ACCOMMODATION: *An arid style of vivarium, with an extensive floor area and a hot spot in which the temperature should be as high as 100°F (38°C)*

(or even slightly higher) is important for their well-being. The temperature should then be allowed to fall off at night, down to about 79°F (26°C). Full-spectrum lighting is vital as well.

BEHAVIOR: *These lizards can produce a surprisingly determined bite, especially if they are not used to being handled. They can also jump well.*

DIET: *A variety of invertebrates.*

BREEDING: *When egg-laying is imminent, females develop reddish blotches on the sides of the body. They lay clutches of up to a dozen eggs, which may take two months or so to hatch.*

SPINY-TAILED IGUANA

Ctenosaura similis   Family Iguanidae (Iguanidae)

As their name suggests, Spiny-tailed Iguanas are protected by rows of sharp spines on their long tail, which they can use to inflict painful blows. They are rather drab in color, varying from dark brown to black, and often displaying a slightly banded appearance. Young hatchlings are green.

DISTRIBUTION: *Central America, ranging from Mexico to Panama.*

SIZE: *Around 35 in (90 cm).*

ACCOMMODATION: *These large lizards spend much of their time off the ground, and this should be reflected in their housing. Branches should be fixed securely in place, to allow them to bask beneath the heat source.*

BEHAVIOR: *In the wild these iguanas tend to live in groups shepherded by a dominant male.*

DIET: *A variety of plant matter, including fruit, which should be laced with a vitamin and mineral preparation. These iguanids also require some invertebrates and will take pinkies. Alternatively, a formulated iguana food can be given.*

▲ GREEN IGUANA (IGUANA IGUANA)

BREEDING: *Females can lay up to 30 eggs in a clutch. The young will usually hatch after about 12 weeks.*

GREEN IGUANA

Iguana iguana　　　　　　Family Iguanidae (Iguanidae)

This used to be a very popular pet lizard, but housing these large iguanas in the home is difficult, and they also frequently become aggressive as they mature. They are typically greenish in color, although they sometimes appear grayish green. Less commonly, they may have a slightly bluish hue to their skin.

DISTRIBUTION: *Extends through Central Mexico down through northern South America.*

SIZE: *May reach up to 6.6 ft (2 m), including the long tail.*

ACCOMMODATION: *Spacious accommodation is important. It should incorporate an area of water, branches and basking facilities. Spray the vivarium to maintain the humidity. It needs to be heated to about 86°F (30°C), dropping back to about 77°F (25°C) at night.*

BEHAVIOR: *These lizards will use their tails to defend themselves and are able to inflict a painful blow with this part of the body. They will also dive off a branch over water and swim away if threatened.*

◄ CHUCKWALLA (SAUROMALUS ATER)

DIET: *Specially formulated diets are now widely available, but Green Iguanas will also feed on a range of plant matter and fruit.*

BREEDING: *Males are generally recognizable by their larger crests. Clutch size is likely to vary between 20 and 40 eggs, with incubation lasting from just over two months up to nearly four months. High humidity—over 85 percent—and a temperature of about 86°F (30°C) are required.*

CHUCKWALLA

Sauromalus ater (obesus)   Family Iguanidae (Iguanidae)

Although they tend to be blackish in color, Chuckwallas may develop reddish areas on their body as they grow older. Dark cross-banding is a feature of younger individuals, while females can usually be distinguished by their smaller size.

DISTRIBUTION: *Southwestern parts of the United States, from southeastern California, southern Nevada and Utah via Arizona down to Mexico.*

SIZE: *Up to 16.5 in (42 cm).*

ACCOMMODATION: *Chuckwallas live in very hot conditions, which should be replicated in the vivarium. The temperature here should be up to 100°F (38°C), with full-spectrum lighting provided. Secure rocky retreats are also important to mimic the lizards' natural surroundings.*

BEHAVIOR: *Chuckwallas inhabit rocky terrain. If threatened, they will retreat under the rocks, anchoring themselves in place by inflating their bodies so they cannot be dislodged.*

DIET: *Herbivorous by nature, eating a variety of plant matter and fruit. Add a vitamin and mineral supplement to this food regularly. Alternatively, offer a specially formulated iguana food.*

BREEDING: *Female Chuckwallas breed only in alternate years. They lay six to 13 eggs, and hatching takes about 11 weeks or so at a temperature of 90°F (32°C).*

DESERT SPINY LIZARD

Sceloporus magister   Family Iguanidae (Phrynosomatidae)

The Desert Spiny Lizard is one of the largest members of the genus and can be identified by the dark spot on each shoulder. It is highly variable in appearance, with nine different subspecies recognized. The body tends to be dark overall, with brighter, rather iridescent colors evident. Males can be distinguished by the bluish violet area on the center of the back.

DISTRIBUTION: *Southwestern United States, from southern Nevada into Baja California. Also occurs in parts of Arizona, New Mexico and Texas, extending across the Mexican border.*

SIZE: *Up to 12 in (30 cm).*

▶ WESTERN FENCE LIZARD (SCELOPORUS OCCIDENTALIS)

ACCOMMODATION: *These spiny lizards are adept at climbing, and this needs to be reflected in their housing. Hot conditions—between 100 and 104°F (38 and 40°C)—must be created in part of the vivarium, although the temperature should be much cooler at night, mimicking their desert home.*

BEHAVIOR: *Frequently occur in rocky areas, where cover is readily available.*

DIET: *Invertebrates of various types. Larger individuals may also eat pinkies.*

BREEDING: *Clutch size can vary from seven to 19 eggs, with incubation likely to take eight to 11 weeks.*

WESTERN FENCE LIZARD

Sceloporus occidentalis   Family Iguanidae (Phrynosomatidae)

The Western Fence Lizard is a brownish shade overall, with some darker markings. Blue areas are evident on the sides of the body, and males can be distinguished by a blue area on the throat, which becomes particularly evident when they are displaying.

DISTRIBUTION: *Western United States, from central Idaho to Nevada. Extends down the Pacific coast to Baja California.*

SIZE: *10 in (25 cm).*

ACCOMMODATION: *Warm surroundings and opportunities for climbing are important. The temperature in their quarters should be up to 95°F (35°C), and a thermal gradient should be created across the vivarium. A full-spectrum light is important.*

BEHAVIOR: *It is not uncommon to see these lizards on fences as well as walls. Being bold by nature, they are often seen in the vicinity of buildings.*

DIET: *A variety of invertebrates, including gut-loaded crickets.*

BREEDING: *Females lay between three and 14 eggs in a clutch. Hatching typically takes seven to 11 weeks.*

OTHER LIZARDS

The vivarium hobby often includes representatives from a number of other lizard families. Their individual care requirements can differ widely, however, as the examples in this section show. Some of these species also produce live young, whereas others reproduce by means of eggs.

▲ EUROPEAN LEGLESS LIZARD (OPHISAURUS APODUS)

EUROPEAN LEGLESS LIZARD
(SCHELTOPUSIK; GLASS SNAKE)

Ophisaurus apodus   Family Anguidae

At first glance the appearance of this lizard is similar to that of a snake, because of its lack of limbs and its size. The fact that it is a true lizard, however, is soon revealed by its ability to blink. European Legless Lizards are brown with pale underparts, while young specimens are ash gray with brown speckling on the body. This species ranks among the longest-lived lizards.

DISTRIBUTION: *From the Balkans in eastern Europe via Turkey to central Asia.*

SIZE: *3.6 ft (1.1 m).*

ACCOMMODATION: *Requires a large vivarium or possibly a secure outdoor enclosure, depending on the temperature. The floor should be covered in part with dry leaves and needs to include areas where these lizards can hide away. The vivarium temperature should be maintained at about 82°F (28°C) during the summer, dropping back at night.*

BEHAVIOR: *The alternative name of Glass Snake arises from the way these lizards will shed their tail readily if handled, as a defensive measure.*

DIET: *Larger invertebrates, especially slugs and snails. Pinkies and formulated foods such as a box turtle diet can be offered occasionally.*

BREEDING: *Cooling for a month in the winter serves as a breeding trigger. The male's head becomes bigger as it matures. Up to a dozen eggs may be laid. Do not try to rear the young with adults, or they will be eaten.*

SOUTHERN ALLIGATOR LIZARD

Elgaria multicarinata (multicarinatus)   Family Anguidae

The prominent large scales of these lizards help explain their common name. They are brownish in color, with black cross-bands edged at the rear with white. The appearance of these lizards differs among individuals, however, and five distinctive subspecies are recognized.

SYNONYM: *Gerrhonotus multicarinatus.*

Distribution: *Western United States, from southern Washington through western Oregon and California down to Baja California.*

SIZE: *Up to 17 in (43 cm).*

ACCOMMODATION: *These lizards favor slightly damp surroundings and need hiding places incorporated in the vivarium. A temperature of 68–77°F (20–25°C) generally suits them, but allow it to drop back slightly at night.*

BEHAVIOR: *Southern Alligator Lizards tend not to climb, but may use their long tail to help them grip if they attempt to do so.*

DIET: *Invertebrates of various types. A small amount of hard-boiled egg may also be eaten.*

BREEDING: *Females often produce several clutches in succession of, on average, 12 eggs each. Hatching may occur after six weeks at 82°F (28°C).*

WARREN'S GIRDLED LIZARD

Cordylus warreni   Family Cordylidae

Striking dark brown and white coloration is typical of these lizards. They also have a rough body surface, caused by projecting scales here and on the tail. Approximately nine subspecies are recognized through this lizard's range, differing from each other slightly in appearance.

DISTRIBUTION: *Southeastern Africa.*

SIZE: *12 in (30 cm).*

ACCOMMODATION: *The daytime vivarium temperature should be about 86°F (30°C), dropping to 68°F (20°F) at night. Humidity should be low, although daily spraying is recommended, and a container of water should be provided. There must also be a full-spectrum light included in the enclosure, since these lizards are diurnal.*

BEHAVIOR: *They anchor themselves with their spiny scales in rocky crevices.*

DIET: *Invertebrates of various types, preferably gut-loaded.*

BREEDING: *Males can be distinguished only by their larger femoral pores. Cooling their quarters for a month is likely to trigger breeding behavior. Females give birth to up to six young.*

▲ *WARREN'S GIRDLED LIZARD (CORDYLUS WARRENI)*

▼ *SOUTHERN ALLIGATOR LIZARD (ELGARIA MULTICARINATA)*

GIANT PLATED LIZARD
(TAWNY PLATED LIZARD)

Gerrhosaurus major   Family Gerrhosauridae

Giant Plated Lizards are mainly brown in color, and some individuals are lighter than others. The scales along the back have a rough texture, while the chin and throat are usually paler than the rest of the body, being cream in color. The underparts are a paler shade of brown.

DISTRIBUTION: *Present in eastern and southeastern parts of Africa.*

SIZE: *20 in (50 cm).*

ACCOMMODATION: *These lizards are found in hot, dry areas and need a vivarium heated to at least 86°F (30°C), dropping back to about 68°F (20°C) at night. They are terrestrial by nature and should be provided with a relatively deep, sandy substrate, in which they are likely to dig. Rockwork providing cover must therefore be securely positioned directly on the vivarium floor to prevent it from toppling over and injuring the lizards.*

BEHAVIOR: *In the wild these lizards often live in termite mounds, which helps protect them from predators and means that they will sometimes feed on these insects.*

DIET: *Omnivorous, eating vegetables, fruit and invertebrates as well as pinkies.*

BREEDING: *Unusual in vivarium surroundings. A cool period of 68°F (20°C) for several weeks may serve as a trigger. Clutches typically consist of two to six eggs.*

FLAT LIZARD

Platysaurus intermedius   Family Cordylidae

Typical coloration for members of this species includes a greenish back with yellow spots. The tail is a dull orange color. The underside of the body is bluish, and males are more brightly colored. The flattened body shape that gives these lizards their common name enables them to hide in rock crevices.

◀ *FLAT LIZARD (PLATYSAURUS INTERMEDIUS)*

DISTRIBUTION: *Southern Africa, present in Zimbabwe, Malawi, Lesotho and northeastern South Africa.*

SIZE: *12 in (30 cm).*

ACCOMMODATION: *These lizards live among rocks, and this habitat needs to be replicated in the vivarium. There should be plenty of retreats, and rocks for climbing over should be securely fixed in place. Hot and dry conditions are required, with a heat lamp providing a temperature of 95°F (35°C), dropping back slightly at night. Full-spectrum lighting is also necessary.*

BEHAVIOR: *Rock lizards generally do not stray far from the security provided by these enclaves. They should be fed in this area, since they may be reluctant to seek food elsewhere. They are very social by nature.*

DIET: *Invertebrates of various types.*

BREEDING: *Females conceal their eggs in crevices, particularly where there is damp material such as leaf mold. A number of females will share a nest site, and each individual will lay two eggs on average. Hatching takes about two months at a temperature of 86°F (30°C).*

▼ *GIANT PLATED LIZARD (GERRHOSAURUS MAJOR)*

GREEN LIZARD
(EMERALD LIZARD)

Lacerta viridis   Family Lacertidae

As its name suggests, the coloration of this lizard is grass green, with a variable pattern of yellow and green dots. Females tend to be a duller shade of green, and sexing is especially straightforward during the breeding season, since males develop a sky blue throat at this stage. The tail of the green lizard is about twice as long as its body.

DISTRIBUTION: *From southern and central parts of Europe to western Asia.*

SIZE: *Up to 16 in (40 cm).*

ACCOMMODATION: *A vivarium moderately heated to a temperature of about 77° F (25° C) is needed, together with full-spectrum lighting. Some decor that also provides hiding places for the lizards should be provided.*

BEHAVIOR: *Green lizards are rather territorial by nature and are therefore best kept in pairs.*

▲ GREEN LIZARD (LACERTA VIRIDIS)

DIET: *Various invertebnrates, including gut-loaded crickets.*

BREEDING: *A winter cooling period is recommended, with the temperature falling to 50° F (10° C). Females may lay a total of up to 20 eggs which are buried. Hatching takes two months or so at 82° F (28° C).*

CHINESE CROCODILE LIZARD

Shinisaurus crocodilurus   Family Xenosauridae

With its broad rounded head and short jaws, the Chinese Crocodile Lizard has a very distinctive shape. It is brownish with some black markings, and the scales along its back are not dissimilar to those of a crocodile. Males can be identified by a slight orange hue on the throat and the sides of the body.

DISTRIBUTION: *Confined to southwestern parts of China.*

SIZE: *16 in (40 cm).*

ACCOMMODATION: *This semiaquatic lizard requires a spacious aquaterrarium. A power filter will help maintain the water quality, but regular water changes will still need to be carried out. Easy access into and out of the water is important. The temperature should be about 68° F (20° C). A full-spectrum light should be incorporated in their quarters.*

BEHAVIOR: *Crocodile lizards have been observed sunbathing on branches above water in the wild, dropping off the branch if danger threatens.*

DIET: *Feeds naturally on fish. May be weaned onto a food specially formulated for garter snakes. Amphibians, including tadpoles, also form part of its natural diet.*

BREEDING: *Usually only one or two young are produced, although up to 10 have been recorded. The female often gives birth in the water.*

TORTOISES AND TURTLES
ORDER TESTUDINES

The protective shells of members of the Order Testudines (formerly Chelonia)—tortoises, terrapins and turtles—make them among the most instantly recognizable of all reptiles. Chelonians, as they are collectively known, represent one of the oldest surviving reptilian lineages, their origins dating back more than 200 million years. Their earliest ancestors were probably not unlike armadillos, in the sense that they had a flexible body and could curl up into a ball to protect themselves. Gradually they sacrificed mobility for a more rigid body armor, and this design has stood the test of time.

Chelonians survived the radical changes on Earth that resulted in the extinction of the dinosaurs and countless other life forms at the end of the Cretaceous Period, around 65 million years ago. At this stage, it was still an aquatic group—the first steps onto land followed during the Eocene epoch, perhaps in the area of present-day North America, although the remains of early tortoises have also been discovered in Africa.

The shells of these land-dwelling chelonians became increasingly domed, partly to protect against predators, and also to provide space for a larger lung capacity. This met the tortoise's raised requirement for oxygen, necessitated by having to carry the weight of its shell on land and, in some cases, by a significant increase in size. Two populations of giant chelonians still exist today and are found on the Aldabran islands close to Africa and also on the Galápagos Islands, off the coast of Ecuador in northern South America.

There were others in the past, notably on Caribbean islands such as Cuba, while the biggest land tortoise ever discovered—with a shell length of some 8 feet (2.4 m)—lived in Asia about 55 million years ago. Even before this, however, the sea turtle *Archaelon* patrolled the oceans during the Cretaceous Period and its shell could grow to a monstrous 12 feet (3.6 m) long, making it the largest chelonian ever recorded.

The figures given for the chelonians covered in the following section also relate to their shell size. Members of this group are measured in a straight line above the vertebral scutes from one end of the shell to the other. This means, therefore, that their maximum size, with head and tail fully extended, will be longer.

◀ *GALÁPAGOS TORTOISE (GEOCHELONE NIGRA)*

TORTOISES
Family Testudinidae

Today representatives of the family Testudinidae are found on all continents except Australia, although they used to occur there in the past. The most recent fossilized remains of the so-called horned tortoises, or meiolaniids, which died out as recently as 120 million years ago, have been found in the region on Lord Howe Island.

Their slow, ponderous gait has done nothing to help tortoises survive in the modern world. Thankfully, however, interest in keeping these reptiles has led to a much greater understanding of their reproductive biology so that even officially endangered species such as the radiated tortoise (*Astrochelys radiata*) are now regularly being bred by enthusiasts. This gives hope for their future of many other species that are under serious threat in the wild.

Not only do tortoises have the greatest life expectancy of any reptile, but they also rank as the longest lived of all vertebrates—there are reliable records showing that they can live for over 150 years. But this does not mean that it will be decades before hatchlings start to breed for the first time; many are likely to be breeding successfully by the time they reach six or seven years of age.

RED-FOOTED TORTOISE

Geochelone carbonaria   Family Testudinidae

Several forms of this wide-ranging tortoise can be identified, the most distinctive being the cherryhead, which is thought to originate from southern Brazil. It is characterized by having more intense and extensive red markings on its head and forelegs than other forms. Cherryheads are also slightly smaller in size than other red-footed tortoises, with mottling often evident on the carapace. In addition, dark areas intermingle right across the plastron, rather than being confined solely to the center.

SYNONYM: *Chelonoidis carbonaria.*

DISTRIBUTION: *Central and South America, from Panama southward to northern Argentina. Also represented on various Caribbean islands, notably Trinidad.*

SIZE: *20 in (51 cm).*

ACCOMMODATION: *In temperate areas, a large heated enclosure is essential, and these tortoises should be allowed outdoors only when the weather is warm. They should be brought in at night to avoid any risk of chilling. A temperature of about 77 to 81°F (25–27°C) is ideal.*

BEHAVIOR: *These tortoises do not hibernate, since they occur on the fringes of forests and in savanna, where food is available throughout the year. Males may fight each other when seeking to mate with a female, and may therefore have to be separated at this stage.*

DIET: *Essentially vegetarian, but should be given restricted amounts of animal protein, which can be in the guise of a formulated food. Will also take fruit, but this should be rationed, since an excess can lead to serious digestive upsets.*

BREEDING: *Females produce clutches of three to five eggs, with the incubation period lasting at least 150 days at 86°F (30°C). They may lay up to three times a year.*

▶ RED-FOOTED TORTOISE (GEOCHELONE CARBONARIA)—CHERRYHEAD.

CHILEAN TORTOISE

Geochelone chilensis   Family Testudinidae

The most southerly of the American tortoises, this is a predominantly brownish colored species. Mature males often tend to be darker than females. This can be helpful in distinguishing the sexes, since the traditional division on the basis of tail length and plastron shape is less clear cut in this species than most.

SYNONYM: *Chelonoidis chilensis.*

DISTRIBUTION: *Southern South America, ranging from Bolivia, Paraguay and Argentina southward as far as the northern Patagonian region of Chile.*

SIZE: *Usually about 10 in (25 cm), but can grow up to 17 in (43 cm).*

ACCOMMODATION: *Requires a relatively dry and arid environment, although drinking water must always be available.*

▲ YELLOW-FOOTED TORTOISE (GEOCHELONE DENTICULATA)

▼ INDIAN STAR TORTOISE (GEOCHELONE ELEGANS)

BEHAVIOR: *The marginals of young Chilean Tortoises are evidently serrated; these sharp projections probably afford some protection against predators.*

DIET: *Largely herbivorous, but may also be given small amounts of fruit. Can also be persuaded to take formulated foods.*

BREEDING: *Females lay clutches of up to six eggs. Eggs have been recorded as hatching after as little as two months at an incubation temperature of 86°F (30°C) and an RH reading of 70 percent. Incubation in the wild might be significantly longer, because young may apparently overwinter in the ground and not emerge until the following spring.*

YELLOW-FOOTED TORTOISE

Geochelone denticulata　　　　　Family Testudinidae

The largest of the mainland South American tortoises, the Yellow-footed Tortoise can be distinguished from its red-footed relative *(Geochelone carbonaria)* by the yellow or orange markings on its head and legs. It is otherwise similar in shape, with a relatively elongated, curved shell, and occurs in rain forest areas where the light is dappled rather than bright.

SYNONYM: *Chelonoidis denticulata.*

DISTRIBUTION: *Ranges discontinuously east of the Andes, being present on Trinidad and through Colombia and Venezuela southward to parts of Bolivia and Brazil.*

SIZE: *Typically 16 in (40 cm) when adult; reputedly can reach twice that size.*

ACCOMMODATION: *Requires warm surroundings with a minimum temperature of 77°F (25°C), and a relatively humid environment to mimic its natural habitat. Ventilation must be good to keep molds from developing.*

BEHAVIOR: *Often likes to bathe. Active by nature.*

DIET: *Requires slightly more fruit (rather than herbage) in its diet than the Red-footed Tortoise—reflecting its natural habitat, which is forest. Will often take prepared tortoise diets readily, too.*

BREEDING: *Has proved less free-breeding overall than the Red-footed Tortoise, but under favorable conditions females will not only lay larger clutches, but also tend to nest more frequently. Hatching periods for both species are similar (i.e., at least 150 days at 86°F/30°C).*

INDIAN STAR TORTOISE

Geochelone elegans　　　　　Family Testudinidae

The common name of this tortoise stems from the the radiating stellar pattern of lines that extend over the carapace and can also be seen on the plastron. These markings are sufficiently distinctive to allow individuals to be recognized.

DISTRIBUTION: *Occurs throughout most of India and the adjacent island of Sri Lanka, but is seemingly less common in Pakistan.*

▲ LEOPARD TORTOISE (GEOCHELONE PARDALIS)—*DARK (TOP) AND LIGHT (ABOVE) FORMS.*

SIZE: *Typically about 11 in (28 cm), but may reach almost 14 in (35 cm).*

ACCOMMODATION: *Maintain in typically warm, dry surroundings. Susceptible to chilling, which is likely to lead to pneumonia.*

BEHAVIOR: *Forages for most of the year in relatively dry areas, and even ventures into human habitats. The monsoon rains throughout the region from June to October trigger a flush of fresh vegetation, which seems to encourage mating.*

DIET: *Mainly herbivorous.*

BREEDING: *Males are typically smaller than females and mature earlier, by five years old. Females can lay three or more clutches of five or six eggs annually. Incubation at 86°F (30°C) takes about 100 days. The young start to develop their markings clearly once they reach a year old.*

LEOPARD TORTOISE

Geochelone pardalis　　　　　Family Testudinidae

This popular species is relatively bold in nature and has a very variable dark and yellowish white shell patterning. Some individuals have a much paler appearance than others. Females generally attain a larger adult size than males.

▲ RADIATED TORTOISE (GEOCHELONE/ ASTROCHELYS RADIATA)

DISTRIBUTION: *The nominate race, with its flatter profile, is restricted to southwestern Africa, with the more commonly kept* Geochelone pardalis babcocki *ranging southward from the southern fringes of the Sahara.*

SIZE: *Usually averages about 14–18 in (35–45 cm), but has been known to grow to nearly 28 in (70 cm).*

ACCOMMODATION: *Can be allowed in a secure outdoor enclosure to forage on warm fine days, but should be brought in at night if the temperature is likely to fall below 59°F (15°C). As for all large tropical species, spacious, heated wintertime accommodation will be required in temperate areas.*

BEHAVIOR: *When kept in groups, males may be aggressive to each other. Can climb well, and may display a homing instinct.*

DIET: *Will consume large quantities of vegetation, and drinks readily, too. Avoid fruit, although tomatoes can be given alongside plant matter such as dandelion leaves. A formulated food will also be eaten.*

BREEDING: *Females can be prolific, laying up to six clutches a year, usually comprising about 10 eggs each, although 20 or more have been documented. Hatchlings may start to emerge after 130 days at an incubator temperature of 86°F (30°C).*

RADIATED TORTOISE

Geochelone radiata   Family Testudinidae

This species has a series of light markings that vary according to the individual. The markings radiate across the carapace from the pale aureoles at the center of the large scutes, forming a contrast with the otherwise dark shell. The patterning is especially bright in young Radiated Tortoises. Roughly symmetrical blackish blotches are evident on the whitish plastron.

SYNONYM: *Astrochelys radiata.*

DISTRIBUTION: *Occurs in southern Madagascar, and has also been*

introduced both to Mauritius and the nearby Reunion Islands.

SIZE: *Can grow up to about 16 in (40 cm).*

ACCOMMODATION: *Must be kept in dry and warm surroundings.*

BEHAVIOR: *Occurs in relatively arid country, consisting of forest and scrubland. Has proved to be very prolific, laying up to seven clutches a year. This has helped ensure that captive-bred stock of this endangered species is relatively widely available.*

DIET: *Browses on vegetation. Fruits of prickly pear cacti (Opuntia sp.) are a natural food and can be offered when available, but they should first be stripped of any thorns.*

BREEDING: *Females lay between three and 14 eggs per clutch. The incubation period is very variable, lasting from about 145 to 230 days in the wild. At 86°F (30°C) hatchlings will emerge after 100 days or so.*

▼ BELL'S HINGEBACK TORTOISE (KINIXYS BELLIANA)

AFRICAN SPURRED TORTOISE

Geochelone sulcata   Family Testudinidae

This is the largest of all the continental land tortoises. The adults can weigh as much as 230 pounds (105 kg), so moving them can present difficulties! They are typically a pale brownish shade overall. This species gets its common name from the prominent spurs present on each thigh, and should not be confused with the Mediterranean species *(Testudo graeca)*.

SYNONYM: *Centrochelys sulcata.*

DISTRIBUTION: *Sub-Saharan Africa, from Mauritania eastward to Ethiopia.*

SIZE: *Can grow up to 33 in (83 cm).*

ACCOMMODATION: *The size of these tortoises means that they require spacious housing. They can be allowed outside into an area of lawn when the weather is dry and sunny.*

BEHAVIOR: *African Spurred Tortoises retreat into underground burrows when the sun is at its hottest, or if there is little food. They dig readily, therefore, and must not be able to tunnel out of their enclosure. In the wild, they have been known to feed at night when it is cooler.*

DIET: *Predominantly herbivorous, requiring a high-fiber diet. These tortoises will consume a wide range of green food, which needs to be laced with a supplement. Will also eat formulated foods.*

BREEDING: *Potentially prolific, with females laying clutches in excess of 30 eggs, and nesting up to six times a year. Calcium supplementation is advised for breeding females in particular. Hatching may take 100 days at 86°F (30°C), and the young grow rapidly.*

ELONGATED TORTOISE
(YELLOW TORTOISE)

Indotestudo elongata   Family Testudinidae

The Elongated Tortoise has a yellowish body color, with variable black blotches on the carapace and plastron. These markings are usually small. Because this species originates from forested surroundings, its eyes appear relatively large.

DISTRIBUTION: *Found across much of southern Asia, from India to southern China.*

SIZE: *When adult, reaches an average of 12–14 in (30–36 cm). Males are slightly larger than females.*

ACCOMMODATION: *Found in tropical forest through much of its range, this species requires relatively shaded, humid surroundings, and is not inclined to bask. Temperature should be in the range of 77–86°F (25–30°C).*

BEHAVIOR: *Becomes most active after heavy rainfall. Both sexes develop pinkish coloration around the eyes at the start of the breeding season.*

DIET: *Feeds on both fruit and green foods as well as invertebrates. These tortoises are omnivorous, so will usually take formulated foods readily.*

BREEDING: *Clutch size averages three to nine eggs, with females laying up to three times a year. Hatching takes about 110 days at an incubation temperature of approximately 86°C (30°C).*

BELL'S HINGEBACK TORTOISE

Kinixys belliana   Family Testudinidae

Bell's Hingeback Tortoise is so highly variable in appearance across its extensive range that some taxonomists have divided it into several races or even split it into separate species. Bell's can be easily identified, however, by the shape of its shell, which is particularly rounded at the rear. Some populations have a mottled carapace, whereas others are brown in coloration.

DISTRIBUTION: *This species is widely represented across much of Africa south of the Sahara.*

SIZE: *Typically ranges from 11–14 in (28–36 cm).*

ACCOMMODATION: *Bell's Hingeback is a relatively active tortoise and tends to occur in more open countryside than the other hingebacks listed here. It will still seek to hide away when resting, however.*

BEHAVIOR: *These tortoises like to bathe, often immersing themselves in a suitable container of water in their quarters.*

DIET: *An omnivorous species, which should be offered mainly herbage, but will also take some fruit and invertebrates. Tomatoes can be a useful food, especially for individuals recuperating from illness.*

BREEDING: *Courtship can be violent in the case of hingebacks, and some males prove to be more aggressive than others. Female Bell's Hingebacks will lay repeatedly, producing eight to 10 eggs per clutch. Hatching is likely to take about three months at 86°F (30°C).*

FOREST HINGEBACK
(ERODED KINIXYS)

Kinixys erosa   Family Testudinidae

This is potentially the largest of the hingebacks, although it is the least commonly seen of the three species in collections. Its shell is a distinctive reddish brown color overall, with the central areas of each tending to appear slightly sunken.

DISTRIBUTION: *Extends from Gambia eastward via the Congo Basin to Uganda, and south to Angola.*

SIZE: *Adult males often reach more than 12 in (30 cm) long; the maximum size for females is approximately 10 in (25 cm).*

ACCOMMODATION: *Originating from areas of tropical forest, this tortoise requires warm, humid conditions in order to thrive in vivarium surroundings.*

BEHAVIOR: *Has been observed hunting for food in shallow streams. In common with related species, it tends to be most active in the early morning and again toward dusk.*

DIET: *As for Bell's Hingeback. Poor appetite in the case of wild-caught hingebacks can often be related to a heavy burden of intestinal worms acquired from feeding on invertebrates.*

BREEDING: *Males of this species are particularly aggressive at mating time. Ideally, a single male should be housed with two or three females. Young hatchlings have sharply serrated marginals, giving them some protection against predators.*

HOME'S HINGEBACK TORTOISE

Kinixys homeana   Family Testudinidae

As with other *Kinixys* species, Home's Hingeback has a distinctive hinge of softer tissue on each side of the carapace. This allows it to seal its hind legs completely within its shell. Compared with the smooth profile of Bell's Hingeback, this species has more of a prominence at the rear of the shell. The shell itself tends to be light brown in color.

DISTRIBUTION: *Confined to West Africa, found in an area extending from Liberia via Côte d'Ivoire to the Congo Basin.*

SIZE: *Attains a maximum size of about 9 in (22 cm). Adult females are slightly larger than males.*

ACCOMMODATION: *Warm, relatively humid surroundings are essential along with a regular opportunity to bathe, all of which mimics rain forest conditions. The surroundings should also be relatively shady, as for K. erosa.*

BEHAVIOR: *A rather shy species; its large eyes suggest that it can see well in forest conditions where the light is relatively poor.*

DIET: *Its feeding need not differ from that of other members of the genus. Formulated foods are often more likely to be eaten if soaked, particularly at first.*

BREEDING: *Its needs are similar to those of K. erosa; as in that species, young Home's Hingebacks have sharp projections around the rear marginals especially, and lack the hinge associated with adults.*

PANCAKE TORTOISE

Malacochersus tornieri   Family Testudinidae

The Pancake Tortoise is one of the most distinctive tortoises. This is because of its flattened body shape and its lightweight shell, which is patterned in such a way that it breaks up the tortoise's outline in its natural habitat.

◄ *HOME'S HINGEBACK TORTOISE (KINIXYS HOMEANA)*

▲ PANCAKE TORTOISE (MALACOCHERSUS TORNIERI)

DISTRIBUTION: *Restricted to parts of central Kenya and nearby Tanzania, where it occurs in rocky areas.*

SIZE: *Measures about 7 in (18 cm) when adult.*

ACCOMMODATION: *A sandy substrate should be devised, with securely fixed rocks that will allow the tortoises to climb and will also provide safe retreats. Dry and warm surroundings are needed, and the temperature should be reduced at night.*

BEHAVIOR: *Having shed the bulk of their shell, these tortoises rely on their speed to escape predators. They run away from danger into rock crevices, anchoring themselves in using their body and legs.*

DIET: *A mixture of fruit and vegetation.*

BREEDING: *Females have just a single egg per clutch, but can lay every six weeks or so. Nesting in the wild occurs mainly in July and August. At 86°F (30°C) incubation may take 150 days, sometimes lasting for as long as 220 days. It is normal for newly hatched young Pancake Tortoises to have a slightly domed appearance.*

BURMESE BROWN TORTOISE

Manouria emys   Family Testudinidae

Two distinctive subspecies exist. The northern form, known as *Manouria emys phayrei*, grows significantly larger than the nominate race; it is also recognizable by its flatter profile. Individuals vary in color from dark brown to almost black.

DISTRIBUTION: *From India and Bangladesh in the north, southward to Malaysia, and parts of Borneo and Sumatra.*

SIZE: Manouria emys emys *grows to nearly 16 in (40 cm) overall, and* M. e. phayrei *reaches 20–24 in (50–60 cm).*

ACCOMMODATION: *Access to bathing facilities is important. Surprisingly, however, these tropical tortoises do not like especially high temperatures. They are active in the range of 68–77°F (20–25°C).*

BEHAVIOR: *In the wild these tortoises become more lively during periods of rainfall, which starts the breeding cycle. After laying, the female will guard her nest site, a behavior most commonly seen in crocodilians but virtually unknown in chelonians.*

DIET: *These tortoises feed mainly on plant matter but can be given fruit in moderation. Will also eat a formulated food.*

BREEDING: *Females lay larger clutches than any other tortoise, producing as many as 50 eggs at a time. At an RH of 90 percent and a temperature of 86°F (30°C) the eggs may starting hatching as soon as 60 days later.*

MEDITERRANEAN SPUR-THIGHED TORTOISE

Testudo graeca   Family Testudinidae

This species should not be confused with the plain-colored African Spurred Tortoise *(Geochelone sulcata)*. The patterning in the Mediterranean Spur-thighed Tortoise depends to a significant degree on locality, which has led to taxonomists dividing the species into a number of races or even different species over recent years. In all forms, however, the relatively small spur is evident between the hind legs and the tail.

DISTRIBUTION: *Occurs on both sides of the Mediterranean coast, as well as the Balearic Islands and Sardinia. Extends to parts of eastern Europe and southwest Asia as well as the Middle East.*

SIZE: *Averages 6–8 in (15–20 cm), with females tending to be bigger. Some geographical variation is apparent.*

ACCOMMODATION: *On warm days during the summer it can be allowed to roam outdoors in a run with an attached shelter. Hibernates in winter.*

BEHAVIOR: *May dig, so the area of the enclosure needs to be secure in order to prevent any escapes.*

DIET: *Feeds largely on vegetation and flowers, but can be given tomatoes and formulated foods.*

BREEDING: *Outdoors females are most likely to show nesting behavior in late summer. Males can become quite persistent in chasing would-be mates during courtship. Clutch size ranges from six to 12 eggs. If incubated at 86°F (30°C), hatching can be anticipated just 60 days later.*

HERMANN'S TORTOISE

Testudo hermanni   Family Testudinidae

This tortoise has a long tip to its tail and lacks thigh tubercles. These features allow it to be distinguished easily from the various forms of *Testudo graeca*. The western subspecies, *T. hermanni hermanni*, can generally be separated from its eastern counterpart, *T. h. boettgeri*, by black coloring that extends over most of its plastron, including the central area. It is also smaller.

DISTRIBUTION: *The nominate race occurs in southern Europe, including southeastern Spain, southern France, and central and southern Italy, as well as on the Mediterranean islands of Corfu, Sicily, and Sardinia. The subspecies T. h. boettgeri is found farther east in the Balkan region, with the largest specimens recorded from Bulgaria.*

▲ *MEDITERRANEAN SPUR-THIGHED TORTOISE. FROM TOP: TESTUDO GRAECA IBERA, T. G. ANAMURENSIS AND T. G. TERRESTRIS.*

▲ *Eastern Hermann's Tortoise* (Testudo hermanni boettgeri)

▶ *Western hermann's tortoise* (Testudo hermanni hermanni)

Size: *About 5–8 in (13–20 cm), but exceptionally to 12 in (30 cm).*

Accommodation: *Will thrive in a secure, warm outdoor enclosure during the summer, hibernating again over the winter. Indoor housing will be needed during periods of bad weather.*

Behavior: *Males will often snap at the females' legs as a preliminary during mating. This may be a way of slowing down a larger female, who might otherwise simply be able to wander off.*

Diet: *These tortoises feed on herbage and will forage outdoors, but extra food such as green foods laced with a vitamin and mineral supplement is recommended, particularly when there is little fresh vegetation available.*

Breeding: *Egg-laying is likely during May and June, with up to a dozen eggs forming a typical clutch. Hatching begins after about 60 days.*

HORSFIELD'S TORTOISE
(RUSSIAN TORTOISE; AFGHAN TORTOISE)

Testudo horsfieldii   Family Testudinidae

This species has a relatively rounded shape and is often lightly marked on the carapace. There is a small horny tip to the tail and a group of enlarged scales in the thigh area.

SYNONYM: *Agrionemys horsfieldii.*

DISTRIBUTION: *Its wide range includes parts of Pakistan, Afghanistan, Iran, areas of the former Soviet Union and western China.*

SIZE: *7–8 in (18–20 cm). Mature females are slightly larger than adult males.*

ACCOMMODATION: *Dry, warm surroundings are important for Horsfield's Tortoise, which occurs in naturally arid areas. These tortoises can dig very effectively, so their enclosure must be reinforced around the perimeter. They are also very adept at climbing up mesh barriers, using their powerful hind legs to support their weight and their front legs rather like arms.*

BEHAVIOR: *In the wild these tortoises may emerge from their burrows only in spring and early summer, when there is plenty of vegetation to eat. They then retreat underground for the rest of the year if food is in short supply.*

DIET: *Grazes readily on a typical mixed lawn and will even eat grass, unlike many tortoises. Will take formulated food and eats tomatoes readily. As always, ensure constant access to fresh drinking water.*

BREEDING: *Clutches of two to six eggs, which start hatching after just two months at approximately 86°F (30°C). Some females will lay two or three clutches in a season.*

MARGINATED TORTOISE
(GREEK TORTOISE)

Testudo marginata   Family Testudinidae

The description "marginated" derives from the way in which the marginal scutes are flared out around the rear end of the carapace—especially in the males of the species. This characteristic gives the Marginated Tortoise an extremely distinctive appearance. It also ranks as the largest of all the *Testudo* species.

DISTRIBUTION: *Central and southern parts of Greece and on various islands, including Sardinia, where it is thought to have been introduced.*

SIZE: *Typically 8–9 in (20–22 cm), but may grow up to 14 in (36 cm).*

ACCOMMODATION: *Can be kept throughout the summer in temperate climates in a secure area of a garden.*

BEHAVIOR: *The breeding period in the wild extends from May to June. At this time males pursue females aggressively by battering their shells and biting at their feet.*

DIET: *Herbivorous. As for all tortoises, do not gather food or allow them to browse where the vegetation has been treated with potentially harmful chemicals.*

BREEDING: *Up to 12 eggs are laid, with two or three clutches being produced in succession. Incubation at 86°F (30°C) should result in the young tortoises starting to emerge about 60 days later.*

▼ MARGINATED TORTOISE (TESTUDO MARGINATA)

OTHER TORTOISE SPECIES

AFRICAN

Aldabran Giant Tortoise (*Geochelone gigantea*)

Range: Aldabran Islands, off Africa's southeastern coast. Also introduced to other nearby islands such as Mauritius.

Size: Up to 55 in (140 cm).

Habitat: Relatively open terrain with bushes.

South African Bowsprit Tortoise (*Chersina angulata*)

Range: Southern Africa and Namibia.

Size: 7 in (18 cm).

Habitat: Ranges from coastal desert to forest.

Speckled Cape Tortoise (*Homopus signatus*)

Range: Southwestern Africa.

Size: Smallest of all living tortoises. Males grow to 3 in (7.5 cm); females to 4 in (10 cm).

Habitat: Woodland and savanna.

Tent Tortoise (*Psammobates tentorius*)

Range: Southwestern Africa, in southern Namibia and northern Cape Province.

Size: 6 in (15 cm).

Habitat: Relatively arid country and savanna.

Madagascar Spider Tortoise (*Pyxis arachnoides*)

Range: Southern Madagascar, off Africa's east coast.

Size: 6 in (15 cm).

Habitat: Woodland areas.

Egyptian Tortoise (*Testudo kleinmanni*)

Range: North Africa. Libya to Israel and Egypt.

Size: 4–6 in (10–15 cm).

Habitat: Arid semidesert.

▼ *Madagascar Spider Tortoise* (Pyxis arachnoides)

▲ *Young Aldabran Giant Tortoise* (Geochelone gigantea)

NORTH AMERICAN

Texas Desert Tortoise (*Gopherus berlandieri*)

Range: From Texas to Tamaulipas, Nuevo Leon and Coahuila, Mexico.

Size: 9 in (22 cm).

Habitat: Scrub and more arid terrain.

Bolson Tortoise (*Gopherus flavomarginatus*)

Range: Northern-central Mexico, between Coahuila, Durango and Chihuahua.

Size: 15 in (38 cm).

Habitat: Arid areas of open country and desert.

Gopher Tortoise (*Gopherus polyphemus*)

Range: Southeastern United States, from Louisiana across much of Florida to South Carolina.

Size: 12 in (30 cm).

Habitat: Sandy areas and prairies.

ASIAN

Forsten's Tortoise (*Indotestudo forstenii*)

Range: Sulawesi, occurring in northern and central parts.

Size: 12 in (30 cm).

Habitat: Tropical forest.

Travancore Tortoise (*Indotestudo travancorica*)

Range: Southern Asia. Kerala and Karnataka states, India.

Size: 13 in (33 cm).

Habitat: Evergreen and deciduous forest.

Impressed Tortoise (*Manouria impressa*)

Range: Southern Asia. Myanmar, Thailand, Vietnam, Malaysia and southern China.

Size: 12 in (30 cm).

Habitat: Montane evergreen forest.

TURTLES AND TERRAPINS
Families Chelidae, Chelydridae, Emydidae, Geoemydidae/ Bataguridae, Kinosternidae, Pelomedusidae, Trionychidae

There is often confusion between the terms "turtle" and "terrapin." Terrapin is a native Amerindian term, applied specifically to the Diamondback Terrapin (*Malaclemys terrapin*) in the family Emydidae, a species that occurs in brackish water.

All other aquatic or semiaquatic chelonians tend to be described as turtles in North America. The word terrapin is sometimes used for certain freshwater species in the United Kingdom, however, particularly the Red-eared subspecies of the Slider (*Trachemys scripta elegans*), also in the family Emydidae.

The habits of turtles differ widely. Some, such as the Wood Turtle (*Clemmys insculpta*), are mainly terrestrial, while at the other extreme there are species that are almost entirely aquatic, such as the snake-necks in the family Chelidae. As a guide, these species tend to have a flattened carapace that lessens water resistance in their aquatic environment, enabling them to swim with less effort. Marine turtles are beyond the scope of the hobbyist, however, because they grow to such a large size and they have highly specialized care needs.

▲ TOAD-HEADED TURTLE (BATRACHEMYS/PHRYNOPS NASUTA)

TOAD-HEAD SIDE-NECKED TURTLE

Batrachemys nasuta   Family Chelidae

Like other turtles from South America, Toad-head Side-necked Turtles are not often available. The head is large, toadlike and gray, while the carapace is a browner shade.

SYNONYM: *Phrynops nasutus.*

DISTRIBUTION: *Northern South America, in southeast Colombia and the Guianas, and southward via Ecuador to eastern Peru and northern Bolivia, extending across the Amazon Basin.*

SIZE: *Up to 13 in (33 cm).*

ACCOMMODATION: *Primarily aquatic, so a large area of water is needed. This can be treated with a blackwater extract (as sold primarily for tropical fish) to mimic the tannins normally present in the water from decaying vegetation. This serves to acidify it, helping protect the turtles against fungal disease to which they can otherwise be susceptible.*

BEHAVIOR: *Occurs in slow-flowing stretches of water, including forest streams.*

DIET: *This turtle is more carnivorous than most of its relatives and will also take formulated foods.*

BREEDING: *Courtship can be aggressive, after which the female will lay six to eight eggs. The hatching period can be very variable, taking anywhere from 140 to 250 days.*

▲ SIEBENROCK'S SNAKE-NECKED TURTLE (CHELODINA SIEBENROCKI)

SIEBENROCK'S SNAKE-NECKED TURTLE

Chelodina siebenrocki   Family Chelidae

There are a number of different turtles of this type occurring in the vicinity of New Guinea and in Australia, but only those from New Guinea are available to hobbyists. It is not always easy to distinguish between these different forms, and their taxonomy is controversial. Individuals of this species typically have a particularly dark carapace that contrasts with the light edging on the sides of the marginals.

DISTRIBUTION: *Southern coastal area of New Guinea to the west of the Fly River. Also present on islands in the Torres Strait.*

SIZE: *Can reach approximately 12 in (30 cm).*

ACCOMMODATION: *In its natural habitat Siebenrock's Snake-necked Turtle inhabits relatively shallow areas of water and will not thrive in a deep aquarium. Ensure that these turtles can lie on the bottom and reach up to the surface with their neck extended.*

BEHAVIOR: *They prowl with their long neck extended, seizing smaller aquatic creatures that come within reach.*

DIET: *Some individuals will take formulated food readily, while others will need to be given a range of invertebrates and similar foods.*

BREEDING: *Females have shorter tails, and a flatter profile. They lay up to 17 eggs, and incubation may take nearly six months in the wild.*

MATAMATA

Chelus fimbriatus   Family Chelidae

Even as a juvenile, the Matamata has an unmistakable appearance. It has a rough, brownish carapace that is readily colonized by algae, while its head is broad, flat and triangular, with flaps of skin to aid its disguise. The nostrils are elongated, allowing the turtle to breathe easily at the surface in shallow water, simply by raising its head.

DISTRIBUTION: *Occurs through much of South America, down to parts of Bolivia and Brazil.*

SIZE: *May grow to 18 in (45 cm).*

ACCOMMODATION: *A shallow tank, with suitable underwater retreats. Matamatas are almost totally aquatic, and do not therefore require a*

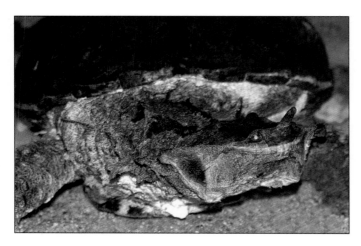

▲ MATAMATA (CHELUS FIMBRIATUS)

large land area. Add a blackwater extract (as sold for tropical fish) to keep the pH of the water slightly acidic.

BEHAVIOR: *This species represents the ultimate passive predator, relying on its leaflike appearance for disguise while it lies in wait for suitable prey to come within reach. The unfortunate creature is then sucked directly into the turtle's mouth and swallowed.*

DIET: *Can be difficult to wean onto inert foods. Various invertebrates need to be offered and possibly small live tropical fish if all else fails, but this can leave the turtles at risk from disease.*

BREEDING: *Males have thicker tails. Females produce clutches typically numbering anywhere from 12 to 28 eggs. Hatching is prolonged—it may take 270 days at a temperature of around 86°F (30°C).*

RED-BELLIED SHORT-NECKED TURTLE

Emydura subglobosa   Family Chelidae

These colorful turtles have become more widely available over recent years as they have been bred with increasing frequency in collections. The carapace is grayish, as is the face—apart from a yellow stripe on the side. The reddish orange coloration is evident on the underparts but tends to fade with age.

DISTRIBUTION: *Southern New Guinea (from where the captive population is descended) and the vicinity of the Jardine River at the northern tip of the Cape York Peninsula in Australia.*

SIZE: *Up to 10 in (25 cm).*

ACCOMMODATION: *Predominantly aquatic by nature, but provide a basking area. The water temperature should be kept at approximately 77°F (25°C), and efficient filtration needs to be in place.*

BEHAVIOR: *Appears to be quite social in the wild, with high population densities recorded in some areas.*

DIET: *Omnivorous. Will take formulated foods readily.*

BREEDING: *Females lay clutches of 10 eggs on average on a regular basis, burying them in a container of sand. Kept under conditions of high humidity, at a temperature of 86°F (30°C), the young may hatch after just 45 days.*

TWIST-NECK TURTLE

Platemys platycephala   Family Chelidae

The colorful Twist-neck Turtle from South America has a predominantly orange top to its head, with a broad back stripe down the center, which reaches almost to the eyes. The edges of both the carapace and the plastron are orange too, with the upper surface of the carapace being a combination of brown and black.

DISTRIBUTION: *Extends from southeastern Colombia, Venezuela and the Guianas southward via the Amazon to Ecuador, Peru and northeast Bolivia.*

SIZE: *7 in (18 cm).*

ACCOMMODATION: *A warm, humid environment suits these rain forest turtles, which wander relatively far from water. They are not powerful swimmers and so do not require deep water in their enclosure, but an easily accessible shallow area should be made available.*

BEHAVIOR: *The onset of the rainy season usually serves to trigger breeding activity in the wild. This can be mimicked in vivarium surroundings by more frequent spraying of their enclosure.*

DIET: *Omnivorous, but often biased toward invertebrates rather than green foods. Will take a formulated food.*

BREEDING: *A female often does not dig a nest, but simply lays her single egg on the surface and then covers it with vegetation. Repeated egg-laying is likely. Hatching may take 180 days.*

▼ *RED-BELLIED SHORT-NECKED TURTLE (EMYDURA SUBGLOBOSA)*

▲ *AMERICAN SNAPPING TURTLE (CHELYDRA SERPENTINA)*

AMERICAN SNAPPING TURTLE

Chelydra serpentina　　　　　　　　Family Chelydridae

American Snapping Turtles have a fearsome reputation, thanks to the large size that they can attain. Even small individuals may inflict a painful bite if handled carelessly. They are brownish in color, with a relatively smooth carapace and a tapering tail.

DISTRIBUTION: *Extends from southern Canada down into the United States east of the Rockies, through Mexico and Central America into Colombia and Ecuador in South America.*

SIZE: *Males can measure up to 19 in (47 cm), with females being slightly smaller.*

ACCOMMODATION: *Requires spacious surroundings in the guise of a pond as they grow bigger. Must not be mixed with smaller individuals, which are likely to be preyed on.*

BEHAVIOR: *A largely aquatic and relatively inactive species, often hiding away or burying itself in mud and seizing prey that comes within reach.*

DIET: *Will eat formulated foods. Naturally feeds on a wide variety of creatures, ranging from invertebrates to waterfowl, depending on the turtle's size.*

BREEDING: *Females can lay viable eggs for several years following a successful mating. Typical clutches consist of 20 to 30 eggs, but large females may lay more than 80 eggs. Incubation at 86°F (30°C) or just over produces female offspring; 77–82°F (25–28°C) gives males. The temperature also affects the time of hatching, which can range from 55 to 125 days. Overwintering in the eggs occurs in the wild.*

EASTERN PAINTED TURTLE

Chrysemys picta picta　　　　　　　　Family Emydidae

This is one of four very distinctive subspecies of the Painted Turtle and is instantly distinguishable by its unmarked yellow

plastron. The carapace is smooth and dark, with red patterning evident on the marginals.

▲ *EASTERN PAINTED TURTLES (CHRYSEMYS PICTA PICTA)*

DISTRIBUTION: *Nova Scotia, southeastern Canada, down the eastern coastal area of the United States as far as northern Georgia and eastern Alabama.*

SIZE: *Up to 8 in (20 cm).*

ACCOMMODATION: *The water temperature should be allowed to drop to 50–59°F (10–15°C) for several weeks in the New Year. It should then gradually be increased in stages to 82°F (28°C) to encourage breeding. Basking facilities are important.*

BEHAVIOR: *These turtles hibernate through the winter under the ice in northern parts of their range.*

DIET: *Will take formulated foods, naturally favoring an omnivorous diet. May uproot and eat aquatic plants growing in the aquarium or pond.*

BREEDING: *Occurs in spring. Incubation temperatures below 80°F (27°C) will yield male hatchlings, and at 86°F (30°C), all-female offspring can be anticipated.*

WESTERN PAINTED TURTLE

Chrysemys picta bellii   Family Emydidae

The western form of the painted turtle has the widest distribution of the four races in the species. In contrast to its eastern cousin, it has a delicate patterning running across its plastron, while that of the Midland Painted Turtle (*Chrysemys picta marginata*) has a dark blotch restricted to the center.

DISTRIBUTION: *Southern Quebec in Canada southward to British Columbia. Ranges to northern Oregon in the United States, and down through Idaho, Wyoming, Nebraska and Missouri. Also at various other localities in the Southwest, and even reported from Chihuahua, Mexico.*

SIZE: *Typically ranges from 7–10 in (18–26 cm).*

ACCOMMODATION: *Can be kept outdoors in most temperate areas throughout the summer in a secure pond that has suitable basking areas. An indoor enclosure requires an area for swimming and an* area of dry land beneath a light should be provided for basking purposes.

BEHAVIOR: *Because the different painted turtles are so closely related, the various subspecies should not be mixed. Otherwise, they are likely to interbreed, producing hybrid offspring.*

DIET: *Young tend to be more active predators by nature, requiring a higher level of protein in their diet. Their nutritional needs can be met by using a formulated food.*

BREEDING: *The western subspecies lays the largest number of eggs in a clutch—typically in excess of 20 in the case of a mature female.*

SOUTHERN PAINTED TURTLE

Chrysemys picta dorsalis   Family Emydidae

This particular painted turtle is the most easily recognizable of all the subspecies, thanks to the reddish yellow stripe that extends down the center of the carapace from the head to the tail. The plastron is yellow and free from any markings.

DISTRIBUTION: *The southern subspecies is not found in Canada. Its range extends from southern Illinois down to the Gulf of Mexico, and from Oklahoma in the west to Alabama in the east.*

SIZE: *Up to 10 in (25 cm).*

ACCOMMODATION: *Painted turtles in general favor slow-flowing stretches of water or ponds where there is plenty of aquatic vegetation to provide cover and a source of food.*

BEHAVIOR: *In suitable localities, large numbers of painted turtles will bask communally. This has the advantage that if one individual spots possible danger and dives back into the water, this will alert the others to take similar action.*

DIET: *Formulated foods provide the simplest way of ensuring these turtles receive a balanced diet.*

BREEDING: *Mature males can be recognized by the longer claws on their front legs. Clutch size is small, consisting of a maximum of seven eggs, but females may lay two or three times a year. Hatching can typically take 55 to 80 days, depending on the incubation temperature.*

SPOTTED TURTLE

Clemmys guttata   Family Emydidae

The blackish carapace of Spotted Turtles is broken up by a series of yellow spots, the size and number of which vary according to the individual. The spots also tend to fade in older turtles. The plastron itself is unspotted. Females have orange eyes, whereas those of males are brown.

DISTRIBUTION: *From southern Canada along the eastern seaboard of the United States down to Florida.*

SIZE : *Up to 5 in (13 cm).*

ACCOMMODATION: *An aquaterrarium is recommended. It should incorporate a significant land area, which should ideally be planted to provide cover. A water temperature of around 72° F (22° C) is recommended, dropping back slightly over the winter, when these turtles would usually hibernate in the wild.*

BEHAVIOR: *A relatively terrestrial species, often encountered out of water. Prefers shallow, slow-flowing stretches of water where there is plenty of vegetation.*

DIET: *Offer a formulated food augmented with invertebrates. May eat some plant matter.*

BREEDING: *Females lay clutches of three to eight eggs, usually in June, which take about two months to hatch. Sometimes, they will lay more than one clutch.*

▲ SOUTHERN PAINTED TURTLE (CHRYSEMYS PICTA DORSALIS)

▼ SPOTTED TURTLE (CLEMMYS GUTTATA)

WOOD TURTLE

Clemmys insculpta   Family Emydidae

The carapace of the wood turtle is brownish. It has a relatively low profile and a rough texture. The skin, especially in the throat area, tends to be pale orange, in contrast to the much darker coloration that can be seen on the head and legs. The male's tail is significantly longer tail than that of the female.

DISTRIBUTION: *Extends from Nova Scotia, Canada, southward through the Unted States as far as northern Virginia. Extends westward to southern Ontario and New York state to Michigan, northeastern Ohio, Wisconsin and eastern Minnesota down to northeastern Iowa.*

SIZE: *Up to 9 in (22 cm).*

ACCOMMODATION: *This turtle needs a spacious land area, since it is highly terrestrial by nature, and also an area of water.*

BEHAVIOR: *Can climb very well, so outdoor enclosures in particular must be adequately covered. Naturally hibernates through the winter, either beneath the water or in a suitable hole nearby.*

DIET: *Omnivorous by nature, will even eat fruits such as blackberries in season. Such items can be offered alongside a formulated food.*

BREEDING: *Mating takes place in water in the spring, with usually about eight eggs being laid, although this number can be as high as 18. Hatching takes some 70 days, and the young are grayish brown, with no orange markings at this age.*

EUROPEAN POND TURTLE

Emys orbicularis   Family Emydidae

These turtles display a wide variation in appearance, with some having a pattern of tiny yellow spots decorating their carapace. In other individuals the area is streaked with yellowish lines.

OTHER TURTLES AND TERRAPINS

ASIA/AUSTRALASIA

Keeled Box Turtle (*Pyxidea mouhotii*)   Family Geoemydidae/Bataguridae

Range: Vietnam to northern Thailand and neighboring Myanmar (formerly Burma). Also on Hainan Island, China.

Size: 7 in (18 cm).

Habitat: Predominantly terrestrial; lives in humid montane forest.

Four-eyed Turtle (*Sacalia quadriocellata*)   Family Geoemydidae/Bataguridae

Range: Southern China and northern Vietnam.

Size: Up to 6 in (15 cm).

Habitat: Woodland streams.

Malaysian Snail-eating Turtle (*Malayemys subtrijuga*)
          Family Geoemydidae/Bataguridae

Range: Southern Vietnam to Thailand and southward down to Java.

Size: 8 in (20 cm).

Habitat: Slow-moving waters, including canals and rice paddies.

▲ KEELED BOX TURTLE (*PYXIDEA MOUHOTII*)

Chinese Yellow-edged Box Turtle
(*Cistoclemmys/Cuora flavomarginata*)   Family Geoemydidae/Bataguridae

Range: Southern, central and eastern areas of China. Also on Taiwan.

Size: 7 in (18 cm).

Habitat: Slow-flowing waters, from forest streams and rice paddies to ponds.

New Guinea Snapping Turtle (*Elseya novaeguineae*)   Family Chelidae

Range: Throughout New Guinea.

Size: 12 in (30 cm).

Habitat: Coastal swamps to larger bodies of inland water.

New Guinea Snake-necked Turtle (*Chelodina novaeguineae*)   Family Chelidae

Range: Southeastern New Guinea and part of northern Australia.

Size: 12 in (30 cm).

Habitat: Shallow lagoons, swamps and streams.

NORTH AMERICA

Barbour's Map Turtle (*Graptemys barbouri*)   Family Emydidae

Range: Southeastern United States, in Florida and Georgia.

Size: Males 5 in (13 cm); females 12 in (30 cm).

Habitat: Occurs in the Apalachicola River.

Yellow Mud Turtle (*Kinosternon flavescens*)   Family Kinosternidae

Range: Southern-central United States and through much of Mexico.

Size: 6 in (15 cm).

Habitat: Slow-flowing or stagnant water.

Mexican Rough-footed Mud Turtle (*Kinosternon hirtipes*)   Family Kinosternidae

Range: Southwest Texas to the valley of Mexico.

Size: 3.75–6.7 in (9.5–17 cm).

Habitat: Ponds, lakes, rivers and marshes.

Their background coloration can be equally variable, ranging from olive brown to black. Males tend to have brighter reddish eyes, whereas those of females are generally brown.

DISTRIBUTION: *Ranges widely from the area of the Caspian Sea westward, and is found as far north as Latvia and Lithuania. To the south, the species is found in countries along the Mediterranean and on islands such as Corsica. It is also present in various countries in North Africa, such as Morocco.*

SIZE: *Up to 8 in (20 cm).*

ACCOMMODATION: *In many areas these turtles can be housed over the summer months in a secure outdoor enclosure with a pond. They favor slow-moving stretches of water where there is plenty of vegetation.*

BEHAVIOR: *European Pond Turtles are very hard to spot in the wild because although they bask for long periods, especially in sunny weather, their cautious nature means they will slip back quietly into the water at the slightest hint of danger, and escape detection.*

DIET: *Essentially carnivorous. Will eat formulated foods readily.*

BREEDING: *Clutch size can vary from three to 16 eggs, but typically averages 10. Incubation temperature influences the gender of the offspring, with virtually all females resulting at 86°F (30°C).*

BOG TURTLE

Glyptemys muhlenbergii   Family Emydidae

Largely as a result of habitat loss, the Bog Turtle now ranks as one of the most endangered turtles in North America. The broad yellowish orange banding at the back of the head is distinctive, although this varies both in depth of color and shape from individual to individual. There are also less conspicuous orange-red markings on the face and legs.

SYNONYM: *Clemmys muhlenbergii.*

DISTRIBUTION: *Now scattered, occurring south of Lake Ontario and also ranging from western Massachusetts to Maryland. Further populations occur south of Lake Erie and in parts of Virginia, the Carolinas, Georgia and eastern Tennessee.*

SIZE: *3–5 in (7–13 cm).*

ACCOMMODATION: *A boglike habitat, with peat sandwiched beneath gravel and shallow water, is recommended. The water must be deep enough to cover the turtles at mating time.*

BEHAVIOR: *The Bog Turtle hibernates over the winter period in the wild, emerging again in April. It hunts prey during the warmer part of the day both in water and on land.*

DIET: *Naturally preys mainly on invertebrates, but also eats fruit and green foods. Could be induced to take a formulated food, augmented with plant matter.*

▲ EUROPEAN POND TURTLE (EMYS ORBICULARIS)

▲ CHINESE YELLOW-EDGED BOX TURTLE (CISTOCLEMMYS/CUORA FLAVOMARGINATA)

Common Mud Turtle (*Kinosternon subrubrum*)   Family Kinosternidae

Range: Eastern side of the United States from Connecticut and Long Island to Texas.

Size: 5 in (13 cm).

Habitat: Streams and slower-flowing stretches of water.

AFRICA

African Mud Turtle (*Pelusios castaneus*)   Family Pelomedusidae

Range: West Africa, from Nigeria to Mauritania. A separate population occurs in the Congo Basin.

Size: 15 in (38 cm).

Habitat: Pools that may disappear in the dry season.

African Forest Mud Turtle (*Pelusios gabonensis*)   Family Pelomedusidae

Range: West Africa, from Liberia and Guinea to Zaire.

Size: 12 in (30 cm).

Habitat: Stretches of water in tropical forests. The young generally avoid fast-flowing streams.

BREEDING: *Females lay clutches of up to half a dozen eggs. Incubator hatching takes about 50 days, but the young may overwinter in nests in the wild.*

MAP TURTLE

Graptemys geographica   Family Emydidae

Map turtles as a group are often described as sawbacks because of the toothlike projections that run down the center of the back, although this characteristic is less apparent in this species. There is a yellow spot evident behind the eye on each side of the head. Young of this species have very evident patterning not just on the carapace but also on the plastron.

DISTRIBUTION: *Extends from southern Quebec, Canada and northwestern Vermont across to southern Wisconsin. Extends south to Arkansas and Georgia, to the west of the Appalachians. Present too in the Delaware River and the Susquehanna River in Maryland and Pennsylvania.*

SIZE: *Males grow up to 6 in (15 cm), while females can measure 7–11 in (18–28 cm) when adult.*

ACCOMMODATION: *Map turtles are social by nature. This species is particularly so, and a group of them can therefore be housed together successfully in suitably spacious surroundings.*

BEHAVIOR: *Communal basking is common, with all the turtles slipping back into the water if an individual is disturbed.*

DIET: *Invertebrates such as aquatic snails are a common food in the wild. Offering formulated foods helps guard against nutritional deficiencies that can arise from a diet lacking in calcium.*

BREEDING: *Laying in the wild occurs from the end of May through July. A typical clutch consists of 10 to 16 eggs.*

BLACK-KNOBBED MAP TURTLE
(BLACK-KNOBBED SAWBACK)

Graptemys nigrinoda   Family Emydidae

One of the most distinctive species of map turtle, the Black-knobbed has black, swollen projections running over the vertebral column. The carapace itself is of an olive hue, more brightly colored in younger turtles. It is a relatively small species.

DISTRIBUTION: *Occurs in the U.S. states of Alabama and Mississippi, in the Tombigbee, Black Warrior and Alabama river systems.*

SIZE: *Males grow to 3–4 in (7–10 cm); females can reach 4–6 in (10–15 cm) when adult.*

ACCOMMODATION: *A suitable area of water for swimming and an area where the turtles can bask are required. Since this species is one of the smallest members of the genus, a pair can be housed easily in a spacious tank even when fully grown.*

▲ *MISSISSIPPI MAP TURTLE (GRAPTEMYS PSEUDOGEOGRAPHICA KOHNII)*

▶ *FALSE MAP TURTLES (GRAPTEMYS PSEUDOGEOGRAPHICA PSEUDOGEOGRAPHICA)—JUVENILES.*

BEHAVIOR: *Although they bask frequently, these turtles will slip back into the water at any hint of danger.*

DIET: *A formulated food is ideal for these turtles. Aquatic snails are a prominent food source in the wild.*

BREEDING: *Incubation temperature will influence the sex of the offspring. Temperatures above 77°F (25°C) and below 80°F (26°C) will result in both sexes being produced—below the lower figure, the clutch will consist of male hatchlings only.*

MISSISSIPPI MAP TURTLE

Graptemys pseudogeographica kohnii   Family Emydidae

Variable yellow markings on the head and a raised area forming a ridge down the vertebral scutes help identify this species. The delicate contourlike shell markings that give this turtle its common name are more evident in hatchlings than in fully grown individuals.

DISTRIBUTION: *The United States, from central Illinois and eastern Nebraska southward to the Gulf, through the Mississippi valley.*

SIZE: *Females up to 10 in (25 cm); males reach about 5 in (13 cm).*

ACCOMMODATION: *A predominantly aquatic setup is needed, but with basking areas. Typical temperature should be around 77°F (25°C).*

BEHAVIOR: *A rather shy species, the Mississippi Map Turtle remains close to water, promptly diving back if disturbed.*

DIET: *A formulated food is usually taken readily by these turtles. Check that females do not monopolize the food offered as they grow larger.*

BREEDING: *Males court females by stroking their faces gently with the long claws on their front legs. Females lay between five and 16 eggs. An incubation temperature of 86°F (30°C) or above produces all-female hatchlings.*

FALSE MAP TURTLE

Graptemys pseudogeographica pseudogeographica

Family Emydidae

The patterning on the carapace of these turtles is variable, with the plastron being a creamy yellow shade in adults. The projections down the center of the carapace are relatively low, and in hatchlings black markings can be seen clearly on the first three vertebral scutes.

DISTRIBUTION: *Found in large streams within the Mississippi area, ranging from Wisconsin southward into Louisiana and eastern Texas.*

SIZE: *Males reach up to 6 in (15 cm) when mature; females can grow to 11 in (28 cm).*

ACCOMMODATION: *This should be similar to that provided for other map turtles. They will instinctively bask for much of the day if left undisturbed.*

BEHAVIOR: *Encountered most frequently in slow-flowing waters, where there is plenty of aquatic vegetation.*

DIET: *Feeds on plant matter, including duckweed (Lemna), which can be provided along with a formulated food and left to grow in the tank.*

BREEDING: *Incubation typically lasts between 60 and 75 days depending on the temperature, which exerts a direct influence on the gender of the hatchlings.*

SPINY HILL TURTLE
(COGWHEEL TURTLE)

Heosemys spinosa

Family Geoemydidae/Bataguridae

Young of this species differ markedly in appearance from adults. They have sharp projections around the edges of the carapace, which resemble cogs. This explains the alternative common

name for the species. The edges of the shell become smoother with age. The shell itself is brownish in color, often with a reddish hue, while the turtle's body is a darker brown.

DISTRIBUTION: *Southeast Asia, in Thailand and Malaysia, and the islands of Sumatra and Borneo.*

SIZE: *Up to 9 in (22 cm).*

ACCOMMODATION: *A large land area should be a feature of the housing for these turtles. Coming from upland forest areas, they also require warm (not hot) and humid conditions, with a relatively shallow area of water, typically heated to about 77°F (25°C).*

BEHAVIOR: *This turtle is largely terrestrial. The sharp projections are thought to deter predators such as snakes, since they probably make the turtle difficult to swallow.*

DIET: *Appears to feed mainly on plant matter and fruit, with banana being a particular favorite. A formulated food can easily be introduced by pressing it into a banana. Some individuals will also take invertebrates. Use a vitamin and mineral supplement regularly if the turtles will not eat a balanced diet.*

BREEDING: *Up to three eggs may be laid. Hatching can take in excess of 100 days.*

DIAMONDBACK TERRAPIN

Malaclemys terrapin　　　　　　Family Emydidae

Up to seven subspecies of this terrapin are recognized. It was heavily hunted for food in the past, but now it is becoming more common again in areas of suitable unpolluted habitat. It has a grayish head, decorated with black spots. Its shell coloration is very variable. It is commonly grayish brown with attractive patterning, but it can sometimes be almost black.

DISTRIBUTION: *Extends from Cape Cod southward in coastal areas down to Texas.*

SIZE: *Males reach nearly 6 in (15 cm), while females grow to 9 in (22 cm).*

ACCOMMODATION: *Diamondback Terrapins occur largely in brackish surroundings and require this type of water in a vivarium. This can be created using marine sea salt, as sold for saltwater aquaria. Check on the water conditions prior to obtaining these terrapins, so you can set up the tank accordingly. They also require a land area.*

BEHAVIOR: *Females excavate their nests above the high water mark in order to avoid exposure to flooding.*

DIET: *Carnivorous by nature. Will feed on formulated foods.*

BREEDING: *Females lay clutches of four to 18 eggs that are likely to hatch after about 90 days. In the wild, however, the hatchlings may overwinter in the nest. Two clutches are often laid in rapid succession.*

EASTERN RIVER COOTER

Pseudemys concinna　　　　　　Family Emydidae

Taxonomists recognize three, four or even five different races of this turtle. It has yellow stripes on the head and also on the carapace, which become less distinct as the turtle grows older. In some areas, however, the different races interbreed, making it impossible to distinguish between them.

DISTRIBUTION: *Ranges widely through much of the southeastern United States as far south as Coahuila, Tamaulipas, and Nuevo León in Mexico, but occurs only in the northwest of Florida.*

SIZE: *Can grow up to 13 in (33 cm).*

ACCOMMODATION: *A large setup is required, featuring an area for swimming and another for basking. It is important that the turtles are able to move in and out of the water easily.*

BEHAVIOR: *This species is often observed basking in mixed groups in the wild, sharing its habitat with map turtles and other species.*

DIET: *Primarily herbivorous in the wild once adult. Young tend to be more predatory, hunting aquatic invertebrates. Provide a formulated food as a basic diet.*

BREEDING: *Males can be recognized by their elongated front claws, which they use for courtship purposes. Up to 19 eggs may be laid, with females often laying more than one clutch during the breeding period. Incubation is likely to last about 70 days.*

FLORIDA RED-BELLIED TURTLE

Pseudemys nelsoni　　　　　　Family Emydidae

The plastron of these turtles is orangish red. The carapace is dark overall, broken by lighter reddish or yellow markings. The head and neck are black with bold yellow stripes.

DISTRIBUTION: *This is more extensive than the common name of the species suggests. It occurs in the Okefenokee swamps of southern Georgia westward to the Appalachian area of Florida.*

SIZE: *May grow to nearly 13 in (33 cm).*

ACCOMMODATION: *It is important to plan ahead when keeping these turtles, in terms of their likely adult size. An indoor pond with a basking area or a spacious aquarium adapted for their needs will be required.*

BEHAVIOR: *Florida Red-bellied Turtles will hybridize with related species such as the Eastern River Cooter (see above) in areas where their range overlaps.*

DIET: *A formulated food is ideal for these omnivorous turtles. Adults will also browse very readily on aquatic plants.*

▶ FLORIDA RED-BELLIED TURTLE (PSEUDEMYS NELSONI)

BREEDING: *Females, which are recognizable by their slightly larger size and shorter front claws, may lay five or even six clutches annually. Each contains up to a dozen eggs. Hatching is likely to take at least 60 days.*

EASTERN BOX TURTLE
(COMMON BOX TURTLE)

Terrapene carolina   Family Emydidae

This species varies significantly in appearance over its wide range. Some individuals have a plain brown carapace, while in other cases it is variegated, often with radial lines or spots. Of the many different races, two—*Terrapene carolina triunguis* and the rarely kept *T. c. mexicana*—can be distinguished by the presence of just three rather than four toes on their hind feet.

DISTRIBUTION: *Extends south from east of Lake Michigan through the southeastern United States, including Florida, down into Mexico, where it occurs in San Luis Potosí, Veracruz and Tamaulipas, as well as on the Yucatán peninsula.*

SIZE: *Up to 8 in (20 cm); the Gulf Coast race (T. c. major) is the largest.*

ACCOMMODATION: *A secure outdoor enclosure will be needed or, in bad weather, an indoor vivarium. Must be able to bathe.*

BEHAVIOR: *Becomes most active after rainfall. Can seal itself in its shell by using the shell hinges to protect against predators and fire.*

DIET: *Omnivorous; eats green foods, berries, and invertebrates. Will readily take formulated food.*

BREEDING: *Males often distinguishable by their reddish eyes—those of females are usually browner. In males the claws on the hind feet tend to be more curved, to provide support during mating, which takes place on land. Females nest several times a year and lay about five eggs in each clutch. Incubation is likely to last a minimum of 75 days.*

SPOTTED BOX TURTLE

Terrapene nelsoni   Family Emydidae

A rarely kept species, the Spotted Box Turtle has a carapace that can vary in appearance from a yellowish shade right through to dark brown. The spotted patterning is also variable, with the spots being smaller and more numerous in the race known as *Terrapene nelsoni klauberti*. Some individuals have no spots.

DISTRIBUTION: *Found in various areas of Mexico, in the states of Nayarit, Sinaloa and Sonora.*

SIZE: *Up to 6 in (15 cm).*

ACCOMMODATION: *Likely to require more warmth than box turtles found farther north.*

BEHAVIOR: *Lives in fairly arid scrublike wooded areas, often retreating underground into burrows.*

▲ *EASTERN BOX TURTLE (TERRAPENE CAROLINA)*

DIET: *Formulated food for this and other box turtles is available. Will also feed on invertebrates and green foods.*

BREEDING: *Females lay one to three eggs in a clutch. They are thought to lay only once over the summer period.*

ORNATE BOX TURTLE

Terrapene ornata   Family Emydidae

Yellow radiating streaks on a dark background help identify this species, which also has a high domed carapace. The patterning is frequently less distinctive in old individuals.

DISTRIBUTION: *Central and southern parts of the United States, extending from Indiana and east Wyoming down to Louisiana and New Mexico. Also present in parts of Texas and Arizona to Mexico, where it occurs in Chihuahua and Sonora.*

▼ *ORNATE BOX TURTLE (TERRAPENE ORNATA)*

SIZE: *Up to 6 in (15 cm). Males tend to be slightly smaller on average.*

ACCOMMODATION: *It is important to prevent this turtle from digging its way out, so a secure outdoor enclosure is recommended. It is primarily terrestrial, but should have the opportunity to enter water as well. A suitable container should be set in the enclosure.*

BEHAVIOR: *Lives in an open, prairie-type landscape, often digging to create a burrow to escape the heat of the day, and rest at night.*

DIET: *Essentially carnivorous, hunting invertebrates. Will take a formulated food, however, and green foods since, like other* Terrapene *species, it feeds on land.*

BREEDING: *Sexing on eye coloration is possible, but the first toe on each hind foot of males curves inward, and is significantly thicker than the others. Breeding details similar to those of the other box turtles described above. Young do not develop the characteristic hinges until they are about four years old.*

RED-EARED SLIDER

Trachemys scripta elegans　　　　Family Emydidae

This is one of the best known of all turtles, although it is prohibited to import it into the European Union at present, because of fears that these turtles might establish themselves in the wild. They are easily distinguished at a glance by the prominent red streaks behind the ears. The carapace is bright green with yellow stripes, becoming darker in older individuals.

DISTRIBUTION: *The range of this subspecies is centered on the Mississippi valley, but there are also populations present in Ohio and in Mexico, close to the border with Texas.*

SIZE: *Males grow to about 8 in (20 cm); females, however, can reach 11 in (28 cm).*

ACCOMMODATION: *A secure outdoor enclosure with a pond will be required or a tank with a land area, complete with a light for basking. Hatchlings will thrive at a temperature of around 75°F (24°C).*

BEHAVIOR: *A male will use his long front claws to caress the face of the female prior to mating. The "slider" part of this species' name comes from its habit of sliding back into the water if disturbed.*

DIET: *Formulated food suits these turtles well.*

BREEDING: *Females lay clutches of 12 to 15 eggs that typically take about 65 days to hatch.*

REEVE'S TURTLE
(CHINESE THREE-KEELED POND TURTLE)

Chinemys reevesi　　　　Family Geoemydidae/Bataguridae

Reeve's Turtles are relatively colorful as hatchlings. Once they mature, however, males tend to darken significantly, becoming blackish, although they do not attain the same size as their mates. The striped neck pattern is most developed in the Taiwanese population.

DISTRIBUTION: *Present on the Japanese islands of Kyushu and Honshu, and on Taiwan. Also occurs in Korea and southern China, including Hong Kong.*

SIZE: *Up to 9.5 in (24 cm).*

ACCOMMODATION: *The water temperature should be around 68°F (20°C), and their quarters should also include a land area where the turtles can bask. Easy access in and out of the water is also required. Reeve's Turtles can often be housed in a secure outdoor pond and enclosure during the summer period.*

BEHAVIOR: *Males can occasionally be somewhat aggressive toward each other.*

DIET: *Can usually be induced to feed on formulated foods quite readily.*

▲ REEVE'S TURTLE (CHINEMYS REEVESI)

BREEDING: *Females may lay several clutches of four to nine eggs in rapid succession. Incubation lasts from 65 to 100 days, although in the wild the young may overwinter in the nest, not emerging until the following spring.*

MALAYSIAN BOX TURTLE

Cuora amboinensis　　　　Family Geoemydidae/Bataguridae

The dome-shaped carapace of the Malaysian Box Turtle is brownish black, but the plastron tends to be paler. The shell is hinged so that these turtles can effectively seal themselves completely in their shells, usually withdrawing in this way when handled. Over time, however, they should become less nervous. A narrow yellow stripe is evident on each side of the head.

DISTRIBUTION: *Occurs through much of Southeast Asia, ranging from Bangladesh, Assam and Myanmar (formerly Burma) through Thailand,*

Cambodia, Vietnam and across Indonesia to the Philippines and Japan.

SIZE: 8 in (20 cm).

ACCOMMODATION: An aquaterrarium will be needed, since these turtles spent much of their time on land. They prefer shallow water, so the aquatic area should not be very deep.

BEHAVIOR: Naturally occurs in small pools and cultivated areas such as paddy fields.

DIET: Will readily take formulated foods as well as plant matter, which forms a significant part of their natural diet. Will also take live food.

BREEDING: Males can become very aggressive during the mating period and may have to be separated to prevent causing injury to the female. Females lay clutches of two or three eggs repeatedly through the year. Hatching can occur just 35 days later.

ASIAN LEAF TURTLE

Cyclemys dentata   Family Geoemydidae/Bataguridae

The Asian Leaf Turtle can be distinguished by having a dark carapace, with paler areas on the plastron that are broken by dark radiating lines, creating a unique patterning. The marginals are slightly serrated, a feature that is particularly noticeable in the young of the species.

DISTRIBUTION: Ranges widely through much of southern Asia, from eastern India across to Yunnan and Guangxi in China, and south via the Malay Peninsula to Indonesia. Also present farther north in the Philippines.

SIZE: Up to 10 in (25 cm).

ACCOMMODATION: Young Asian Leaf Turtles tend to be more aquatic by nature than adults, and this should be reflected in the design of their housing. The water must not be too deep, allowing the turtle to reach the surface easily, and must also provide good access to a basking area.

BEHAVIOR: This species frequents slow-flowing, relatively shallow stretches of water where there is plenty of aquatic vegetation.

DIET: Omnivorous; the young turtles in particular have very healthy appetites and grow fast. Offer a formulated food as a basic diet.

BREEDING: Females, often recognizable by their slightly larger size when adult, lay small clutches of two or three eggs several times during the year. At 86°F (30°C), hatching can occur after 75 days.

▼ *MALAYSIAN BOX TURTLE (CUORA AMBOINENSIS)*

▲ *ASIAN LEAF TURTLE (CYCLEMYS DENTATA)*

VIETNAMESE WOOD TURTLE
(BLACK-BREASTED WOOD TURTLE)

Geoemyda splengeri   Family Geoemydidae/Bataguridae

The carapace is brownish, which probably helps these turtles blend in with leaf litter, and there are projections around the rear of the carapace. There are yellow markings behind the eye. The plastron, apart from its pale-colored margins, is black. The tail is long, especially in males.

DISTRIBUTION: *Extends from southern China, including Hainan Island, to Vietnam in Southeast Asia. Also present on the islands of Sumatra, Borneo and Okinawa.*

SIZE: *5 in (13 cm).*

ACCOMMODATION: *This species generally roams on land; in vivarium surroundings therefore it requires access to only a relatively small, shallow area of water. A temperature range of 68 to 77°F (20–25°C) is recommended.*

BEHAVIOR: *Occurs in mountain forest through its range, spending little time in the streams present in this type of habitat.*

DIET: *Omnivorous; eats vegetable matter and invertebrates. Can be offered a formulated food.*

BREEDING: *A female is likely to lay about two eggs in a clutch. They are elongated in shape. A relatively low incubation temperature of about 77°F (25°C) is recommended, and the relative humidity in the incubator should be kept high. The young turtles should then emerge after approximately 70 days.*

CASPIAN TURTLE

Mauremys caspica   Family Geoemydidae/Bataguridae

A narrow pattern of yellow stripes around the head, with no spot behind the eyes, helps identify this species. The edges of the marginals can be pale orangish yellow, broken by black markings. Young hatchlings are often more brightly colored than adults.

DISTRIBUTION: *Eastern Mediterranean region, extending from the southwest of the former Soviet Union and Iran across to Saudi Arabia and Israel. Also ranges from Turkey to Bulgaria. Found on the Ionian peninsula and the islands of Crete and Cyprus, to the vicinity of the former Yugoslavia.*

SIZE: *Up to 9 in (22 cm).*

ACCOMMODATION: *A secure outdoor enclosure with a pond may be suitable for these turtles, certainly on sunny days during the summer period, which will provide them with an opportunity to benefit from the sun's rays outside.*

BEHAVIOR: *Adaptable, colonizing irrigation canals. Generally inhabits relatively large, permanent stretches of water.*

DIET: *Carnivorous by nature. A formulated food should prove to be a good alternative.*

BREEDING: *Females are larger than males, with shorter tails, which means that the vent region does not extend beyond the border of the shell. They lay clutches of four to six eggs during the summer. The young should hatch about 70 days later.*

◄ ORNATE WOOD TURTLE (RHINOCLEMMYS PULCHERRIMA)

▼ RED-CHEEKED MUD TURTLE (KINOSTERNON SCORPIOIDES CRUENTATUM)

MEDITERRANEAN TURTLE
(SPANISH TURTLE)

Mauremys leprosa   Family Geoemydidae/Bataguridae

This species has a flat, dark, brownish carapace, but its most distinctive characteristic is the presence of a small yellowish orange spot behind each eye. The top of the head is brown, and there are yellow stripes on the sides of the face and on the throat.

DISTRIBUTION: *Has declined dramatically over recent years, especially in Europe, where it is present in Spain and Portugal. Also occurs more widely through North Africa. It is now strictly protected in the European Union.*

SIZE: *8 in (20 cm).*

ACCOMMODATION: *A tank enabling the turtle to bask on land is necessary. This helps prevent the shell from becoming badly damaged by algae that may otherwise colonize the plastron.*

BEHAVIOR: *Will frequently empty its bladder when picked up, which is a response often more commonly associated with tortoises than turtles.*

DIET: *Omnivorous by nature. Takes formulated foods without problems.*

BREEDING: *Males have longer tails and are smaller than females. Mating can occur on land rather than in water. The female then lays six to nine eggs, which are likely to take at least 65 days to hatch.*

GOLDEN THREAD TURTLE
(CHINESE STRIPE-NECKED TURTLE)

Ocadia sinensis   Family Geoemydidae/Bataguridae

Narrow yellow stripes, faintly reminiscent of golden threads, extend back along the head and neck of this turtle. They are also present on the legs, especially where they meet the body, and are set against an olive background. The carapace is blackish, and the plastron is hinged.

DISTRIBUTION: *Much of southern China, including the area of Shanghai and Hainan. Also present on Taiwan and in northern Vietnam.*

SIZE: *Up to 10 in (25 cm).*

ACCOMMODATION: *This should be designed to enable the turtles to swim and bask. A water temperature of around 75°F (24°C) should be adequate.*

BEHAVIOR: *This species inhabits well vegetated stretches of water in the wild, where the water is slow-flowing.*

DIET: *Primarily herbivorous, particularly when older. Will eat aquatic plants, or even pieces of dandelion dropped on the water's surface.*

BREEDING: *Not well documented. Females, distinguishable by their shorter tails, may lay clutches of three eggs.*

ORNATE WOOD TURTLE
(PAINTED WOOD TURTLE)

Rhinoclemmys pulcherrima   Family Geoemydidae

These very attractive wood turtles are brightly colored, with narrow red stripes on the face and orange areas on the shell. The most striking form, however, is *Rhinoclemmys pulcherrima manni*, with its red and yellow ocelli on the pleural scutes.

DISTRIBUTION: *Central America, ranging from Sonora on the western side of Mexico southward via Nicaragua as far as Costa Rica.*

SIZE: *Up to 8 in (20 cm).*

ACCOMMODATION: *A largely terrestrial species, the Ornate Wood Turtle must also have a permanent area of water in its enclosure in which it can bathe and even swim. Regular spraying will help maintain the humidity, while the vivarium lighting should be diffuse.*

BEHAVIOR: *The bright patterning may give some defense against predators, since it resembles that of a coral snake.*

DIET: *Omnivorous, but more inclined toward a herbivorous diet, eating greenstuff such as dandelions readily. Will also eat invertebrates and can be persuaded to take a formulated food.*

BREEDING: *The vent area on the male's tail is outside the line of the carapace, and the females are slightly larger overall. Clutches consist of three to five eggs, with two or three clutches likely to be laid in succession. The hatching period can be very variable, from 60 days to over six months.*

RED-CHEEKED MUD TURTLE

Kinosternon scorpioides cruentatum   Family Kinosternidae

This relatively colorful mud turtle is now regarded as a subspecies of the Scorpion Mud Turtle. As its name suggests, it has red coloration on the sides of its face, but the extent of the red markings varies significantly according to the individual.

DISTRIBUTION: *Central America, from Veracruz and Tamaulipas, Mexico, southward as far as northeast Nicaragua and Honduras.*

SIZE: *Up to 11 in (28 cm).*

ACCOMMODATION: *A water temperature of 75 to 79°F (24–26°C) is generally recommended.*

BEHAVIOR: *Can seal itself totally within its shell by moving the hinges on the plastron. The keels on the carapace wear down with age, giving the shell a smoother profile.*

DIET: *Formulated foods can be recommended. Try different brands if palatability is an issue at first.*

BREEDING: *Males can be recognized by their longer tails. Clutch size can vary from six to 12 eggs, and hatching takes place about 90 days later.*

SCORPION MUD TURTLE

Kinosternon scorpioides   Family Kinosternidae

The coloration of the carapace in the Scorpion Mud Turtle varies from light brown through black. The taxonomy of the species is confused, with a number of subspecies or possibly distinctive species having been identified through its wide range. Some have much more colorful facial markings than others.

DISTRIBUTION: *Central America from southern Tamaulipas, Mexico, down across South America to northern Peru, Bolivia and northern Argentina.*

SIZE: *Up to 11 in (28 cm).*

ACCOMMODATION: *As for other mud turtles. A water temperature of 75 to 79°F (24–26°C) is generally recommended.*

BEHAVIOR: *A hinge on the plastron gives these turtles increased protection from predators. They will bury into the mud if the water dries up in stretches of water where they are resident.*

DIET: *Carnivorous. Will readily take a formulated food.*

BREEDING: *A spine at the tip of the tail helps identify the male. Clutch size can vary from six to 12 eggs, and hatching takes place about 90 days later.*

GIANT MEXICAN MUSK TURTLE
(CHIAPAS GIANT MUSK TURTLE)

Staurotypus salvinii   Family Kinosternidae

This species not only grows to a relatively large size, but it also develops three characteristic longitudinal keels running in parallel down its back. Its coloring varies from olive grayish to dark brown, sometimes with some spotting evident on the carapace.

▼ SCORPION MUD TURTLE (KINOSTERNON SCORPIOIDES)

DISTRIBUTION: *Central America, from the Mexican states of Oaxaca and Chiapas southward as far as Guatemala and El Salvador.*

SIZE: *Can grow to 10 in (25 cm).*

ACCOMMODATION: *A large aquarium is required, with an easily accessible dry area for basking. Water temperature, as for other species, should be 75 to 79°F (24–26°C).*

BEHAVIOR: *Has a reputation for being rather aggressive by nature.*

DIET: *Carnivorous. Feeds on a range of aquatic creatures. Will take a formulated food.*

BREEDING: *Males have long tails, and rough scales on their hind legs, helping them anchor themselves while mating. Courtship is often rough. Females lay clutches of six to 10 eggs. Incubation period is variable, from 80 days onward, with the young sometimes overwintering in the nest.*

RAZORBACK MUSK TURTLE

Sternotherus carinatus   Family Kinosternidae

The carapace of the Razorback Musk Turtle has steep sloping sides. This feature is particularly evident in hatchlings, which can appear to have a shell deformity as a result. The skin tends to be grayish in color, while the plastron is yellow. Males have a much longer and thicker tail, ending in a spiny tip.

DISTRIBUTION: *Centered on the Gulf coastal plain of the United States, from southeast Oklahoma, central Arkansas and Mississippi to the Gulf of Mexico.*

SIZE: *6 in (15 cm).*

ACCOMMODATION: *The small size of this species even when adult means that it can quite easily be housed in a large aquarium with a land area that is equipped with a basking light.*

BEHAVIOR: *It favors slow-flowing stretches of water, where there is lush aquatic vegetation.*

DIET: *Omnivorous. Offer a formulated food.*

BREEDING: *Females usually lay two clutches over the summer, containing on average four to seven eggs. Incubation may take more than 100 days.*

COMMON MUSK TURTLE
(STINKPOT)

Sternotherus odoratus   Family Kinosternidae

Young hatchlings tend to display brighter coloration than adult Common Musk Turtles. As the turtle grows, the yellow markings on the head become less distinct, and the black background coloration becomes grayish. The nose is quite prominent when the head is seen in profile, and the carapace is noticeably domed.

DISTRIBUTION: *Ranges widely across the southeastern United States, occurring as far north as southern Ontario in Canada. Extends via Florida along the Gulf Coast to Texas. Also recorded from Chihuahua, Mexico.*

SIZE: *Just over 5 in (13 cm).*

ACCOMMODATION: *Must have both an area for swimming and also dry land where it is possible to walk around and bask.*

BEHAVIOR: *Musk turtles are so called because of the unpleasant musky odor they can release from special glands when caught and handled. Once tame, however, they tend not to react in this way.*

DIET: *A formulated food is ideal for this omnivorous species.*

BREEDING: *Rough patches on the thighs of males may help them grip when mating. Females lay up to four clutches a year, usually of two to five eggs. Hatchlings should start to emerge after about 75 days.*

AFRICAN HELMETED TURTLE

Pelomedusa subrufa   Family Pelomedusidae

These turtles have a relatively flat carapace, which can vary from brown to olive in color, contrasting with the yellowish cream plastron. The head is brown and spotted, paler on the underside, as are the limbs.

DISTRIBUTION: *Ranges widely across Africa, from Ethiopia and Sudan across to West Africa, including Ghana, Senegal, Mali and Nigeria, extending to the Cameroons and as far south as Cape Province in South Africa. Also represented on the island of Madagascar.*

SIZE: *Usually does not exceed 8 in (20 cm), but may attain 13 in (33 cm).*

ACCOMMODATION: *A relatively large land area is important for these turtles, because they naturally roam widely out of water.*

BEHAVIOR: *Found in more arid areas than Pelusios species, often in temporary water holes. Here the turtles bury themselves in the mud and estivate until the rains return, filling the pool again. They can emit an unpleasant musky odor if frightened.*

DIET: *Omnivorous. Offer a formulated food.*

BREEDING: *A single clutch—typically of up to 16 eggs but sometimes more than 40—will be laid. Hatching usually takes between 75 and 90 days.*

EAST AFRICAN MUD TURTLE
(BLACK MARSH SIDE-NECK TURTLE)

Pelusios subniger   Family Pelomedusidae

These turtles have a relatively smooth oval carapace that is dark brown in color. The head is also brown, but the area around the jaws is paler. The legs, tail and neck are gray. There are two sensory swellings, or barbels, on the underside of the chin.

DISTRIBUTION: *Confined to East Africa, from Burundi and Tanzania to parts of eastern Zaire, Zambia and northern Botswana, extending southward to Mozambique. Also present on Madagascar and other offshore islands.*

SIZE: *Up to 8 in (20 cm).*

ACCOMMODATION: *Requires both an area of water and land. A power filter is recommended to keep the water clean.*

BEHAVIOR: *Sometimes occurs in pools, and may be encountered wandering over land at night during the wet season.*

DIET: *Omnivorous. Offer a formulated food.*

BREEDING: *Females—distinguishable by their shorter tails—lay eight to 12 eggs that hatch after at least 58 days when incubated at 86°F (30°C).*

FLORIDA SOFTSHELL TURTLE

Apalone ferox   Family Trionychidae

The leathery carapace is brownish, sometimes gray, with dark spots evident in some young hatchlings. The nasal area is elongated, as in related species, to allow the turtles to breathe while remaining essentially submerged.

▲ FLORIDA SOFTSHELL TURTLE (APALONE FEROX)

DISTRIBUTION: *Central-southern and eastern parts of the United States.*

SIZE: *Males vary from 6–12 in (15–30 cm); females are larger, from 8–24 in (20–60 cm).*

ACCOMMODATION: *Relatively shallow water is necessary so that the turtle can rest on the bottom and still extend its long neck to the surface to breathe through its snout. Sandy substrate allows it to bury itself. Water quality is very important, since these turtles can be prone to fungal infections.*

BEHAVIOR: *Largely aquatic. Also able to extract oxygen from water sucked into the mouth, in the pharyngeal region, and via the cloaca, at the end of the intestinal tract, as well as directly from the air.*

DIET: *Will take live foods and prepared foods. Bullying, especially at feeding time, is not uncommon, and these turtles need spacious accommodation. In some circumstances they may even need to be housed individually.*

BREEDING: *Females have shorter tails than males and are larger overall. They lay up to 23 eggs, and the incubation period lasts for a minimum of 60 days.*

AMPHIBIANS

▲ *Strawberry Dart Frog (Dendrobates pumilio)*

NEWTS AND SALAMANDERS
ORDER CAUDATA

▲ BANDED NEWT PAIR (TRITURUS VITTATUS)—MALE (TOP) AND FEMALE.

The Caudata—literally "tailed amphibians"—includes the world's largest amphibian species, namely the giant salamanders (*Andias*) from China and Japan, which can grow to about 5 feet (1.5 m) long. Today they are likely to be seen only in zoological collections, partly because they have been designated as endangered.

Some of the primitive species of salamanders from North America with their narrow, eel-like bodies can, reach more than 3 feet (1 m) in length. Overall, though, the Caudata is a relatively small group, both numerically and in terms of the individual size of the species. They tend to be most common across North America, Europe and Asia, but there are representatives of this order farther south, in north Africa, for example.

The reproductive biology of this group holds a number of surprises. In some cases the female displays remarkable parental care toward her developing brood, while climatic considerations mean that some populations of certain species, for example, the Fire Salamander (*Salamandra salamandra*), have evolved distinct reproductive strategies in different parts of their range. In the case of the Fire Salamander, development of the eggs can occur within the female's body. She gives birth to live young rather than laying eggs. The eggs then hatch into larvae, which are known as tadpoles, and they in turn metamorphose into miniature adults.

Like some other amphibians, many newts and salamanders have protective skin toxins. They often also have remarkably long life expectancies, of 20 years or more in some cases.

NEWTS

Family Salamandridae (part)

The two main divisions within the Caudata are described as newts and salamanders. Unfortunately, distinguishing between the two groups is far from straightforward. As a general guide, newts are perceived as being more closely dependent on water, with some species spending most of their lives in an aquatic environment, rather than simply returning to water to reproduce. This is not entirely true—some newts spend their early life on land, perhaps not returning to water until they are ready to breed after two or three years.

▲ BLUE-TAILED NEWT (CYNOPS CYANURUS)—FEMALE.

BLUE-TAILED NEWT

Cynops cyanurus   Family Salamandridae

The distinctive blue tail of this species is seen only in mature males as they come into spawning condition, but there are other features that help distinguish these newts from other *Cynops* species. There may be a pale orange stripe running down the back, and there is invariably a spot of similar color behind each eye. Males are generally smaller in size than females.

DISTRIBUTION: *Southwestern China, in the provinces of Yunnan and Guizhou.*

SIZE: *3.5–4.5 in (8.5–11 cm).*

ACCOMMODATION: *These newts require an aquaterrarium, enabling them to emerge onto land. The temperature in their quarters during the summer*

can be as high as 75°F (24°C) but can be allowed to fall back as low as 50°F (10°C) in late winter, to condition the newts for breeding purposes.

BEHAVIOR: *Like related species, these newts are social by nature and can be kept together in groups.*

DIET: *Amphibian pellets when in water, and small live foods.*

BREEDING: *Occurs in the spring. Details similar to other* Cynops. *Young in this case can vary very widely in color at first—some are completely orange, whereas others display a combination of orange and black mottling over the body.*

JAPANESE SWORD-TAILED NEWT

Cynops ensicauda   Family Salamandridae

These colorful newts have orange underparts and a black body. In the case of the subspecies *Cynops ensicauda popei*, it often seems to be dusted with distinctive golden specks. As their name suggests, Japanese Sword-tailed Newts can also be identified by the distinctive shape of the tail.

DISTRIBUTION: *Restricted to southern parts of Japan and the Ryukyu Islands that lie to the south.*

SIZE: *Typically 4.25–5.5 in (11–14 cm).*

ACCOMMODATION: *Keep relatively warm, in water heated to about 75°F (24°C) during the summer, allowing this to drop back over the winter to around 59°F (15°C) in the case of adults. A predominantly aquatic setup, as for other* Cynops, *is required.*

▲ JAPANESE SWORD-TAILED NEWT (CYNOPS ENSICAUDA POPEI)

BEHAVIOR: *Males release scents known as pheromones into the water to attract females when they are ready to mate.*

DIET: *Invertebrates of suitable size, although amphibian pellets provide a better diet.*

BREEDING: *Occurs in the spring. Only males of the nominate race develop a bluish hue to their tails at this stage. The female carefully deposits her eggs individually on plants such as Canadian Pondweed (Elodea). The eggs must be transferred elsewhere before the tadpoles hatch.*

CHINESE FIRE-BELLIED NEWT
(DWARF FIRE-BELLIED NEWT)

Cynops orientalis   Family Salamandridae

The small size of these distinguishes them from other *Cynops* species. They are otherwise similar in color, with brownish black upper parts and an individual orange patterning on their under-parts. Males are usually recognizable by their proportionately shorter tails.

DISTRIBUTION: *The southeastern region of China, including the Yangtse River delta.*

▼ CHINESE FIRE-BELLIED NEWT (CYNOPS ORIENTALIS)

SIZE: *About 4 in (10 cm).*

ACCOMMODATION: *This predominantly aquatic species requires an aquarium filled with up to 3 in (7.5 cm) of water, and stocked with pondweed. There should be an opportunity for them to leave the water, however, in the form of some rocks. No heating is normally required.*

BEHAVIOR: *These newts agree well in a group, but take care when feeding them, because they may snap at each other's legs.*

DIET: *Small amphibian pellets, augmented with small worms and similar live food.*

BREEDING: *Slight cooling over the winter is likely to trigger breeding in the spring. Males have a characteristic swollen cloacal area at the start of the spawning period. The eggs need to be hatched in a separate aquarium, filled with dechlorinated water. Hatching may take anywhere from two to four weeks, depending on the water temperature.*

JAPANESE FIRE-BELLIED NEWT

Cynops pyrrhogaster   Family Salamandridae

One of the most widely kept members of the genus, the Japanese Fire-bellied Newt is brownish black on the upper parts, with a relatively fiery reddish pattern on its underparts. However, there is individual variation, as well as some subspecific variation.

DISTRIBUTION: *Japan.*

SIZE: *3.5–5 in (8.5–13 cm).*

ACCOMMODATION: *As recommended for related species. No heating is necessary but, as with other aquatic amphibians, perform water changes once or twice a week, especially at first. This will maintain the water quality until the filtration system is functioning effectively, which may take two months or more.*

BEHAVIOR: *Will shed their skin, with the body becoming paler shortly beforehand. The old skin is then usually eaten.*

DIET: *Amphibian pellets are usually taken readily, along with various worms and other invertebrates.*

BREEDING: *Expect 150 to 300 eggs, laid individually. The resulting tadpoles should hatch between two and four weeks later, before completing their transformation into young newts about three months after that.*

▼ JAPANESE FIRE-BELLIED NEWT (CYNOPS PYRRHOGASTER)

EASTERN NEWT
(RED-SPOTTED NEWT)

Notophthalmus viridescens   Family Salamandridae

The Eastern Newt varies widely in appearance through its range, and only certain populations have red spots on each side of the body, typically between the front and hind legs. Adults otherwise have brownish upper parts, broken up with small black spots, and they are yellowish below. Their newly metamorphosed young are reddish and are known as "red efts."

DISTRIBUTION: *Ranges widely through eastern North America, extending down from Nova Scotia and southwest Ontario in Canada to Florida, and west as far as Texas.*

SIZE: *2.5–5.5 in (6.5–14 cm).*

ACCOMMODATION: *Adults require an aquaterrarium, which provides easy access to an area of water, where they are likely to hunt for food. Red efts are essentially terrestrial, although their enclosure should include a pot of water. A typical mossy setting, with small logs and stones to provide cover, will be needed, and should be sprayed regularly.*

BEHAVIOR: *Known to feed on the eggs of fish and other amphibians in the wild.*

DIET: *Amphibian pellets may be eaten by adults, but red efts require smaller live foods—an individual may eat 2,000 springtails at a time if hungry.*

BREEDING: *Females lay up to 400 eggs, in typical newt fashion. Hatching takes up to two months, depending on the water temperature.*

BLACK-SPOTTED STOUT NEWT
(SPOTTED PADDLE TAIL NEWT)

Pachytriton breviceps   Family Salamandridae

The color of these newts is variable, but generally dark chocolate brown above with orangish coloration elsewhere, broken by dark spots. Some individuals are much paler than others. Black-spotted Stout Newts are stocky in appearance, with short legs and small eyes. The tail is thick and paddlelike in appearance.

DISTRIBUTION: *Restricted to southeastern parts of China, typically at altitudes of 300–2,400 ft (100–700 m).*

SIZE: *5.5–7.5 in (14–19 cm).*

ACCOMMODATION: *Shallow, relatively cool water—about 59°F (15°C)—and an area of dry land will be required. An airstone to create water movement, or even a power filter, is recommended.*

BEHAVIOR: *These newts naturally occur in shallow, well-oxygenated, flowing streams.*

DIET: *These newts can be persuaded to eat amphibian pellets in addition to invertebrates.*

BREEDING: *Females will lay up to about 70 eggs, depositing them individually on aquatic plants. Males develop blue spots on the sides of the tail at the start of the spawning period.*

▲ EASTERN NEWT (NOTOPHTHALMUS VIRIDESCENS)

▼ PADDLE-TAILED NEWT (PARAMESOTRITON HONGKONGENSIS)

PADDLE-TAILED NEWT
(HONG KONG WARTY NEWT)

Paramesotriton hongkongensis   Family Salamandridae

The upper parts of this newt are chocolate brown, sometimes with an olive hue. Their underparts are blackish, broken by orange spots. Their skin is not as smooth as that of many other newts, which explains why members of this genus are described as warty.

DISTRIBUTION: *Restricted to Hong Kong.*

SIZE: *Up to 5.5 in (14 cm).*

ACCOMMODATION: *This particular species is predominantly aquatic, and should be housed accordingly. The water temperature needs to be heated up to 68° F (20° C) in summer—an undertank heating pad is helpful for this purpose.*

BEHAVIOR: *These newts can be found throughout the year in slow-flowing mountain streams in which aquatic vegetation is well established.*

DIET: *Amphibian pellets and invertebrates can be provided.*

BREEDING: *In the wild, the breeding season extends from November to February. Females may lay as many as 120 eggs, depositing them on water plants. Metamorphosis can take up to eight months.*

SPANISH RIBBED NEWT

Pleurodeles waltl   Family Salamandridae

The Spanish Ribbed Newt is the largest European newt, so called because of its prominent ribs. These ribs may form protective spines on each side of the body adjacent to the backbone, actually breaking through the skin. The newts are dark olive in color, with blackish spots and a relatively broad, flat head.

DISTRIBUTION: *Occurs in the southwestern area of the Iberian Peninsula and across the Mediterranean, in northwestern Morocco.*

SIZE: *8–12 in (20–30 cm).*

ACCOMMODATION: *Predominantly aquatic, these newts require a spacious aquarium, with up to 12 in (30 cm) of water and aquatic plants. The temperature should be up to 77°F (25°C) in the summer, falling back to about 59°F (15°C) over the winter.*

BEHAVIOR: *Will strike out viciously when feeding. Do not overcrowd these newts; allow them plenty of space in order to prevent injuries to their limbs.*

DIET: *Amphibian pellets and a range of invertebrates.*

BREEDING: *Females may lay 800 to 1,000 eggs, carefully concealing them not just on plants but also on rocks and other tank decor. The eggs need to*

be transferred to a separate tank, where the tadpoles can then hatch safely about a week later.

ALPINE NEWT

Triturus alpestris   Family Salamandridae

A dark bluish black back with orange underparts and spotted patterning on the sides of the body are features of this species, although there is some marked variation in appearance through its range. Females can be distinguished by their yellower underparts, while males become particularly striking at the start of the breeding season, with the sides of their body and tail becoming violet. They also develop a low crest.

DISTRIBUTION: *Represented widely in western, central and southeastern Europe, from Spain via Italy to Greece.*

SIZE: *Up to 5 in (13 cm).*

ACCOMMODATION: *Being hardy by nature, these newts can be housed in a secure outdoor pond with a small adjacent land area, also enclosed.*

BEHAVIOR: *Some subspecies, such as the Italian race* Triturus alpestris apuanus, *are more aquatic by nature than others.*

DIET: *Amphibian pellets and invertebrates, especially small worms of various types.*

BREEDING: *Occurs in the spring. Females may produce 300 eggs or more, which may not hatch for a month. The young newts develop slowly, leaving the water after three months.*

▲ *ALPINE NEWT (TRITURUS ALPESTRIS)—MALE (ABOVE) AND FEMALE (RIGHT).*

ITALIAN CRESTED NEWT
(SOUTHERN CRESTED NEWT)

Triturus carnifex   Family Salamandridae

Current thinking suggests that this form of the crested newt is a separate species from the more northern Great Crested Newt *(Triturus cristatus)*. It can be distinguished at a glance, since its flanks are black, lacking the pearly white spots seen in its cousin. Females also have a distinctive orangish yellow stripe running down the center of the back.

DISTRIBUTION: *Southern Europe, occurring throughout Italy.*

SIZE: *Up to 7 in (18 cm).*

ACCOMMODATION: *A water temperature of around 68°F (20°C) is needed.*

◄ *SPANISH RIBBED NEWT (PLEURODELES WALTL)*

▼ *ITALIAN CRESTED NEWT (TRITURUS CARNIFEX)—JUVENILE.*

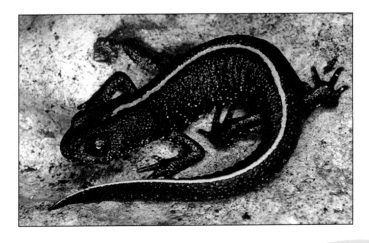

A pair should be accommodated in a spacious aquarium with suitable broad-leaved aquatic plants, such as watercress, included for spawning purposes. A land area with retreats is also important, and the temperature should be dropped back over the winter.

BEHAVIOR: *Males start to develop their distinctive crest after emerging from winter hibernation, and spawning takes place soon afterward.*

DIET: *Will eat amphibian pellets as well as suitable invertebrates.*

BREEDING: *Expect 200 eggs or so. Do not allow the tadpoles to hatch in the same tank as the adults, or they will be eaten. The young should be mature by two years old.*

ITALIAN NEWT

Triturus italicus   Family Salamandridae

A very small species, the Italian Newt is fairly subdued in terms of its coloring, being grayish brown on the upperparts, often with blackish spots evident here. The underparts are whitish with smaller pale orange areas in the center.

DISTRIBUTION: *Central and southern areas of Italy; especially common at lower altitudes.*

SIZE: *2–3 in (5–7.5 cm) when adult.*

ACCOMMODATION: *Conditions similar to those recommended for the Italian Crested Newt* (Triturus carnifex) *will suit these newts.*

BEHAVIOR: *Italian Newts are often encountered in temporary, shallow areas of water, retreating into cooler forested areas when on land.*

DIET: *Amphibian pellets or a range of invertebrates, especially small worms.*

BREEDING: *Males are usually smaller than females. Eggs are disguised on the leaves of aquatic plants. Fry foods as recommended for fish and powdered flake food are useful for rearing the resulting tadpoles.*

MARBLED NEWT

Triturus marmoratus   Family Salamandridae

One of the most beautifully colored of all the European species, the Marbled Newt is a combination of mossy green and black markings. Females can be recognized easily by the reddish stripe running down the center of the back from behind the head.

DISTRIBUTION: *The Iberian Peninsula, extending eastward into France.*

OTHER NEWTS

Palmate Newt (*Triturus helveticus* **)**

Range: Present in the United Kingdom (but not Northern Ireland) and western parts of Europe, from northern Spain.

Size: 3.5 in (9 cm).

Habitat: Damp areas.

Banded Newt (*Triturus vittatus* **)**

Range: Extends from the area of the western Caucasus and Anatolia south to Israel.

Size: About 6 in (15 cm).

Habitat: Occurs at relatively high altitudes, above 3,000 ft (900 m).

SIZE: *Up to 7 in (18 cm).*

ACCOMMODATION: *The vivarium should consist mainly of a land area, with a relatively large, easily accessible water bowl. Hiding places, such as small pieces of cork bark, should be incorporated.*

BEHAVIOR: *Spends most of its time on land outside the breeding period.*

DIET: *Amphibian pellets in water or various invertebrates of suitable size on land.*

◀ *MARBLED NEWT (TRITURUS MARMORATUS)*

▶ *EUROPEAN SMOOTH NEWT (TRITURUS VULGARIS)*

BREEDING: *Males develop a crest at the start of the breeding period in spring. Exposing the tank to the gentle rays of morning sunshine helps encourage spawning. Females may lay as many as 250 eggs.*

CARPATHIAN NEWT
(MONTANDON'S NEWT)

Triturus montandoni   Family Salamandridae

This species is characterized by brownish tan coloration with darker lines running along the body. The underparts are a variable shade of orangish yellow. At the start of the spawning period, males develop a low crest and two ridges, one running down each side of the body.

DISTRIBUTION: *Occurs in both the Carpathian and the Tatra mountain regions in central Europe, particularly in Ukraine.*

SIZE: *4 in (10 cm).*

ACCOMMODATION: *This should be similar to that described for the Alpine Newt (Triturus alpestris).*

BEHAVIOR: *In its natural range it survives the cold weather in the winter by hibernating, but may breed in temporary areas of water.*

DIET: *Amphibian pellets, worms or other suitable invertebrates.*

BREEDING: *Males are slightly smaller in size than females and may develop a bluish or white area on the tail at the start of the spawning period. Females lay on plants, and the resulting tadpoles can be reared separately on fry foods, powdered flake and small invertebrates.*

EUROPEAN SMOOTH NEWT

Triturus vulgaris   Family Salamandridae

The body color of the European Smooth Newt is brown with darker blackish spotting. The underparts are paler. Sexing is straightforward in the spring, at which time males grow a prominent crest when they return to water. They also tend to have more prominent spotting.

DISTRIBUTION: *Extends very widely across western Europe, ranging as far north as Scandinavia.*

SIZE: *4 in (10 cm).*

ACCOMMODATION: *A largely terrestrial setup is required for much of the year, since these newts return to the water only to breed. They can be kept outdoors in a secure pond.*

BEHAVIOR: *In the wild adults will prey on frog tadpoles when in their aquatic breeding phase.*

DIET: *Amphibian pellets as well as invertebrates such as worms.*

BREEDING: *Between 200 and 300 eggs are deposited individually on the leaves of aquatic plants. The female folds over the leaf after laying, to conceal her egg. The tadpoles will hatch in about two weeks, and the young newts emerge onto land after two months or so.*

◀ *ITALIAN NEWT (TRITURUS ITALICUS)*

SALAMANDERS

Families Ambystomatidae, Plethodontidae, Salamandridae (part)

Salamanders are generally adept at hunting invertebrate prey on land, but they are usually secretive. This is not so much a reflection of the fact that they are shy—many are well protected by skin toxins—but when they emerge under cover of darkness, the temperature is cooler. As a result, they are at less risk from dehydration, which would seriously restrict their ability to breathe through the skin. Because not all salamanders develop lungs, skin breathing is vital for many species—oxygen enters and carbon dioxide diffuses out through their skin. Young amphibians extract oxygen from water using their gills but, once on land, the gills are usually lost.

SPOTTED SALAMANDER

Ambystoma maculatum   Family Ambystomatidae

Spotted Salamanders can be identified by a variable pattern of yellow or sometimes orange spots roughly arranged in two rows, running from the head to the tail. The body itself is blackish in color, while the underside is gray.

DISTRIBUTION: *From south-central Ontario east to Nova Scotia in the north, and then south throughout the eastern United States to Georgia and eastern Texas; absent from Florida.*

SIZE: *6–10 in (15–25 cm).*

ACCOMMODATION: *An outdoor vivarium can be used for these salamanders. If they are housed indoors, ensure the enclosure has some drier areas, a shallow container of water, and moist areas with moss.*

BEHAVIOR: *These amphibians are secretive by nature and spend much of their time hidden.*

DIET: *A range of invertebrates of suitable size.*

BREEDING: *Increasing the temperature slightly and flooding the water area will trigger breeding. Females lay eggs in clumps of about 100 or more, which stick on to aquatic plants. The eggs should hatch within a month or so, and the young salamanders will leave the water after another two months.*

AXOLOTL

Ambystoma mexicanum   Family Ambystomatidae

The Axolotl is, in fact, a giant tadpole, complete with gills. It has evolved the ability to reproduce in this seemingly immature state. Axolotls are extensively bred around the world. The most common colors are the native black form and a white variant. Other color varieties such as golden, pied and olive are less common.

DISTRIBUTION: *Restricted to Lake Xochimilco and Lake Chalco in Mexico.*

SIZE: *Up to 12 in (30 cm).*

◄ COLOR FORMS OF AXOLOTL (AMBYSTOMA MEXICANUM), CLOCKWISE FROM LEFT: WHITE; BLACK; PIED; GOLDEN.

measuring about 0.5 in (1.25 cm) long. Powdered fish food and small aquatic creatures such as Daphnia can be used initially for rearing purposes, but ensure the water does not become polluted. Young can breed once they are about one year old, and Axolotls can live for over 20 years.

MARBLED SALAMANDER

Ambystoma opacum   Family Ambystomatidae

This species is distinctively colored, with variable silvery gray markings over the entire length of the body. Males are more brightly colored, with a whiter tone to their markings.

DISTRIBUTION: *South of Lakes Erie and Michigan, and from southern New Hampshire along the Gulf Coast to eastern Texas. Absent from Florida.*

SIZE: *3.5–5 in (8.5–13 cm).*

ACCOMMODATION: *Somewhat drier conditions are favored by these salamanders. Secure outdoor accommodation is ideal, particularly for breeding purposes.*

BEHAVIOR: *Mating takes place in the fall on land. The female remains with the eggs in hollows under leaf litter, waiting for the rains to fill up these dried-up areas. At this juncture the young hatch and survive the winter*

ACCOMMODATION: *An aquatic setup with a water depth of about 12 in (30 cm) will suffice, with coarse gravel or stones used as a floor covering.*

BEHAVIOR: *It is possible to encourage the development of Axolotls into adult salamanders if required, by gradually lowering the water level in their quarters and adding some drops of iodine to the water. This affects the hormonal output of the thyroid glands, triggering metamorphosis.*

DIET: *Worms and other invertebrates.*

BREEDING: *Female Axolotls lay 200 to 300 eggs among aquatic plants. They will need to be transferred to a separate aquarium, preferably one with gentle aeration. Hatching takes about two weeks, with the young Axolotls*

even under ice. During dry periods, however, development of the young continues in the eggs, and hatching may not take place until spring.

DIET: *Invertebrates of various types, including worms and small slugs.*

BREEDING: *Females lay a clutch of up to 200 eggs. In water, tadpoles change into small salamanders up to six months after egg-laying occurs.*

TIGER SALAMANDER

Ambystoma tigrinum   Family Ambystomatidae

This is the largest terrestrial species of salamander. Its striped patterning accounts for its common name, although individuals vary significantly in their markings, with some having spots rather than stripes. Six different subspecies have been identified, all of which have broad heads.

DISTRIBUTION: *Extends southward from central Alberta and Saskatchewan down to Mexico, with a narrow range along the eastern seaboard of the United States; absent from Florida.*

SIZE: *6–13.5 in (15–34 cm).*

ACCOMMODATION: *For breeding purposes a secure enclosure outdoors is most likely to give the best results. A relatively deep pond and some aquatic plants should be incorporated.*

BEHAVIOR: *These salamanders are reasonably bold and will soon learn to anticipate food, although they seek burrows to hide in during the day.*

DIET: *Invertebrates of suitable size; larger individuals will take pinkies too.*

▼ *TIGER SALAMANDER (AMBYSTOMA TIGRINUM)*

BREEDING: *Females lay up to 250 eggs, which they entwine around aquatic plants. It is a good idea to rear the young in groups consisting of individuals of similar size, because cannibalism can sometimes be a problem. Certain western populations are neotenic, with females giving birth to live young.*

DUSKY SALAMANDER

Desmognathus fuscus   Family Plethodontidae

There are two distinctive subspecies based on the appearance of their young. The northern population quickly loses the yellow spotted patterning seen in immature animals, and the adults are dusky brown with black spots and some indistinct striping. The yellow spotted coloration persists in the other race.

DISTRIBUTION: *Extends from southeastern Quebec and southern New Brunswick in a southwesterly direction as far as Louisiana in the United States. Absent from the southeastern area, including Florida.*

SIZE: *2.5–5.5 in (6.5–14 cm).*

ACCOMMODATION: *Damp surroundings are essential for these salamanders, along with places to hide in the vivarium. Leaf litter is often favored as a substrate. They need to be kept relatively cool.*

BEHAVIOR: *Members of this family have no lungs and breathe entirely through their skin, which must be kept moist for this purpose.*

DIET: *Suitable invertebrates, including earthworms, which are the natural prey of these salamanders.*

▲ *Dusky Salamander (Desmognathus fuscus)*

▲ *Two-Lined Salamander (Eurycea bislineata)*

BREEDING: *Females lay small clutches numbering 30 eggs or so, close to water. The young may take up to 13 weeks to emerge, and then may not metamorphose until they are a year old. It may take them four years to reach sexual maturity.*

TWO-LINED SALAMANDER

Eurycea bislineata   Family Plethodontidae

These lungless salamanders are quite colorful, with yellowish and blackish bands running along the length of their body. There may also be a series of fine spots on the upper parts, on an olive-yellow background. In the case of the Blue Ridge sub-species (*Eurycea bislineata wilderae*), the overall coloration is orange rather than yellow.

DISTRIBUTION: *Extends from southeastern Ontario and the St. Lawrence River in Quebec southward across the U.S. border down to the Gulf states, although present only in northern Florida.*

SIZE: *2.5–4.75 in (6.5–12 cm).*

ACCOMMODATION: *A cool, moist environment is needed, with the floor of the vivarium incorporating moss and leaf litter and an area of standing water.*

BEHAVIOR: *Tadpoles that do not metamorphose have been recorded in the wild, this phenomenon possibly being the result of an iodine deficiency.*

DIET: *A range of invertebrates, including small worms and slugs.*

BREEDING: *The female may guard her eggs after spawning. Clutch size is variable and can number up to about 100 eggs. Metamorphosis is slow, being likely to last between one and three years.*

LONG-TAILED SALAMANDER
(THREE-LINED SALAMANDER)

Eurycea longicauda   Family Plethodontidae

The southern form typically has a blackish stripe running down the center of the back, and another on each side of the body. Northern forms have scattered black spots. Body color varies from yellowish brown to a striking orange-red, with widespread regional differences. The tail is noticeably longer than the body.

DISTRIBUTION: *Southern parts of New York State, down along the Gulf Coast into southern Texas, but absent from most of Florida. Northwesterly range extends to Arizona and Utah.*

SIZE: *4–8 in (10–20 cm).*

ACCOMMODATION: *These salamanders prefer a temperature below 61°F (16°C). If they are kept in outdoor accommodation, it needs to be located in a shady spot.*

BEHAVIOR: *They may hide away during the day but emerge to hunt after dark, particularly during periods of rainy weather.*

DIET: *Various invertebrates, which should be dusted as necessary with a vitamin and mineral powder.*

BREEDING: *Only up to about 25 eggs are likely to be laid, which hatch in six to eight weeks. It may take up to seven months for the young salamanders to emerge onto land.*

FIRE SALAMANDER

Salamandra salamandra   Family Salamandridae

Highly variable in appearance, the Fire Salamander's patterning can range from black with yellow spots to populations that are almost entirely yellow. At least 13 different subspecies have been proposed. Some also display orange-red coloration, but this tends to be more a characteristic of individuals rather than a recognizable geographical variance.

DISTRIBUTION: *Occurs widely through Europe, from the Iberian Peninsula eastward up to northern Germany and south to Greece and Turkey. Also present in North Africa and parts of the Middle East.*

SIZE: *Can grow to about 12 in (30 cm).*

ACCOMMODATION: *Damp surroundings generally suit these salamanders, although some prefer drier conditions than others. Pieces of cork bark and other similar retreats should be provided.*

BEHAVIOR: *Often tend to be nocturnal, but they are protected against would-be predators by toxins in their skin. Always wear gloves when handling these salamanders.*

DIET: *Will eat a range of worms, slugs and other invertebrates.*

BREEDING: *Mating occurs on land. The female often lays 25 to 75 eggs in*

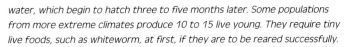

▲▲ *FIRE SALAMANDER* (SALAMANDRA SALAMANDRA)

▲ *EMPEROR SALAMANDER* (TYLOTOTRITON VERRUCOSUS)

◀ *LONG-TAILED SALAMANDER* (EURYCEA LONGICAUDA)

DISTRIBUTION: *Northern parts of India, Myanmar (formerly Burma), Nepal, Thailand, and Vietnam, extending into western Yunnan, China. Tylototriton shanjing is restricted to Yunnan, but ranges more widely here.*

SIZE: *About 7 in (18 cm).*

ACCOMMODATION: *Originating from cool, upland areas, these salamanders require a moist, moss-lined vivarium with hiding places and an easily accessible bowl of water for most of the year. They should be maintained at a temperature of about 64°F (18°C).*

BEHAVIOR: *Emperor Salamanders are primarily terrestrial, returning to the water only in the spring to breed.*

DIET: *Feed on an array of suitable invertebrates, which should be dusted with a vitamin and mineral powder as required.*

BREEDING: *Up to 50 eggs may be deposited on the leaves of plants by the female. The adults should be removed, and the tadpoles will hatch about four days later. They may remain in this larval stage for up to 11 months before emerging onto land. Powdered flake and live foods should be provided as rearing foods.*

water, which begin to hatch three to five months later. Some populations from more extreme climates produce 10 to 15 live young. They require tiny live foods, such as whiteworm, at first, if they are to be reared successfully.

EMPEROR SALAMANDER
(MANDARIN NEWT)

Tylototriton verrucosus Family Salamandridae

There has been some dispute over the taxonomy of Emperor Salamanders recently, and some people believe this species should be split into two. These salamanders are brightly colored with orange head markings, a central orange stripe, orange tail and a series of spots running down the sides of the body. The form now known as *Tylototriton shanjing* is accepted as being the more brightly colored of the two.

AMPHIUMAS, MUDPUPPIES, AND SIRENS
Families Amphiumidae, Proteidae, Sirenidae

TWO-TOED AMPHIUMA

Amphiuma means   Family Amphiumidae

The dark grayish skin of this amphibian is slippery, so the safest way to catch or move them is by using a net. They have four small legs, each equipped with two toes, which explains their common name.

DISTRIBUTION: *Seaboard of southeastern United States, extending from southeastern Virginia through Florida to eastern Louisiana.*

SIZE: *18–46 in (45–117 cm).*

ACCOMMODATION: *A large setup is recommended, with a secure barrier outdoors to prevent the amphiumas from straying. Service their quarters with care, since they are potentially aggressive and will bite.*

BEHAVIOR: *They sometimes leave the water, particularly during periods of rainfall, although their limbs do not help them move over land.*

DIET: *Natural prey consists of crustaceans, fish, and other amphibians. Offer suitably sized invertebrates.*

BREEDING: *Their breeding season is influenced by their distribution, occurring later in the year in more northerly areas. The female constructs a hidden nest in shallow water and coils around her eggs, guarding them until they hatch approximately five months later. Amphiumas, unlike most amphibians, have internal fertilization.*

▼ MUDPUPPY (NECTURUS MACULOSUS)

MUDPUPPY
(WATERDOG)

Necturus maculosus   Family Proteidae

Mudpuppies are totally aquatic and cannot survive long out of water. Adults take the form of larvae, with three pairs of external gills, and tail fins. Their brown speckled body is flattened. The young have two yellow stripes down the back.

DISTRIBUTION: *Southern Quebec to southeastern Manitoba in Canada, extending southward as far as northern Georgia and Louisiana. An introduced population occurs in rivers in New England.*

SIZE: *8–17 in (20–43 cm).*

ACCOMMODATION: *Entirely aquatic by nature, mudpuppies may benefit from gentle filtration to improve the oxygenation of their water. This should be relatively cool, typically no warmer than 61°F (16°C).*

BEHAVIOR: *These amphibians are so called because of the sounds they can make, which have been likened to a puppy barking.*

DIET: *A variety of invertebrates, including crustaceans and aquatic snails. They will also catch fish and should not be kept alongside them in an outdoor pond.*

BREEDING: *Mating occurs in the fall, with the female laying in early summer. She chooses a quiet place where the eggs will be hidden, such as the underside of a submerged log. Hatching takes between five and nine weeks. The young themselves will not be fully mature until they are at least six years old.*

WESTERN LESSER SIREN

Siren intermedia   Family Sirenidae

Sirens are often mistaken for eels, in spite of the fact that they have external gills. They are dark in color and also possess very small limbs. Males attain a larger size overall than females.

DISTRIBUTION: *Extends down the Eastern Seaboard from the southern area of North Carolina down to central Florida and along the Gulf Coast to Texas. Also extends northward to southwestern Michigan.*

SIZE: *Typically around 16 in (40 cm). Larger individuals, up to 27 in (69 cm) are known, often being recorded from Texas.*

ACCOMMODATION: *Sirens need a relatively shallow but spacious aquarium that offers space for swimming as well as cover in the form of plants and caves.*

BEHAVIOR: *They can survive drought in the wild by burrowing down into the mud; their gills shrink in size during this period.*

DIET: *In the wild the sirens feed on crustaceans, aquatic snails, worms, and small fish; also eats some plant matter.*

BREEDING: *Females lay up to 200 eggs early in the year. The young tadpoles measure about 0.5 in (1.25 cm). Reducing the water temperature over the winter may help trigger spawning in the spring. Sexual maturity is reached at two years of age.*

▼ *WESTERN LESSER SIREN (SIREN INTERMEDIA)*

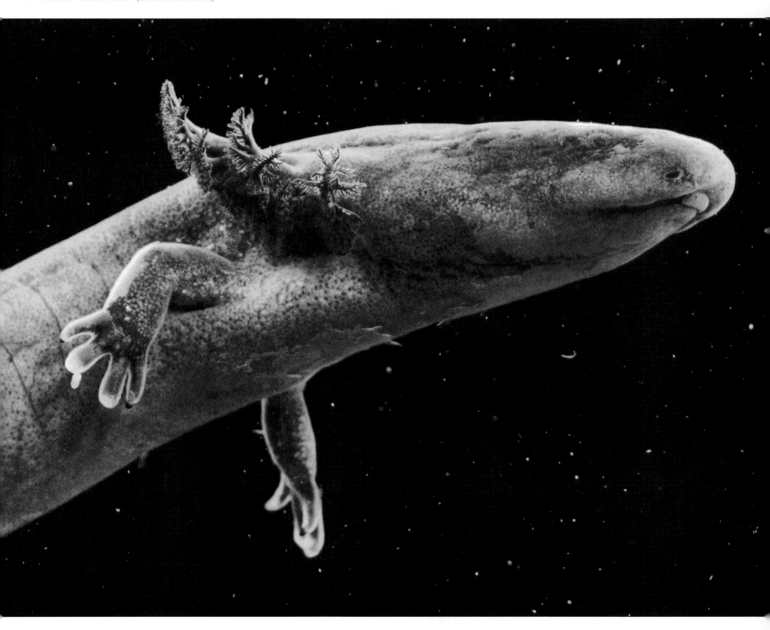

FROGS AND TOADS
ORDER ANURA

Frogs and toads are the major group in the Class Amphibia. They form the Order Anura, which means "tail-less." The fact that they have no tails distinguishes them immediately from newts and salamanders, and from the caecilians. They represent the largest subdivision, numbering some 3,500 out of a total of about 4,000 amphibian species.

Representatives of the group are found on every continent and have colonized virtually every type of habitat, with the exception of true deserts and frozen wastelands—they are even found within the Arctic Circle. Anurans vary in size from less than 1 inch (2.5 cm) in length up to the Goliath Frog (*Conraua goliath*) from Africa, which can reach 12 inches (30 cm) long or more.

Perhaps surprisingly, there is no definitive way of distinguishing between frogs and toads themselves.

As a general guide, frogs tend to live a more aquatic existence than toads, although the African Clawed Toad (*Xenopus laevis*) is, in fact, almost entirely aquatic. It is usually said that toads have a rather warty appearance, and this has given rise to a number of myths about these amphibians. But there again, some types of frog, such as the horned frogs (*Ceratophrys* species) also have a rough skin. While true toads are well protected against predators by skin toxins, this also applies to a number of frogs, especially the often highly colorful dart frogs (family Dendrobatidae) from Central and South America. All frogs and toads, aside from a single known exception, are predatory when adult, with invertebrates playing a prominent part in the diets of most species.

▼ *DYEING DART FROGS (*DENDROBATES TINCTORIUS*)*

TREE FROGS

Families Hylidae, Hyperoliidae, Rhacophoridae

As their name suggests, the majority of tree frogs are adept at climbing, thanks to the suction provided by their expanded toe pads. They tend to be confined primarily to tropical areas and will leap between branches to escape danger, although their camouflage coloration often helps conceal their presence.

Tree frogs require a relatively tall vivarium, decorated with suitable plants—real or artificial—on which they can climb. Their food should also be offered off the ground, since that is where these frogs normally hunt. The provision of water in a shallow container on the floor of the enclosure is very important, partly because many species spawn on leaves above water. Once they hatch, the resulting tadpoles will drop down into the water below to complete their metamorphosis.

RED-EYED TREE FROG

Agalychnis callidryas   Family Hylidae

The most distinctive characteristic of these frogs is their striking red eyes. Their overall coloration is a bright grass green, with signs of cream barring—sometimes mixed with a bluish color—on the sides of the body. The expanded toes, which are characteristic of tree frogs in general, are pale orange.

DISTRIBUTION: *Central America, from southern Mexico via Guatemala and Belize down through El Salvador and Honduras; through Nicaragua and Costa Rica to Panama.*

SIZE: *Up to 3 in (7.5 cm) long; adult females are larger than males.*

ACCOMMODATION: *A warm, humid, spacious vivarium is required for these tree frogs, which can be housed in a small group if required. A temperature of about 75° F (24° C) will be adequate. Brief spraying to mimic daily periods of rainfall is recommended.*

BEHAVIOR: *Unfortunately, this species is nocturnal, so the frogs only become active under cover of darkness. They hide away during the daytime.*

DIET: *Feeds on insects, rarely descending to the ground in search of food. May be reluctant to feed at first for a few days after a move, being*

▲ RED-EYED TREE FROG (AGALYCHNIS CALLIDRYAS)

nervous and shy by nature. Crickets are normally eaten readily though, especially off vivarium vegetation.

BREEDING: *Decreasing the relative humidity in the vivarium and then increasing it again, mimicking the onset of tropical rains, can trigger breeding. Ensure there is a broad leaf for spawning above an area of water, into which the tadpoles can fall when they hatch about five days later. Powdered flake food can be used as a first food for the tadpoles; the transition to small frogs takes about 100 days.*

MARSUPIAL FROG

Gastrotheca riobambae   Family Hylidae

These unusual frogs are fairly variable in appearance, ranging from all-green to green with various bronze markings or stripes on the body. They display the typical expanded foot pads that characterize tree frogs in general.

DISTRIBUTION: *Upland areas of Ecuador in northwest South America.*

SIZE: *Up to 3 in (7.5 cm).*

ACCOMMODATION: *Despite originating from near the equator, this species does not thrive in typically tropical temperatures, since it lives at relatively high altitude. Its vivarium does not need to be particularly tall either, because these frogs tend to live on or near the ground.*

BEHAVIOR: *Females carry the eggs—numbering up to 100—in a pouch on their back, which is why these frogs are popularly known as Marsupial Frogs.*

DIET: *Feeds readily on a wide range of invertebrates.*

BREEDING: *Calls of the male have been likened to the clucking sounds of a chicken. Mating occurs on land, with the male helping steer the eggs into the female's pouch. It will then be about 10 weeks before the female releases her tadpoles into the water, if necessary scooping them out of the pouch with her long hind toes.*

EUROPEAN GREEN TREE FROG

Hyla arborea   Family Hylidae

These tree frogs are normally bright green with dark blackish stripes running from the eyes down the sides of the body, while the underparts are whitish. Color variants are known, however, in which brown markings replace the green on the back. There is an even more unusual blue morph. Males have a brownish yellow vocal sac in the throat area.

DISTRIBUTION: *Widely distributed across mainland Europe, from Scandinavia southward to the Mediterranean and eastward into Russia.*

SIZE: *Up to 1.75 in (4.5 cm).*

ACCOMMODATION: *These tree frogs are relatively hardy and can be housed outdoors through the summer in a secure greenhouse with shade available, where they will help control insect pests. They can also be housed indoors in an unheated planted vivarium, but are less likely to breed there.*

BEHAVIOR: *Males will call when in breeding condition; several of them together can be surprisingly noisy, competing in a chorus with each other.*

DIET: *Takes a wide variety of invertebrates.*

BREEDING: *Starts in the spring. Females produce up to 200 eggs at each spawning, which they will lay among aquatic plants. In an aquarium in which the water is heated to 68°F (20°C), the tadpoles are easy to rear and will*

metamorphose in about eight weeks. The young tree frogs can be fed on hatchling crickets from the outset, and may be mature by two years of age.

GREEN TREE FROG

Hyla cinerea   Family Hylidae

Not to be confused with its European cousin *Hyla arborea*, this species is also an attractive shade of grass green. The vast majority of individuals have a cream-colored line extending from the jaw down the flanks. Occasional red-eyed, bright yellow individuals have been recorded.

DISTRIBUTION: *Southern United States, extending from Delaware west to Texas and south to Florida.*

SIZE: *1.2–2.5 in (3–6.5 cm).*

ACCOMMODATION: *The vivarium should be well stocked with tall plants and have a substantial area of water on the floor, surrounded by moss as a floor covering. As with other tree frogs, this species can very agile, using its*

▲ MARSUPIAL FROG (GASTROTHECA RIOBAMBAE)

▼ BARKING TREE FROG (HYLA GRATIOSA)

suckerlike toes to climb up glass without difficulty. Its housing must therefore be adequately covered to prevent escapes.

BEHAVIOR: *The loud calls of males of this species have been likened to the sound of a dog barking and are usually uttered through the mating period during spring and summer.*

DIET: *A wide variety of invertebrates will be eaten. As always, use a vitamin and mineral supplement if the prey is not gut-loaded.*

BREEDING: *A similar breeding setup as recommended for the European Green Tree Frog should suffice, but this American species has not proved as ready as its relative to spawn in collections.*

BARKING TREE FROG

Hyla gratiosa   Family Hylidae

Barking Tree Frogs tend to be green, with a variable pattern of darker markings over their bodies, along with white blotches. In addition, the appearance of an individual can vary somewhat depending on its mood and its surroundings. The males have a yellow or green throat.

▲ GREEN TREE FROG (HYLA CINEREA)

DISTRIBUTION: *Eastern seaboard of the United States, from southern New Jersey via Florida to northeastern Louisiana.*

SIZE: *Up to 3 in (7.5 cm).*

ACCOMMODATION: *Ensure that the frogs can submerge themselves in a bowl of water with some aquatic plants such as Canadian Pondweed (Elodea) included. The vivarium itself should have branches, allowing the frogs to climb.*

BEHAVIOR: *Barking Tree Frogs are social by nature and are best kept in small groups. They are usually nocturnal. As the temperature falls in the wild, they leave the trees and tend to burrow.*

DIET: *They can prove to be gluttonous feeders. Aside from invertebrates, large individuals may occasionally eat newborn pinkies, more commonly sold as snake food.*

BREEDING: *The calls of males are exceptionally loud during the spawning period and resemble a dog's bark—to the extent that dogs have been known to bark back! Breeding details are similar to those of related species.*

EUROPEAN STRIPELESS TREE FROG

Hyla meridionalis   Family Hylidae

This species is very similar to the European Green Tree Frog (*Hyla arborea*) in terms of appearance, although it is larger in size. The dark stripe on the sides of the body is also less pronounced, and usually begins only from the eyes, not the nostrils.

DISTRIBUTION: *Through the Mediterranean region in France, Spain and Portugal, with a more restricted range than* H. arborea.

SIZE: *About 2.5 in (6.5 cm).*

ACCOMMODATION: *Occurs farther south than its close relative, so this tree frog is less hardy. Like many species, these frogs may benefit from the presence of an ultraviolet light, especially in the case of young individuals that have recently metamorphosed and are still growing.*

BEHAVIOR: *They often like to rest on broad-leaved plants, especially where the leaves come into contact with the sides of the vivarium.*

DIET: *As in other cases, these tree frogs naturally prey on flying insects. Crickets—which can be gut-loaded to improve their nutritional value—will be eaten without problems.*

BREEDING: *Females can often be persuaded to spawn more than once through the spring and summer, particularly if food is readily available. Mating starts on land, with egg-laying occurring subsequently in the water.*

COMMON GRAY TREE FROG

Hyla versicolor   Family Hylidae

Although individuals are very variable in their markings, the distinctive gray appearance of these tree frogs is a good identifier. The frogs' thighs are an attractive contrasting yellowish orange color. A characteristic light spot with a dark border is present below each eye.

▼ COMMON GRAY TREE FROG (HYLA VERSICOLOR)

DISTRIBUTION: *Eastern North America. Ranges from southern Ontario and Manitoba in Canada southward via Maine to northern Florida and westward to central Texas.*

SIZE: *1.2–2.5 in (3–6.5 cm).*

ACCOMMODATION: *A setup similar to that used for other* Hyla *species from this part of the world is recommended. An attractive yet practical way of decorating the sides and back of the aquarium is to use cork bark, which can be easily sawn to fit and allows these tree frogs to climb easily.*

BEHAVIOR: *Found in association with trees, clambering high up and resting during the day, but becoming more active at night. Usually seen close to areas of water.*

DIET: *Hunts invertebrates and is nocturnal in its feeding habits. Moths are a favored prey, but this tree frog is generally unfussy.*

BREEDING: *Northern populations breed only during the warmer months of the year; southern populations may spawn at any stage.*

GOLDEN BELL FROG
(GREEN AND GOLDEN BELL FROG)

Litoria aurea   Family Hylidae

The coloration of these frogs is variable, ranging from emerald green to dull olive green, broken up by blotches of bronze. There is a cream-colored area extending backward from close to the snout, below each eye. A blackish stripe runs through the eyes and above the very prominent tympanum.

DISTRIBUTION: *Australia, restricted to eastern and southeastern Victoria and eastern New South Wales.*

SIZE: *Up to 3.5 in (8.5 cm).*

ACCOMMODATION: *This is a highly aquatic species, so a large area of water needs to be provided in its enclosure. Hiding places, such as cork bark, need to be included.*

BEHAVIOR: *Hunts during the day. Can be cannibalistic, so avoid keeping individuals of different sizes together.*

DIET: *Eats an array of invertebrates.*

BREEDING: *Extends from October to January in the wild. The pigmented eggs are laid in a clump, which sinks before the tadpoles hatch. They are pinkish gray and have contrasting yellowish fins.*

WHITE'S TREE FROG

Litoria caerulea   Family Hylidae

One of the most popular tree frogs as a vivarium subject, the natural form of White's Tree Frog is bright green with pale underparts, although bluish variants are known, as are pied individuals, with whitish areas on the upper part of their bodies.

▲ *Golden Bell Frog* (Litoria aurea)

◀ *European Stripeless Tree Frog* (Hyla meridionalis)

▼ *White's Tree Frog* (Litoria caerulea)

DISTRIBUTION: *Much of southeast Australia, extending through northern parts of the Northern Territory and Western Australia. Also present in southern New Guinea and neighboring smaller islands.*

SIZE: *Usually up to 4 in (10 cm). Can weigh as much as 8 oz (227 g).*

ACCOMMODATION: *Provide a large enclosure with a water bowl, and a basking light under which the frogs can rest during the day. Surroundings should not be especially humid, but spray regularly. Large plants such as philodendrons are necessary to support the weight of these tree frogs, and retreats should also be included.*

BEHAVIOR: *One of the longest lived of all tree frogs, White's have a typical life expectancy of 10 years, and some individuals have been known to live twice as long. They can also become very tame, which helps explain their popularity.*

DIET: *Will eat a wide range of invertebrates. Can be prone to obesity, so encourage the frogs to hunt for their own food by scattering it around the vivarium.*

BREEDING: *Although these tree frogs are easily obtainable, thanks to artificial spawning, natural breeding is less easy to achieve in vivarium surroundings. Cooling the vivarium down to 68° F (20° C) once the frogs are in good condition, and then raising the temperature to 77° F (25° C) can help, especially if the humidity is increased dramatically at the same time. Calling starts shortly afterward, and females each produce up to 3,000 eggs. Use natural fluorescent tubes over the tadpoles to encourage healthy development. This may also improve the color of the young frogs, which will start to leave the water once they are a month old. Only keep those of similar size together, in order to deter cannibalism.*

WHITE-LIPPED TREE FROG

Litoria infrafrenata   Family Hylidae

Although similar to White's Tree Frog *(Litoria caerulea)*, this species has a far less dumpy shape. It too is green in color, with a very distinctive white line around the lower jaw. Once again, the depth of green coloration differs among individuals, with some being more brightly colored than others.

▼ WHITE-LIPPED TREE FROG (LITORIA INFRAFRENATA)

DISTRIBUTION: *Indonesia and the former region of East Timor. Also occurs in lowland areas of New Guinea, eastward to New Ireland in the Bismarck Archipelago. Present in Australia through the Cape York Peninsula down to northeastern Queensland.*

SIZE: *Up to 4 in (10 cm).*

ACCOMMODATION: *A similar setup to that of White's Tree Frog is required. Occurs in a wide range of different habitats in the wild.*

BEHAVIOR: *Nocturnal in its habits.*

DIET: *Will take a range of invertebrates, but newly acquired individuals may be reluctant to feed at first.*

BREEDING: *Similar to that of White's Tree Frog, but natural spawnings are hard to achieve. Metamorphosis of the tadpoles typically takes about two months.*

CUBAN TREE FROG

Osteopilus septentrionalis   Family Hylidae

The coloration of these tree frogs varies from shades of brown through to green. This may be combined with a slight reddish coloring along the back. The large size of Cuban Tree Frogs may account for their pronounced toe pads, which serve to anchor them as they climb. The Cuban Tree Frog has become the largest tree frog on the North American mainland.

SYNONYM: *Hyla septentrionalis.*

DISTRIBUTION: *Occurs naturally on Cuba, the Bahamas and the Cayman Islands. Accidentally introduced to Florida about a century ago, and now well established there.*

SIZE: *1.5–5.5 in (4–14 cm).*

ACCOMMODATION: *A large enclosure is needed, with plenty of branches and suitable plants for these arboreal amphibians to clamber around on.*

◄ GIANT MEXICAN TREE FROG (PACHYMEDUSA DACNICOLOR)

A temperature of around 77°F (25°C) will be needed.

BEHAVIOR: *Their large size means that these tree frogs will readily prey on smaller companions. Males when calling sound as if they are snoring.*

DIET: *Will feed readily on a wide range of invertebrates.*

BREEDING: *Easily accomplished, with females proving prolific. They may lay as many as 2,000 eggs in a single spawning. The tadpoles develop rapidly, and some may emerge from the water as froglets in as little as six weeks.*

HAITIAN GIANT TREE FROG

Osteopilus vastus   Family Hylidae

The upper parts of these very large tree frogs are a greenish gray shade, with darker blackish or gray markings on their body. There may be an outline of a T-shaped marking on the head, with the underparts being pale. Young of this species tend to be dark gray in color, with a slight greenish suffusion.

DISTRIBUTION: *Restricted entirely to the Caribbean island of Hispaniola, where it occurs in both Haiti and the Dominican Republic.*

SIZE: *Females grow up to 5.5 in (14 cm); males do not exceed 4 in (10 cm).*

ACCOMMODATION: *A tall and relatively spacious vivarium is required for these large tree frogs. A temperature of about 77–82°F (25–28°C) will be required.*

BEHAVIOR: *Encountered in close proximity to streams in its natural habitat.*

DIET: *Eats a variety of invertebrates.*

BREEDING: *Gentle aeration of the water will be beneficial after spawning occurs. In this species the tadpoles' gills are naturally small relative to their overall size, suggesting that the water in which they hatch is naturally well oxygenated.*

GIANT MEXICAN TREE FROG
(MEXICAN LEAF FROG)

Pachymedusa dacnicolor   Family Hylidae

The upper parts of this tree frog are greenish, with scattered white spots also evident. The underside of the body is white, but the toes and often the legs as well are orange. The pupils are yellowish with black reticulations. The tympanum behind the eye is prominent and tends to be paler in color than the surrounding skin.

DISTRIBUTION: *Restricted to the western side of Mexico, ranging from southern Sonora to the Isthmus of Tehuantepec.*

SIZE: *Up to 4 in (10 cm); females are larger than males.*

▲ WAXY MONKEY TREE FROG (PHYLLOMEDUSA SAUVAGII)

DISTRIBUTION: *Occurs widely in South America, in Colombia, Venezuela, French Guiana, Surinam and Guyana, southward to Argentina, Brazil, Bolivia and Paraguay.*

SIZE: *About 2.5 in (6.5 cm).*

ACCOMMODATION: *The vivarium needs to be hot and dry. Create a thermal gradient across the vivarium, with a basking spot at one end where the temperature is around 95° F (35° C), falling back slightly at night. That is when the frogs become more active, descending to the ground in search of food. A water dish should also be provided for them. They should not be sprayed.*

BEHAVIOR: *These frogs can be observed sleeping in curled leaves or hollow branches that give them protection. They will spawn off the ground as well, in the central water-filled cup of various bromeliads.*

DIET: *Feed these frogs at dusk and offer a range of invertebrates.*

BREEDING: *Similar to that the Waxy Monkey Tree Frog.*

ACCOMMODATION: *A relatively dry, warm environment is required for these frogs, but with standing water always available. The vivarium should include burrows, which can be created using a broken flowerpot or tubing buried in the substrate, allowing the frogs to retreat here during the day. These burrows can obviously be covered with moss to disguise them.*

BEHAVIOR: *Does not have a dormant period; remains active through the dry season.*

DIET: *Feeds mainly on invertebrates.*

BREEDING: *Creates a foamy nest for its eggs on vegetation in a shady spot. After hatching, the tadpoles slide down into the water below, where they complete their metamorphosis. Powdered flake food can be used for rearing purposes.*

TIGER-LEGGED MONKEY TREE FROG

Phyllomedusa hypochondrialis   Family Hylidae

These attractive frogs are a bright green color, with white or pale yellow underparts. Their distinctive characteristic is the striped patterning on the inside of their legs, which explains their common name. As with related species, they produce a unique waxy substance from their body, made up of lipids. They use this secretion to coat themselves, thereby slowing water loss from their body. This allows them to thrive under relatively arid conditions.

WAXY MONKEY TREE FROG

Phyllomedusa sauvagii   Family Hylidae

This is one of the largest member of the genus. It is bright green in color with white areas on the underparts and a white stripe. Waxy Monkey Tree Frogs move through the branches effectively by walking rather than hopping, in a similar way to monkeys.

DISTRIBUTION: *Restricted to central South America, occurring in Brazil, Argentina, Bolivia and Paraguay.*

SIZE: *Up to 4.5 in (11 cm).*

ACCOMMODATION: *Similar to that recommended for the Tiger-legged Monkey Tree Frog. Their surroundings must not be humid. A warm daytime basking spot is essential, with a special night light so that you can observe these frogs as they become active.*

BEHAVIOR: *This species roosts in the open on branches during the day, rather than hiding away. Their waxy body covering protects them against dehydration.*

DIET: *Offer vitamin- and mineral-enriched invertebrates in the evening.*

BREEDING: *May use bromeliad cups for spawning in the wild. Eggs are laid above water, in leaves that are stuck together for this purpose. They are protected by foam and, after hatching, tadpoles will develop in the water beneath.*

ASIAN TREE FROG

Polypedates leucomystax   Family Rhacophoridae

The basic color of these widely kept tree frogs is brown, but it can vary from a creamy shade through reddish brown to dark brown. Lighting conditions can affect the coloration, with these frogs becoming paler when they are in bright light.

DISTRIBUTION: *Ranges widely through Southeast Asia, not just in the countryside but often even in city centers.*

SIZE: *2–4 in (5–10 cm); females are significantly larger than males.*

ACCOMMODATION: *A well planted, tall vivarium is required, with a temperature of between 77 and 86°F (25–30°C).*

BEHAVIOR: *This is another foam-nesting species that lays its eggs out of the water.*

DIET: *Assorted invertebrates, especially crickets, which will jump onto the vegetation.*

BREEDING: *Increasing the relative humidity by spraying with tepid dechlorinated water will trigger spawning. The eggs are deposited in a nest overhanging water, usually attached to the side of the vivarium rather than on plants. Hatching takes about five days, and the tadpoles fall into the water at this stage. They often develop at different rates, with the first young frogs emerging on to land about a month later.*

PACIFIC TREE FROG

Pseudacris regilla   Family Hylidae

The coloration of the Pacific Tree Frog is very variable, ranging from shades of green through brown. In all cases, however, there is a prominent black stripe extending on each side of the head from the snout through the eyes down to the top of the forelegs. Males have dusky throats.

SYNONYM: *Hyla regilla.*

DISTRIBUTION: *Extends from Mount Scriven, British Columbia, southward along the Pacific coast to the tip of Baja California, and east to Montana and Nevada. Also occurs on islands off southern California and introduced to various localities in this region, including a desert population at Soda Springs.*

SIZE: *Up to 2 in (5 cm).*

◀ *ASIAN TREE FROGS (POLYPEDATES LEUCOMYSTAX)—TWO COLOR FORMS.*

ACCOMMODATION: *A relatively arid yet warm vivarium setup is required for these small tree frogs. They tend not to climb to any great height, so the area of the enclosure is more important than its height.*

BEHAVIOR: *Generally breed in standing areas of water. Males call very frequently, every second or so, with the call note being made up of two distinctive parts.*

DIET: *Offer relatively small invertebrates.*

BREEDING: *Occurs naturally between November and July, with eggs being laid in batches of 10 to 70. Large females may produce more than 1,000 eggs in total. The tadpoles can be reared easily on powdered flake.*

MEXICAN MASKED TREE FROG

Smilisca baudinii   Family Hylidae

Individuals may range in coloration from golden green through to a brownish shade of gray. One distinctive feature, however, is the mask, which is in the form of a dark band extending from the snout through the eyes to the top of the forelegs. Females tend to have a more rounded profile overall and a shorter snout.

DISTRIBUTION: *Occurs widely through Central America, from Mexico south via Guatemala and Belize through El Salvador, Honduras and Nicaragua to Costa Rica. Also present in the extreme south of Texas.*

SIZE: *Females grow to 3 in (7.5 cm); males are about 1 in (2.5 cm) smaller.*

ACCOMMODATION: *A large enclosure is recommended. It should be heated to about 83°F (28°C), but the temperature should be reduced a little at night.*

BEHAVIOR: *Hides away during the dry season in hollow trees and similar retreats.*

DIET: *Feeds on invertebrates.*

BREEDING: *Dark vocal sacs become more prominent in males at the start of the spawning period. Males also develop nuptial pads at this stage. Females may lay up to 2,000 eggs in standing areas of water. Rearing of the tadpoles is relatively straightforward.*

MAYAN CASQUE-HEADED FROG

Triprion petasatus   Family Hylidae

The unusual head shape of these frogs helps identify them, looking somewhat like a shovel when viewed from above. Their eyes are very prominent. They are brownish in color, sometimes displaying an olive tinge, with pale underparts.

DISTRIBUTION: *From the Yucatán Peninsula of Mexico southward to El Peten in Guatemala.*

SIZE: *Typically 2.5–3 in (6–7.5 cm), but can reach 4.75 in (12 cm).*

ACCOMMODATION: *These frogs are very fast moving and will leap with little provocation, sometimes even injuring themselves. Keep disturbances in their quarters to a minimum and always move slowly to avoid disturbing them. Temperatures during the day should be around 80°F (27°C), dropping back a little at night. Water for swimming should also be available.*

BEHAVIOR: *The unusual head shape of this frog is vital to its survival. When it gets dry the frog squeezes into a cool hollow—for example, within a tree branch—and plugs the entrance with its head. In this way its surroundings remain more humid, preventing the frog from becoming seriously dehydrated—little water is lost from its bony head.*

DIET: *Requires small invertebrates, supplemented with vitamins and minerals.*

BREEDING: *Spawning occurs from June through September in the wild, linking with the rainy season.*

◀ MEXICAN MASKED TREE FROG (SMILISCA BAUDINII)

▼ AFRICAN REED FROG (HYPEROLIUS MARMORATUS)

STRIPED SPINY REED FROG

Afrixalus dorsalis   Family Hyperoliidae

These small frogs are dark brown, and they have intervening lighter stripes on the back. In common with other tree frogs, they have swollen tips on their digits, which help them climb more effectively, even up vertical surfaces and on glass. All the members of this genus have vertical pupils, distinguishing them from *Hyperolius* species.

DISTRIBUTION: *Found in central parts of Africa, including Cameroon and Angola.*

SIZE: *About 1–1.5 in (2.5–4 cm).*

ACCOMMODATION: *A setup mimicking a tropical rain forest is ideal for these frogs. A temperature between 77 and 83°F (25–28°C) should be maintained during the day, falling back a little at night.*

BEHAVIOR: *Striped Spiny Reed Frogs are also known as Banana Frogs because they often hide in the leaves of these plants during the daytime.*

DIET: *Will feed on a range of small invertebrates, which should be supplemented with a vitamin and mineral preparation.*

BREEDING: *Eggs are laid in folded leaves just above the water surface. Hatching takes about 10 days, with the tadpoles slipping down into the water. They will then emerge as froglets after about 10 weeks.*

AFRICAN REED FROG
(MARBLED REED FROG; PAINTED REED FROG)

Hyperolius marmoratus   Family Hyperoliidae

The taxonomy of reed frogs, which occur across much of sub-Saharan Africa, is the subject of considerable controversy. This is reflected by their highly variable appearance. The underlying background color of African Reed Frogs can vary from cream through green, with patterns including both spots and stripes in a wide range of colors having been identified. The underparts are paler, often whitish.

DISTRIBUTION: *East Africa southward, from Tanzania, Swaziland and Mozambique to South Africa.*

SIZE: *1–1.5 in (2.5–4 cm).*

ACCOMMODATION: *A well planted, tall vivarium that provides space for climbing is needed. Typical daytime temperature should be around 77°F (25°C). This can be allowed to drop back very slightly at night.*

BEHAVIOR: *Males will start calling toward dusk; their calls sound a little like a wheelbarrow with a squeaky wheel.*

DIET: *A range of relatively small live foods such as mini-mealworms should be offered.*

▲ AMANI FOREST TREE FROG (LEPTOPELIS VERMICULATUS)

BREEDING: *Can vary depending on the origins of the frogs. Java moss serves as a good spawning medium, and is easily transferred with the eggs to a tank, where hatching should take place about three days later. Each spawning may consist of as many as 200 eggs, laid in clumps. The tadpoles can be reared on powdered fry food, emerging as young brown-colored frogs two months later.*

RED-LEGGED KASSINO FROG
(RED-LEGGED PAN FROG)

Kassina maculata   Family Hyperoliidae

Although members of this genus are often described collectively as African striped frogs, this species tends to be spotted. It is gray overall, with black spots that have lighter borders.

DISTRIBUTION: *Present in East Africa, from the coastal region of Kenya southward; extends down to South Africa.*

SIZE: *Up to 2.5 in (6.5 cm).*

ACCOMMODATION: *Since it occurs naturally in areas of rain forest, this species requires a typically warm, humid environment. A temperature of 77–83°F (25–28°C) is therefore recommended, dropping back slightly at night. Moss and leaf litter will provide a good covering on the floor of the vivarium, along with some larger plants.*

BEHAVIOR: *Nocturnal by nature, these frogs are unusual because they rarely jump, preferring to escape danger by running instead.*

DIET: *Take a wide variety of prey. Can display cannibalistic tendencies, so keep only individuals of similar size together.*

BREEDING: *Increase relative humidity to condition the frogs. Males start calling and are likely to become increasingly aggressive at this stage. Expect*

up to 400 eggs, laid among aquatic plants. As the tadpoles grow older they will feed on live foods too, such as mosquito larvae and whiteworm, before metamorphosing at about three months old.

AMANI FOREST TREE FROG
(BIG-EYED TREE FROG)

Leptopelis vermiculatus   Family Hyperoliidae

There are two distinctive color phases recognized in this species. One is bright green with black speckling over the back, and more evident black streaks and white areas on the sides of the body. The other is predominantly brown with a darker triangular patch on the back, and spots elsewhere. In both cases the underparts are creamy white.

DISTRIBUTION: *Occurs in the Usambara and Rungwege mountain area of Tanzania.*

SIZE: *Up to 2.75 in (7 cm). Males may be only half this size.*

ACCOMMODATION: *A tall vivarium is very important, since these frogs prefer to rest at the highest available vantage point. They are nocturnal by nature.*

BEHAVIOR: *Although agile and active, Amani Forest Tree Frogs will seek refuge during the dry season by burrowing into the ground, at which stage they become inactive.*

DIET: *Will eat invertebrates and are also cannibalistic.*

BREEDING: *Smaller males should be housed only with well-fed females for spawning purposes. Egg-laying usually occurs in a muddy bank, with the tadpoles wriggling down into the water. Increasing the humidity should help encourage breeding behavior.*

OTHER NORTH AMERICAN TREE FROGS

Mountain Tree Frog (Hyla eximia)

Range: Occurs in the mountainous areas of central Arizona and western New Mexico, southward to Guerrero in Mexico.

Size: 0.75–2.25 in (2–6 cm).

Habitat: Areas of pine woodland and grassland, above 5,000 ft (1,520 m).

Pinewoods Tree Frog (Hyla femoralis)

Range: Around the southeastern coastal area, from southeastern Virginia and much of Florida, apart from the south, to eastern Louisiana.

Size: 1–1.5 in (2.5–4 cm).

Habitat: Pinewoods and cypress swamps. A high-climbing species.

Little Grass Frog (Pseudacris ocularis)

Range: Southeastern seaboard of the United States, extending throughout Florida.

Size: 0.4–0.7 in (1–1.7 cm), making this the smallest North American frog.

Habitat: Grassy areas near ponds and cypress.

GROUND-DWELLING FROGS

Families Leptodactylidae, Megophryidae, Microhylidae, Pelodytidae, Ranidae

A wide variety of species with different lifestyles are included in this group, and it is very important to be aware of their individual needs. Some will spend much of their time in water, whereas others will only return here essentially to breed. Certain species may be able to survive shortages of water by burrowing into damp soil, remaining there until the return of the rains, which usually also serve as a trigger for spawning.

Ranid frogs, in particular, can prove to be rather nervous in new vivarium surroundings at first. It is therefore very important to include suitable retreats for them where they will feel secure, to prevent the risk of any injuries. Also, always take care that these frogs do not leap out of the vivarium when you are attending to their needs. On the other hand, others such as the Horned Frogs (*Ceratophrys* species) can become surprisingly tame, soon learning to recognize when food is being offered. Unfortunately, they are also aggressive by nature, to the extent that trying to breed them in a typical vivarium is difficult. Many other frogs, however, will reproduce readily in these surroundings.

▲ COLOMBIAN HORNED FROG (CERATOPHRYS CALCARATA)

GAY'S FROG
(HELMETED WATER TOAD)

Caudiverbera caudiverbera   Family Leptodactylidae

These frogs are olive brown in color, with some variable paler spotting over the back, emphasizing their rather warty appearance. Their underparts are grayish white. Males develop prominent black nuptial pads, and also become more vocal when they are in breeding condition.

DISTRIBUTION: *Restricted to Chile in South America, in the area between 30° and 42° of latitude.*

SIZE: *Males grow to about 5 in (13 cm), but females can exceed 12 in (30 cm).*

ACCOMMODATION: *A large, mainly aquatic vivarium is required, usually without heating—room temperature is acceptable. There must also be an area where the frogs can burrow. Avoid keeping Gay's Frogs of widely differing sizes together, because of their cannibalistic nature.*

BEHAVIOR: *These frogs will defend themselves ferociously against potential predators, inflating their bodies to make themselves appear larger in size, and lunging aggressively as a further deterrent.*

DIET: *An avid hunter, preying not only on invertebrates but also on fish, small mammals and birds in the wild. Larger individuals can be offered pinkies.*

BREEDING: *The natural spawning period for these frogs is September and October, when males will call loudly. Females are likely to produce as many as 10,000 eggs, with hatching taking about three weeks. Tadpoles are slow to metamorphose, remaining in this form for up to two years. They become very large, up to 6 in (15 cm) long.*

COLOMBIAN HORNED FROG

Ceratophrys calcarata   Family Leptodactylidae

Thanks to their resemblance to the popular computer game icon, this group of frogs is often known as Pacman Frogs. Their taxonomy is confused—most herpetologists accept that there are about seven distinct species. The Colombian Horned Frog is greenish gray with tan and whitish markings, and its horns are relatively indistinct.

DIET: *Will basically consume any creature that is small enough to be swallowed, including others of their own kind, which precludes keeping them in groups.*

BREEDING: *Up to 1,000 eggs are laid among aquatic vegetation and hatch within a day. Small live foods such as daphnia and whiteworm can be used for rearing the tadpoles.*

SURINAM HORNED FROG

Ceratophrys cornuta   Family Leptodactylidae

The huge head is a distinctive feature of this and other horned frogs, with its capacious mouth making it a formidable predator. It is often a colorful shade of reddish brown, and the patterning is highly individual. The distinctive horns above the eyes are especially prominent in this species. Males develop pale brown nuptial pads.

DISTRIBUTION: *Northern South America, in the Amazon Basin, with a range including Guyana, northeastern Brazil and Ecuador.*

SIZE: *Can reach up to 8 in (20 cm).*

ACCOMMODATION: *A typical rain forest setup, with forest soil as a floor covering for burrowing purposes, is recommended, along with a large water bowl.*

BEHAVIOR: *These frogs prove very sedentary, burrowing down to disguise their presence. They leave their head exposed, to grab any prey that comes within reach.*

DIET: *Will eat both invertebrates and pinkies, as well as smaller companions.*

BREEDING: *The reproductive cycle in the wild is linked to the onset of the rainy season, which triggers the males to call. The tadpoles are highly predatory by nature and will be cannibalistic. Separating them into groups of similar size is therefore necessary, and rearing them individually is the safest option.*

▲ SURINAM HORNED FROG (CERATOPHRYS CORNUTA)

DISTRIBUTION: *Northern South America, in Colombia and Venezuela.*

SIZE: *4–6 in (10–15 cm).*

ACCOMMODATION: *Housing for these frogs must be carefully planned without the use of gravel or small pieces of bark, which could be swallowed when the frogs snap up food, resulting in a potentially life-threatening obstruction in the intestinal tract.*

BEHAVIOR: *Horned frogs generally are equipped with very powerful jaws and will instinctively snap if they sense movement near their head. They do not discriminate if your finger is within reach, and are capable of inflicting a painful bite. These frogs cannot be fed very safely by hand. Blunt-ended forceps, as recommended for snakes, can be used instead if you want to tame them to feed in this way.*

▼ CHACO HORNED FROG (CERATOPHRYS CRANWELLI)—NORMAL FORM (BELOW); LEUCISTIC FORM (BELOW RIGHT).

▲ *ORNATE HORNED FROG (CERATOPHRYS ORNATA)*

CHACO HORNED FROG
(CRANWELL'S HORNED FROG)

Ceratophrys cranwelli   Family Leptodactylidae

This species resembles the Ornate Horned Frog *(Ceratophrys ornata)*, although young frogs are not so brightly colored at first. The horns of Chaco Horned Frogs tend to be larger than those of the Ornate Horned Frog, and their gape may be slightly wider. They are normally bright green and brown, but there is also a leucistic variant with orange and yellow markings, which is often sold incorrectly as an albino.

DISTRIBUTION: *Restricted to Argentina, in the grassland area known as the Gran Chaco.*

SIZE: *3–5 in (7.5–13 cm).*

ACCOMMODATION: *A setup similar to that for other horned frogs is recommended, with a temperature of about 77° F (25° C), dropping back slightly at night. They also need a container of dechlorinated water, which should be changed every day or so.*

BEHAVIOR: *Nocturnal by nature. Will also estivate under adverse conditions, with a thick layer of skin covering its body to prevent further dessication.*

DIET: *Invertebrates, which should be suitably enriched with a vitamin and mineral supplement, as well as pinkies. Avoid overfeeding, which leads to obesity.*

BREEDING: *Hormonal injections are often used to achieve spawning in this and other horned frogs. There has also been cross-breeding between different species, giving rise to hybrid offspring.*

ORNATE HORNED FROG
(BELL'S HORNED FROG; ARGENTINE HORNED FROG)

Ceratophrys ornata   Family Leptodactylidae

Currently this is one of the more readily available species of horned frogs. As in other cases, their appearance can be highly individual. They can vary from shades of green with red markings to darker combinations of black with only relatively small areas of green being evident. The horns in this species tend to be low triangular swellings.

DISTRIBUTION: *Eastern parts of Brazil and Argentina.*

SIZE: *4–6 in (10–15 cm).*

ACCOMMODATION: *It is usual to keep these frogs on their own to prevent any injuries arising from attempts at cannibalism.*

BEHAVIOR: *Young frogs can breed from about 18 months old. As they grow, they shed their skin, taking on a glassy appearance beforehand and temporarily losing interest in their food. On average, their life span is seven years.*

DIET: *Invertebrates of a size suitable for the frog to swallow easily should be a mainstay of its diet, although pinkies can be given occasionally. Feed young frogs only two to three times a week to prevent obesity.*

BREEDING: *Males are smaller than females, as in other species. Cooling their surroundings over several weeks down to 68°F (20°C) and then raising the temperature and humidity by placing them in an enclosure with a sprinkler system can result in successful natural spawning.*

SMOKY MOUNTAIN JUNGLE FROG
(SOUTH AMERICAN BULLFROG)

Leptodactylus pentadactylus   Family Leptodactylidae

The coloration of Smoky Mountain Jungle Frogs is highly individual. They are yellowish brown in color, with darker reddish brown patterning superimposed. The underside of the body is cream with darker markings. Males tend to be bigger than females, and they develop swollen forearms prior to spawning.

DISTRIBUTION: *From northern Honduras south via Panama through to Ecuador in South America, and eastward across the Amazon region to the Guianas.*

SIZE: *Up to 8 in (20 cm).*

ACCOMMODATION: *A large enclosure is recommended. It should have plenty of retreats, such as logs and leaf litter, and a substrate that allows them to burrow. An area of water needs to be included as well, and the temperature should range between 77 and 82°F (25–28°C).*

BEHAVIOR: *This is a rather secretive species that tends to hide away through the day. These frogs possess an alarming high-pitched call which they utter if restrained, sounding a little like a scream.*

DIET: *Feeds readily on a range of invertebrates.*

BREEDING: *Males start honking at the start of the breeding season. Females lay their eggs in nests of foam at the water surface.*

DWARF LEAF FROG

Megophrys montana   Family Megophryidae

As its name suggests, this species is smaller in size than its better known cousin, the Asian Leaf Frog (*Megophrys nasuta*), which it otherwise resembles. Its upper parts are brownish, often with a touch of red. Even the pupil is brown in color, emphasizing its leaflike appearance.

DISTRIBUTION: *Occurs through much of Southeast Asia, from Thailand and Malaysia on the mainland to Java, Natuna, Borneo and the Philippines.*

SIZE: *Males grow to 3.5 in (8.5 cm); females are about 1 in (2.5 cm) larger.*

ACCOMMODATION: *A terrestrial setup with plenty of cover will be ideal, as recommended for the Asian Leaf Frog. It should be maintained at a temperature between 77 and 82°F (25–28°C) and can incorporate suitable plants. Living naturally on the forest floor, these frogs require only a low light intensity in their quarters.*

BEHAVIOR: *They are ambush predators, grabbing invertebrates that come within reach of their hiding places.*

DIET: *Offer a range of invertebrates that have been gut-loaded or dusted with a vitamin and mineral powder.*

BREEDING: *Spawning takes place in the vicinity of forest streams, with females attaching their eggs to rocks or logs directly above the water.*

ASIAN LEAF FROG
(MALAYSIAN HORNED FROG; LONG-NOSED HORNED FROG)

Megophrys nasuta   Family Megophryidae

The striking appearance of these frogs, which are brown in color and have prominent hornlike projections above the eyes and a similarly shaped snout, provides them with superb camouflage in their forest home. In their natural environment they live on the ground among dead leaves.

DISTRIBUTION: *Occurs through much of Southeast Asia, from Thailand and Malaysia on the mainland to Sumatra and Borneo.*

SIZE: *Up to 5.5 in (14 cm), with males usually significantly smaller.*

ACCOMMODATION: *A rain forest environment, with leaf litter and also dry leaves (which may be available from specialized suppliers) will help these frogs settle in well. Incorporate areas of cork bark to serve as additional retreats. A bowl of water is also required.*

◀ *ASIAN LEAF FROG (*MEGOPHRYS NASUTA*)*

BEHAVIOR: *These frogs emerge from their hiding places to hunt under cover of darkness, so they should be fed only in the evening.*

DIET: *Prey naturally on relatively large invertebrates, including snails. Waxworms are a good restorative food that can be used to help new arrivals settle in, but a varied diet is important.*

BREEDING: *Often more difficult to obtain the larger females. Try lowering both temperature and humidity slightly in the vivarium, and raising it again after three weeks. Females lay in a similar fashion to the Dwarf Leaf Frog (Megophrys montana). The tadpoles slide into the water and grow rapidly if given a varied diet. Beware of cannibalism, however—they may even need to be reared individually.*

SPECIES: *D. antongilii; D. guineti; D. insularis.*

DISTRIBUTION: *Restricted to the island of Madagascar, off the southeast coast of Africa.*

SIZE: *Up to 4.5 in (11 cm).*

ACCOMMODATION: *A good layer of a rain forest soil or leaf litter should be used on the floor of the vivarium for these frogs, which will burrow into the substrate. Their quarters can also be decorated with tropical plants and moss, and a bowl of water should be provided. A temperature of about 77° F (25° C) will be adequate.*

TOMATO FROGS

Dyscophus species   Family Microhylidae

Of the three species known popularly as tomato frogs, it is only *Dyscophus antongilii* that has the distinctive bright reddish coloration. *Dyscophus insularis* is a much duller shade of reddish brown with dark markings over its body, and is significantly smaller in size, averaging about 2 in (5 cm). Another relative, *D. guineti*—sometimes called the False Tomato Frog—is also not as brightly colored as *D. antongilii*.

▼ ▶ BELOW: *TOMATO FROG (DYSCOPHUS ANTONGILII); RIGHT: FALSE TOMATO FROG (D. GUINETI).*

BEHAVIOR: *The bright coloring of these frogs conveys a warning—their skin secretes a sticky substance that temporarily gums up the would-be predator's mouth when it catches the frog, usually causing it to let go.*

DIET: *Will feed on vitamin- and mineral-enriched invertebrates of suitable size.*

BREEDING: *Reducing the relative humidity for a month and then effectively showering them off is likely to trigger spawning. The eggs, numbering up to 1,000, start to hatch after six weeks. Be sure that the young frogs can clamber out of the water easily, otherwise they may drown.*

RED-BANDED CREVICE CREEPER
(BANDED RUBBER FROG)

Phrynomantis bifasciatus   Family Microhylidae

This brightly colored species displays red and black banding across its entire body. The smooth, shiny nature of its skin helps explain why members of this genus are known as rubber frogs. This may make them less vulnerable to dehydration, since they are often found far away from water.

DISTRIBUTION: *Extends through Africa from Somalia in the north down to South Africa in the south, occurring westward as far as Zaire.*

SIZE: *Up to 3 in (7.5 cm).*

ACCOMMODATION: *A warm vivarium—heated to about 75°F (24°C)—with retreats in which the frogs can hide, will be required. The substrate should be deep, allowing the frogs to burrow. It must not be left to dry out completely.*

BEHAVIOR: *The lack of webbing between the toes indicates that these frogs are well equipped for life on land. They may seek the relative safety of termite nests, into which they often retreat during the dry season.*

DIET: *Their natural food consists mainly of ants and termites, but they will readily eat small crickets and similar live foods in the vivarium.*

BREEDING: *Stimulated by the rains. Let the vivarium dry out slightly more than usual. Next, transfer the frogs to a shallow aquarium with aquatic plants, and increase the water level. At this point males will utter their calls, which have an almost musical quality.*

RED-BACKED CREVICE CREEPER
(GHANA FIRE FROG)

Phrynomantis microps   Family Microhylidae

The bright coloration of members of this genus may appear attractive, but in reality it serves as a warning. Their skin can cause irritation because of the presence of protective toxins, so these frogs should be handled only with gloves. Males have deep black throats.

DISTRIBUTION: *Western and central parts of Africa, from Senegal to Nigeria and south to the Central African Republic and the Congo Basin.*

▲ RED-BANDED CREVICE CREEPER (PHRYNOMANTIS BIFASCIATUS)

SIZE: *Up to nearly 2.5 in (6 cm); males are smaller than females.*

ACCOMMODATION: *As for the previous species. An area of water must be included. They are rather shy by nature, becoming more active at night.*

BEHAVIOR: *These frogs will walk rather than run and are able to burrow backward directly into the ground.*

DIET: *Smaller invertebrates, which should be dusted with a vitamin and mineral powder or gut-loaded to maximize their nutritional value.*

BREEDING: *Is not often achieved in vivarium surroundings, but if you proceed as for the Red-banded Crevice Creeper, you may have some measure of success. Females may lay as many as 1,500 eggs. The young hatch within a few days and emerge from the water as small frogs about 40 days later. From this stage onward they require plenty of small live foods, including fruit flies and aphids.*

MARBLED HOPPER
(RAINBOW BURROWING FROG)

Scaphiophryne gottlebei   Family Microhylidae

The Marbled Hopper is a particularly colorful species. It has variable orange and yellow markings, prominently bordered by black areas, over the back and sides of the body. The rest of the body is white, again broken up by a random pattern of black stripes.

DISTRIBUTION: *Confined to the central southern area of Madagascar, off Africa's southeastern coast.*

SIZE: *Up to 1.5 in (4 cm); males are slightly smaller than the females.*

ACCOMMODATION: *It is important to provide a thick substrate, which will allow these frogs to dig. A shallow area of water should be provided, because these frogs cannot swim well.*

BEHAVIOR: *Its enlarged toe pads suggest that it may climb occasionally, perhaps to escape fierce flash floods that sweep through the forested area in which it lives.*

DIET: *Will feed on a variety of invertebrates.*

BREEDING: *Males have a more slender appearance than females. They spawn in pools of rainwater, with as many as 500 eggs being laid. The young frogs are small when they first emerge from the water, but they grow rapidly if well fed on live foods of suitable size. They reach maturity at one year old.*

MADAGASCAR GREEN HOPPER
(MADAGASCAR BURROWING FROG)

Scaphiophryne marmorata   Family Microhylidae

This species has iridescent green and dark brownish markings on its body, interspersed with paler cream areas. There is a series of small protective spines here too. Their long legs help them climb in the woodland areas they inhabit.

DISTRIBUTION: *The eastern region of the island of Madagascar.*

SIZE: *Males average 1.2 in (3 cm), while the females are about 0.5 in (1 cm) larger.*

ACCOMMODATION: *Its needs are similar to those of the Marbled Hopper. The temperature requirement is approximately 77°F (25°C).*

BEHAVIOR: *The so-called spades on the hind feet of members of this genus help the frogs burrow rapidly away from danger, as does the rounded shape of the nose. They can prove aggressive if cornered and may strike out to defend themselves.*

DIET: *Will eat a variety of small invertebrates.*

BREEDING: *Allowing the humidity in their quarters to fall along with the temperature, and then reintroducing warmer, wetter conditions (mimicking the situation in the wild) should trigger spawning. The tadpoles metamorphose after about 70 days. To encourage their development, their water temperature should be kept to around 79°F (26°C).*

PARSLEY FROG

Pelodytes punctatus   Family Pelodytidae

The common name of these frogs originates from the green speckling on their otherwise brown backs, which suggests they have been decorated with chopped parsley leaves. The classification of parsley frogs is controversial—some taxonomists regard them as forming a family on their own.

DISTRIBUTION: *Ranges across parts of Europe, from Belgium through France and Luxembourg to northern and eastern parts of Spain, as well as northwestern Italy.*

SIZE: *About 1.5 in (4 cm).*

ACCOMMODATION: *Their temperate distribution means that these frogs can be housed in secure enclosures outdoors, where they may spawn in a suitable area of water.*

BEHAVIOR: *These frogs are secretive by nature, hiding away and only leaving their retreats at night after rainfall. Depending on their origins they may hibernate over the winter period.*

DIET: *They will feed on a variety of invertebrates, with crickets featuring in their natural diet.*

BREEDING: *Triggered by rainfall, usually in spring. Females may produce up to 300 eggs per spawning and can lay several times in succession. Tadpoles develop slowly, growing to almost 2.5 in (6.5 cm) so, unusually, they are larger at this stage than the adult frogs. Metamorphosis is slow, likely to take about eight months.*

AFRICAN BULLFROG
(AFRICAN BURROWING FROG)

Pyxicephalus adspersus   Family Ranidae

These frogs can potentially grow to a large size, and their lifestyle is very similar to that of the South American horned frogs (*Ceratophrys* species). The young African Bullfrogs are more colorful than the adults, displaying green and brown spotted markings that become less distinctive with age, and a stripe running from the snout down the center of the back.

DISTRIBUTION: *Found in tropical parts of Africa, from Nigeria eastward and southward into the Congo Basin.*

SIZE: *Can reach up to 8 in (20 cm).*

ACCOMMODATION: *A deep substrate is essential, which will allow these frogs to burrow. The frogs' hind feet are adapted for this purpose. They need to*

▼ *MADAGASCAR GREEN HOPPER (SCAPHIOPHRYNE MARMORATA)*

be maintained at a temperature of 77–82° F (25–28° C), dropping back at night, and in relatively humid surroundings. An area of water should be present.

BEHAVIOR: *These frogs are highly predatory, which means they should generally be kept on their own.*

DIET: *Can be maintained easily on invertebrates of suitable size, as well as*

pinkies. Take care not to overfeed, because otherwise they will rapidly become obese.

BREEDING: *Males have yellow throats and tend to be larger than females. Spawning follows a dry period, occurring naturally when the rains return to form temporary pools. Having mimicked the environmental changes, feed members of a pair so that each is sated before introducing them, to decrease the risk of aggression. Cannibalism is also likely among the young.*

OTHER NORTH AMERICAN RANID FROGS

American Bullfrog (*Rana catesbeiana*)

Range: From New Brunswick and Nova Scotia southward through southeastern United States. Introduced to western areas.

Size: Up to 8 in (20 cm). The largest North American species.

Habitat: Ponds, lakes and other relative large areas of still water.

Northern Leopard Frog (*Rana pipiens*)

Range: From Canada southward across much of the United States, although absent from the southeastern and western coastal regions.

Size: 3.5 in (9 cm).

Habitat: Adaptable, but usually prefers slow-flowing areas of permanent water.

Wood Frog (*Rana sylvatica*)

Range: From Alaska down across much of Canada into eastern United States. The only species of North American frog found within the Arctic Circle.

Size: Around 3 in (7.5 cm).

Habitat: Can be found in tundra, grassland and woodland areas.

▲ WOOD FROG (RANA SYLVATICA)

▼ NORTHERN LEOPARD FROG (RANA PIPIENS)

DART FROGS AND MANTELLAS
Families Dendrobatidae and Mantellidae

Dart frogs and mantellas are similar in appearance, although they come from widely separated parts of the world and belong to different families. Dart frogs (family Dendrobatidae) originate from Central and South America, whereas mantellas (family Mantellidae) are confined to the island of Madagascar, off the southeastern coast of Africa.

Members of both groups are small in size but brightly colored. They are armed with a range of protective skin toxins, which means they should not be touched with bare hands. Dart frogs are named for their lethal venom, which is used to tip the arrows of native peoples. Another characteristic linking these frogs is that members of both groups usually have very limited distributions in the wild, and their individual populations often vary enormously in their coloration and patterning.

GREEN AND BLACK DART FROG

Dendrobates auratus   Family Dendrobatidae

This is one of the most variable of all members of the family, in terms of both size and appearance. Not all of these frogs are even green and black—for example, the population found on the Panamanian island of Taboga is brown with golden stripes.

DISTRIBUTION: *Central and northern South America. Extends from southern Nicaragua down through Costa Rica and Panama into Colombia. Also introduced to Oahu in the Hawaiian Islands.*

SIZE: *Varies from 1–2.5 in (2.5–6 cm) long.*

ACCOMMODATION: *The floor area of the vivarium is important because this species is terrestrial in its habits. The substrate should include dry leaves, with which these frogs are always associated in the wild. The temperature should be around 77° F (25° C).*

BEHAVIOR: *These frogs tend to be found either in pairs or groups, usually in slightly drier regions of forest. A rather shy species, it lives alongside other* Dendrobates *species, such as D. pumilio, in the wild and can be housed with them in vivarium surroundings.*

DIET: *Small invertebrates such as* Drosophilia.

▲ GREEN AND BLACK DART FROG (DENDROBATES AURATUS)—COLOR MORPHS. TOP: GREEN AND BLACK; CENTER: BLUE AND BLACK; BOTTOM: YELLOW AND BLACK.

SIZE: *Up to 1.75 in (4.5 cm), making this one of the larger dart frogs.*

ACCOMMODATION: *Terrestrial, living in savanna with small streams nearby. Requires a temperature of about 79°F (26°C) during the day, dropping back to no lower than 68°F (20°C) at night.*

BEHAVIOR: *A bold, conspicuous species. The female approaches the male when she is ready to spawn, using her front legs to stroke his back.*

DIET: *Small invertebrates, including hatchling crickets.*

BREEDING: *The eggs must not be totally covered by water. Hatching is likely to take about 18 days. The tadpoles need to be reared separately, since they are highly predatory. Powdered flake and similar foods, augmented with tiny live food, should see them metamorphose in three months.*

HARLEQUIN DART FROG

Dendrobates histrionicus   Family Dendrobatidae

Displaying very variable coloration, the Harlequin Dart Frog is often seen in shades of brown offset with red and yellow markings. Some individuals have green markings too, while others display bold yellow and black markings.

DISTRIBUTION: *Restricted to western Colombia and northwestern Ecuador.*

SIZE: *Up to 1.5 in (3.75 cm).*

ACCOMMODATION: *The ideal temperature range is a maximum of 79°F (26°C), dropping back to about 68°F (20°C) at night. A high relative humidity, typically of about 70 percent, will be needed.*

◀ *BLUE DART FROG (DENDROBATES AZUREUS)*

▶ *BUMBLEBEE DART FROG (DENDROBATES LEUCOMELAS)*

▼ *HARLEQUIN DART FROG (DENDROBATES HISTRIONICUS)*

BREEDING: *Increase the relative humidity and keep these dart frogs in a small group to ensure that you have at least a pair. Egg-laying will occur in the substrate, either among the leaves or in pieces of coconut shell.*

BLUE DART FROG

Dendrobates azureus   Family Dendrobatidae

As its name suggests, the strikingly colored Blue Dart Frog is predominantly blue. It has variable darker spotting on the head and back, and the legs are a duller shade of blue. On close examination males can be distinguished by the flattened tips of their front feet.

DISTRIBUTION: *Known only from the Sipaliwini area of Surinam, at an altitude of between 1,300 and 1,400 ft (400–430 m).*

DISTRIBUTION: *Upland forest areas of Colombia in South America, from 2,600–4,000 ft (800–1,200 m), occupying a total area of just 4 square miles (10 sq. km).*

SIZE: *About 1.5 in (3.75 cm).*

ACCOMMODATION: *Requires a slightly cooler temperature than the Harlequin Dart Frog, of about 75° F (24° C) during the day, dropping back to 64° F (18° C) at night. The height of the vivarium is important in this case because Lehmann's Dart Frog is not completely terrestrial by nature.*

BEHAVIOR: *These dart frogs may climb up to 2 ft (60 cm) off the ground. In the wild, females rear their young in bromeliad cups filled with rainwater, and provide infertile eggs for them to eat.*

DIET: *Small invertebrates.*

BREEDING: *Not all females will instinctively care for their eggs in the vivarium, even if there are bromeliads here. Under these circumstances, the young will need to be reared on egg yolk.*

BUMBLEBEE DART FROG

Dendrobates leucomelas   Family Dendrobatidae

The color scheme of these dart frogs is black with three yellow stripes evenly spaced over the back, giving them their common name. Their patterning is nevertheless sufficiently individual to allow particular frogs in a group to be distinguished easily. Bumblebee Dart Frogs make an excellent introduction to this fascinating family, since they are relatively easy to maintain in vivarium surroundings.

DISTRIBUTION: *Venezuela, occurring in rain forests up to an altitude of 2,600 ft (800 m).*

SIZE: *May reach 1.5 in (3.75 cm); males are slightly smaller.*

ACCOMMODATION: *Keep relatively warm, between 75 and 79° F (24–26° C), in humid surroundings. These frogs are primarily terrestrial in their habits, and leaves should be incorporated on the vivarium floor to provide cover.*

BEHAVIOR: *Males would normally carry the tadpoles to water once they hatch, but commonly do not display this behavior in vivaria.*

DIET: *Small invertebrates such as Drosophila.*

BREEDING: *As they come into breeding condition males will become vocal. The female approaches the male initially. Then the pair will spawn in a cave, which can be created from a small flowerpot disguised by leaves. Typically about half a dozen eggs are laid. Hatching takes a little less than two weeks, and the resulting tadpoles will need to be transferred to shallow water, with a temperature of about 77° F (25° C). The young can be reared as a group, being fed on powdered flake. After about 10 weeks their metamorphosis is complete, although they will be less colorful than the adults. The young frogs must then have almost constant access to tiny live foods in order to thrive.*

BEHAVIOR: *Occurs in tropical lowlands and up to an altitude of 3,300 ft (1,000 m), where it prefers shady areas and lives on the ground.*

DIET: *Small invertebrates.*

BREEDING: *When spawning, females produce between four and nine eggs, which they lay on bromeliad leaves.*

LEHMANN'S DART FROG

Dendrobates lehmanni   Family Dendrobatidae

Lehmann's Dart Frog is very similar to the Harlequin Dart Frog (*Dendrobates histrionicus*), and the two species will hybridize if kept together, although this should be avoided. Its coloration is also very variable, ranging from red and white combinations to individuals displaying yellow and black colors.

▲ MORPHS OF STRAWBERRY DART FROG (DENDROBATES PUMILIO): *1 SIQUERRES;*
2 BLUE JEANS; 3 ISLA COLÓN; 4 BASTIMENTOS; 5 SHEPHERD ISLAND; 6 RIO BRANCO;
7 SAN CRISTÓBAL; 8 CAUCHERO.

STRAWBERRY DART FROG

Dendrobates pumilio   Family Dendrobatidae

The typical forms of this dart frog found in Costa Rica are red with black markings, but there are other forms—found notably in western Panama—such as the plain purple variant known as "Cauchero," that display totally different coloring.

DISTRIBUTION: *Extends down through Central America from the northern part of Nicaragua via Costa Rica into Panama.*

SIZE: *Relatively small, ranging from 0.75 in (2 cm) to 1 in (2.5 cm).*

ACCOMMODATION: *A relatively tall vivarium is needed. Bromeliads should be included, since it is in the cups of these plants that the frogs deposit their eggs. The temperature needs to be warm, averaging 77–86°F (25–30°C), and falling back to about 68°F (20°C) at night, with high humidity.*

BEHAVIOR: *Strawberry Dart Frogs are active during the day, hunting for food both on the ground and on vegetation.*

DIET: *Small invertebrates such as hatchling crickets and* Drosophila.

BREEDING: *Spawning may take place on the bromeliad leaves, with the eggs kept moist by the male until they hatch after about 10 days. They are then carried to the water-filled cups of bromeliads. The female returns to them regularly, depositing infertile eggs in the water as food for the tadpoles. Trying to substitute for this with fine powdered chicken egg yolk is not totally satisfactory, partly because this food will pollute the water very rapidly, and also because the tadpoles metamorphose much more slowly than usual, suggesting it is not an ideal food.*

DYEING DART FROG
(DYE DART FROG)

Dendrobates tinctorius   Family Dendrobatidae

These large, colorful dart frogs occur in various forms depending on their area of origin. They tend to be a combination of black with highly variable streaks or bands of pale lemon to yellow running along the upper parts of their bodies. The "Nikita" morph is one of the most colorful. Their legs are usually mottled.

DISTRIBUTION: *Northern South America, from Guyana through Surinam to French Guiana, and south into adjacent areas of Brazil.*

SIZE: *May reach nearly 2.5 in (6.5 cm); males are smaller.*

ACCOMMODATION: *A tropical rain forest environment with a relative humidity reading of at least 60 percent is essential. A waterfall should be incorporated into the vivarium for this reason, and the enclosure should be densely planted.*

BEHAVIOR: *These dart frogs tend not to climb, usually remaining well hidden in their surroundings, from where they will soon start to emerge at feeding time.*

DIET: *The larger size of the Dyeing Dart Frogs means they can be given slightly bigger prey than related species.*

BREEDING: *Spawning occurs as for the Bumblebee Dart Frog (D. leucomelas). Males can be recognized not just by their size but also by the heart-shaped swellings on the tips of their toes. Clutch size can vary from five to 20 eggs. The male would normally care for the eggs, keeping them moist, with hatching taking place about two weeks later. Powdered flake makes a good rearing diet for the tadpoles.*

KOKOE DART FROG

Phyllobates aurotaenia   Family Dendrobatidae

The Kokoe Dart Frog is predominantly matt black in color, with a pair of yellowish or green stripes running across the back. The underparts are marbled with bluish green markings.

DISTRIBUTION: *Occurs west of the Andes, and is restricted to the Chocó region of Colombia.*

SIZE: *Up to nearly 1.5 in (4 cm).*

ACCOMMODATION: *Hot and humid conditions are required. The ideal temperature is around 82°F (28°C), dropping back slightly at night.*

BEHAVIOR: *This species has a particularly potent skin toxin, which is sought by native peoples through its range in order to tip their arrows.*

DIET: *Small invertebrates.*

BREEDING: *Males trill to females when in spawning condition. They are likely to spawn in a cave, which can be replicated by using a small clay flowerpot. The young are subsequently carried to water by the male, who returns when the eggs are due to hatch some two weeks after spawning.*

BLACK-LEG DART FROG

Phyllobates bicolor   Family Dendrobatidae

A brightly colored species, the Black-leg Dart Frog has a back that can vary from yellow to red, contrasting with its dark legs and underparts when adult. Young froglets, however, have black backs with yellow stripes. Their striking coloration is matched by their toxicity.

DISTRIBUTION: *Northern South America, occurring in western Colombia.*

SIZE: *Up to 1.5 in (4 cm).*

ACCOMMODATION: *These dart frogs are a terrestrial species, so a tall enclosure is not necessary for them. They require warm, humid surroundings. Moss makes an attractive floor covering, and pieces of wood provide hiding places for the frogs, recreating the impression of the forest floor.*

BEHAVIOR: *Some individuals have golden yellow underparts, mimicking the appearance of the Golden Dart Frog* (Phyllobates terribilis).

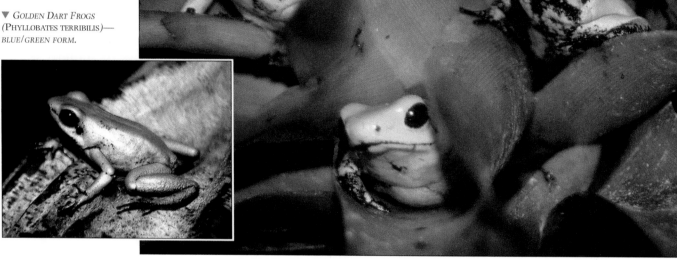

▶ *Golden Dart Frogs* (Phyllobates terribilis)— yellow/orange form.

▼ *Golden Dart Frogs* (Phyllobates terribilis)— blue/green form.

DIET: *A range of small invertebrates.*

BREEDING: *The eggs are concealed in a dark locality. The tadpoles can be reared as a group, but regular water changes are essential to their well-being. The water must be dechlorinated and returned to vivarium temperature before it is used.*

GOLDEN DART FROG

Phyllobates terribilis   Family Dendrobatidae

These dart frogs can vary from orange to yellow or yellowish green in color, and their legs are slightly darker. As its scientific name suggests, this is potentially one of the most deadly of the poison dart frogs, and as with all of them, handling should be kept to an absolute minimum. Disposable gloves must be worn when attending to their needs within the vivarium, even though the level of poison generally decreases dramatically in captive-bred stock.

DISTRIBUTION: *Northern South America, in the vicinity of the Rio Saija in western Colombia.*

SIZE: *Up to 2 in (5 cm).*

ACCOMMODATION: *Similar conditions to those recommended for the Black-leg Dart Frog* (Phyllobates bicolor) *suit these dart frogs, which occur farther south in Colombia.*

BEHAVIOR: *In the wild the Golden Dart Frog does not occur in high densities and is usually found close to water.*

OTHER DART FROGS

Panama Rocket Frog (*Colostethus inguinalis*)

Range: Extends from Panama in Central America southward as far as Colombia.

Size: May grow to nearly 1.5 in (4 cm).

Habitat: Lives in close proximity to fast-flowing streams.

Red-back Dart Frog (*Dendrobates reticulatus*)

Range: The Cordillera Central region, northeastern Peru.

Size: About 0.5 in (1 cm)—one of the smallest species.

Habitat: Below 2,600 ft (800 m) in rain forest.

Splendid Poison Dart Frog (Lovely Poison Dart Frog) (*Phyllobates lugubris*)

Range: Eastern areas of Costa Rica and Panama, and offshore islands.

Size: About 1 in (2.5 cm).

Habitat: Lowland and mountain areas, to about 2,100 ft (640 m).

DIET: *A variety of small live foods that have been dusted or gut-loaded with a vitamin and mineral supplement will be necessary.*

BREEDING: *Having spawned in a suitable receptacle, it ultimately falls to the male to transport the young tadpoles on his back to water. Flake food or a similar substitute, augmented with small live food, can be used for rearing purposes.*

▶ *Golden mantella* (Mantella aurantiaca)

GREEN STRIPED DART FROG

Phyllobates vittatus   Family Dendrobatidae

Not only is this dart frog attractively colored, with orange and black stripes down its back and iridescent green legs with black markings, but it also makes an ideal introduction to this group of amphibians. It is relatively undemanding in terms of its care needs, and will breed readily.

DISTRIBUTION: *Central America, in lowland forests on the western side of Costa Rica.*

SIZE: *Reaches a little over 1 in (2.5 cm) in length; males are smaller.*

ACCOMMODATION: *A typical tropical rain forest setup is recommended, complete with a waterfall to help maintain the humidity. Bromeliads are essential because they are used for spawning, but they need to be placed close to the ground, since these little frogs do not stray far above the forest floor.*

BEHAVIOR: *Males are very territorial and will fight each other. They can be recognized by their slightly smaller size and their constant trilling call notes.*

DIET: *A range of small invertebrates will be needed.*

BREEDING: *After the female has laid eggs on the bromeliad leaf, the male fertilizes the eggs and remains with them until they hatch about two weeks later. He then carries them around on his back until he finds a suitable area of water in which to deposit them. This may take over a week in the wild, with the tadpoles growing throughout this period. The water needs to be about 1 in (2.5 cm) or less in depth. The tadpoles will then metamorphose after about six weeks and should be mature by one year old.*

GOLDEN MANTELLA

Mantella aurantiaca   Family Mantellidae

The best-known members of the genus, Golden Mantellas display some variation in color, which can range from a yellowish shade through to a vibrant reddish orange, depending on the locality of the ancestral stock. This bright coloration contrasts with their vibrant black eyes.

DISTRIBUTION: *The central-eastern area of the island of Madagascar.*

SIZE: *Up to 1 in (2.5 cm); males are smaller than females.*

ACCOMMODATION: *A daytime temperature range of 65–72°F (18–22°C) is recommended, with a relative humidity figure of about 85 percent. The enclosure should include a number of retreats, the substrate should be moist, and leaves should be provided on the floor.*

BEHAVIOR: *These mantellas live well in small groups. They should be given a rest period each year, during which time the temperature should fall back several degrees and the vivarium should be kept slightly drier, to replicate conditions in the wild. This can help trigger breeding.*

DIET: *A wide range of small invertebrates, which should be dusted regularly with a vitamin and mineral supplement.*

BREEDING: *The eggs are concealed close to water, usually in shaded areas. Females can be prolific, producing clutches of more than 100 eggs on occasion. The water for hatching purposes needs to be about 1 in (2.5 cm) deep initially. The temperature should be about 68°F (20°C) and slightly acidic. The young leave the water from about 15 weeks onward and are brown in color. They start to gain adult coloration about six weeks later.*

COPPER MANTELLA
(YELLOW MANTELLA; EASTERN MANTELLA)

Mantella crocea   Family Mantellidae

A very variable species, with the upper parts varying in color from yellow and yellowish green to a coppery shade, with black markings on the sides of the body and red markings on the hind legs. The underside of the body may be paler in some individuals than in others.

DISTRIBUTION: *Central-eastern region of Madagascar, in the vicinity of Andasibe.*

SIZE: *Up to nearly 1 in (2.5 cm); males are smaller.*

ACCOMMODATION: *Housing should be similar to that recommended for the Golden Mantella* (Mantella aurantiaca), *which is found in the same area as the Copper Mantella. High temperatures can rapidly prove fatal, so keep within the range of 62–70°F (17–21°C).*

BEHAVIOR: *Shallow water with easy access is required, since these frogs are not powerful swimmers and can otherwise drown easily.*

DIET: *Will eat small invertebrates, including* Drosophila *and aphids when available.*

BREEDING: *Lays clutches usually of less than 30 eggs, close to water. Hatching will take eight days, and metamorphosis about four months. Tiny invertebrates are needed when the froglets first emerge onto land.*

BLUE-LEGGED MANTELLA

Mantella expectata   Family Mantellidae

In spite of its name, many examples of this species have gray rather than blue legs. The central area of the upper parts of the body is yellowish, and there is a black area on the sides of the body that passes through the eyes.

DISTRIBUTION: *The southwestern area of Madagascar, extending as far north as Morondava.*

SIZE: *Up to 1.2 in (3 cm).*

ACCOMMODATION: *Temperature range can be up to 84°F (29°C), dropping back at night to as low as 62°F (17°C). Originating from an arid area, these mantellas require relatively dry surroundings, with a relative humidity of about 75 percent.*

BEHAVIOR: *The coloration of the legs becomes brighter when the frogs are active, especially during the spawning period.*

DIET: *A range of invertebrates of suitable size. Prey should be dusted regularly with a vitamin and mineral supplement.*

BREEDING: *Increase the vivarium temperature slightly and the relative humidity by misting to encourage spawning some weeks later. Spawning takes place above water, with clutches consisting of as many as 80 eggs. Hatching should then occur within about three days. In a shallow aquarium the young tadpoles will emerge as frogs in as little as five weeks. The young mantellas gain adult coloration within about four months.*

▼ *BLUE-LEGGED MANTELLA (MANTELLA EXPECTATA)*

HARALD MEIERI'S MANTELLA
(TOLAGNARO GOLDEN MANTELLA)

Mantella haraldmeieri   Family Mantellidae

This mantella has a relatively dark body with whitish areas at the shoulders and red on the hind legs. The spotted patterning on the throat is more extensive and distinctive in males.

DISTRIBUTION: *Restricted to the southeastern corner of Madagascar, in areas of humid rain forest, such as the Bezavona region around Fort Dauphin.*

SIZE: *Around 1 in (2.5 in). There is relatively little difference in size between the sexes, although females may be slightly bigger.*

ACCOMMODATION: *Requires warm conditions, up to 75°F (24°C), with a high relative humidity. Adding a mister to the vivarium can be beneficial for this purpose.*

BEHAVIOR: *Shy, and therefore requires plenty of retreats in the vivarium.*

▲ PAINTED MANTELLA (MANTELLA MADAGASCARIENSIS)

DIET: *Not always an easy species to feed. Normally preys largely on ants. Reluctant individuals can be persuaded to take hatchling black crickets instead, and then a wider range of invertebrates.*

BREEDING: *Often problematic. Infertility may be high, and those that hatch can often prove challenging to rear. Keep the relative humidity high. Up to 50 eggs are laid, hatching after just four days. Young froglets have beige areas on their front legs at first.*

PAINTED MANTELLA
(MADAGASCAN MANTELLA)

Mantella madagascariensis   Family Mantellidae

Individuals of this species can be distinguished by their highly distinctive patterning. It consists of black stripes and blotches, all interspersed with yellowish or yellowish green areas. The hind legs of the Painted Mantella are a combination of orange and black, with the undersurface of the feet also being a distinctive shade of reddish orange.

DISTRIBUTION: *Central-eastern Madagascar, over a wide area.*

SIZE: *Up to nearly 1.2 in (3 cm); males are smaller.*

ACCOMMODATION: *It is vital not to keep these mantellas too hot because, like other members of the genus, they can succumb rapidly to heatstroke.*

BEHAVIOR: *When seeking mates, males sit and call in prominent positions just off the ground in the vivarium. They will often wrestle with each other at this stage.*

DIET: *A selection of small invertebrates will be required.*

BREEDING: *A female may lay clutches of more than 40 eggs. Increasing the amount of food can play a part in encouraging spawning. Tiny live foods are essential for the rearing of the froglets once they emerge onto land, but they are unlikely to start eating until their tails have been fully absorbed into their bodies.*

GREEN MANTELLA
(LIME MANTELLA)

Mantella viridis   Family Mantellidae

As its name suggests, this mantella is a lime green shade, often appearing more yellowish over the back. There is a whitish stripe in the vicinity of the jaws, and a prominent black stripe running from the snout through the eye and tympanum to just behind the front legs.

DISTRIBUTION: *The range of the Green Mantella is restricted to the extreme northern tip of Madagascar.*

SIZE: *Up to 1.25 in (3.5 cm); females are markedly larger.*

ACCOMMODATION: *Requires a temperature range of 68–75°F (20–24°C)*

and a relative humidity figure of over 80 per cent. Spraying the vivarium is therefore likely to be beneficial.

BEHAVIOR: *These mantellas may climb on occasion, sometimes concealing themselves in plants up to 8 in (20 cm) off the ground.*

DIET: *Provide a range of small invertebrates.*

BREEDING: *Clutches can contain up to 60 eggs, which hatch in less than two days. Relatively shallow water—about 5 in (13 cm) deep—with a slightly acid pH is ideal. For rearing purposes, it should be heated to the vivarium temperature. Frequent water changes are needed. Watch also for signs of cannibalism—powdered flake food is useful for rearing the tadpoles. They leave the water as froglets after 10 weeks or so. Rearing them from this stage to adulthood is often the trickiest phase, with a wide range of small live foods, such as springtails, being required. The young mantellas lose their brown coloration and start to resemble adults after about six months.*

OTHER MANTELLAS

Bronze Mantella (*Mantella betsileo*)

Range: Fairly widely distributed in Madagascar through the coastal region from the central-western area around to the northeast side of the island.

Size: Grows to just over 1 in (2.5 cm).

Habitat: Lowland species, often associated with forests, but also seen in agricultural areas.

Cowan's Mantella (*Mantella cowani*)

Range: Central parts of Madagascar.

Size: 1.2 in (3 cm).

Habitat: Occurs at a higher altitude than other species, typically above 4,500 ft (1,400 m).

Black-eared Golden Mantella (*Mantella milotympanum*)

Range: Exact distribution unclear, but present in the Fiherenana valley in central-eastern Madagascar.

Size: Up to about 0.8 in (2 cm), with some females being larger.

Habitat: Humid, upland rain forest.

▲ BRONZE MANTELLA (MANTELLA BETSILEO)

▲ COWAN'S MANTELLA (MANTELLA COWANI)

▲ BLACK-EARED GOLDEN MANTELLA (MANTELLA MILOTYMPANUM)

AQUATIC FROGS
Families Leptodactylidae and Pipidae

There are relatively few truly aquatic frogs. Most species have emerged onto land and developed a range of strategies to cope with water loss and avoid dessication. Budgett's Frog *(Lepidobatrachus leavis)* provides an unusual example of a lifestyle that evolved out of necessity—it lives underground during the dry winter months in a cocoon made of layers of shed skin.

Caring for most aquatic frogs is straightforward, but maintaining good water quality is extremely important to their well-being. This means that their care may be a little more time-consuming for than in the case of more terrestrial species.

▼ *DWARF AFRICAN CLAWED FROG (HYMENOCHIRUS BOETTGERI)*

DWARF AFRICAN CLAWED FROG

Hymenochirus boettgeri   Family Pipidae

The popular Dwarf African Clawed Frogs have a flattened body shape. They are dark brown in color with blackish spots on their back, and there are slight spiny projections evident along the sides of the body. There is also an albino form which has been bred and is now widely available.

DISTRIBUTION: *West Africa, from Nigeria and the Cameroons south to Zaire..*

SIZE: *Up to 1.5 in (4 cm).*

ACCOMMODATION: *Requires an aquarium with a depth of water of about 8 in (20 cm), heated to about 75°F (24°C), planted with aquatic vegetation. Floating plants will help diffuse the light, and there should also be some bogwood or rockwork to provide retreats. The tank must also be covered to prevent any escapes.*

BEHAVIOR: *The streamlined shape of these frogs makes them powerful swimmers.*

DIET: *Will feed on a variety of small invertebrates. May also prey on fish fry, which is one reason why they should not be housed with fish.*

BREEDING: *Compared with males, females appear more rounded in shape when viewed from above; they also have a smaller tympanum. The male grabs the female's hindquarters, and the pair flip over at the surface, with spawning occurring there. Up to 100 eggs may be laid and must be moved to a separate rearing tank. Rearing foods composed of fish fry can be a useful starter food for the young tadpoles, which are carnivorous. Small live foods, such as newly hatched brine shrimp nauplii, can then be given, with cultures being set up in succession to maintain a constant supply.*

BUDGETT'S FROG

Lepidobatrachus laevis   Family Leptodactylidae

With their rounded faces and prominent eyes, these stocky frogs are not easily overlooked. The upper parts of the body are a dark shade of greenish gray, with blotching in this area highlighted by orange edges. The underparts are cream in color. Only the male has a dark throat (see page 28).

DISTRIBUTION: *Southern parts of South America, in Argentina, Paraguay and Bolivia.*

▼ SURINAM TOAD (PIPA PIPA)

SIZE: *Grows to nearly 6 in (15 cm).*

ACCOMMODATION: *The housing needs of these frogs change through the year. For six months they should be housed in a primarily aquatic setup, in which water temperature is maintained at about 77°F (25°C). For the remainder of the year they will need to be transferred to an aquarium that has a layer of substrate at least 12 in (30 cm) deep so that the frogs can bury into it and undergo a period of estivation. A water bowl is necessary though, and the surface of the substrate must not be allowed to dry out.*

BEHAVIOR: *The way in which these frogs estivate reflects the way they survive through the dry period in their native habitat, reemerging when the rains return.*

DIET: *Invertebrates such as earthworms can be given, although larger individuals will feed on pinkies. It may also be worth trying to wean them onto floating foodsticks intended for reptiles and amphibians.*

BREEDING: *Hormonal injections are normally used to encourage spawning in this species. Tadpoles are predatory and will need to be kept in groups containing individuals of similar size, to prevent cannibalism. Small live foods such as brine shrimp nauplii can be used as a first food for them.*

SURINAM TOAD
(PIPA TOAD)

Pipa pipa   Family Pipidae

This is a truly bizarre amphibian, not just in terms of its appearance, but because of its breeding habits. It is brownish in color, becoming more of a reddish brown shade around the extremities of its flattened body. It has long digits and a sharply triangular head shape, with tiny eyes. The underside of the body is a pale grayish white.

DISTRIBUTION: *Northern South America, ranging through the Amazon region. Present in Peru and Brazil to Surinam and Guyana.*

SIZE: *Up to 8 in (20 cm).*

ACCOMMODATION: *A similar but larger setup to that suggested for the African Clawed Toad (Xenopus laevis) is recommended. There needs to be adequate space for these frogs to swim without being hindered by the tank decor, and the water level can be deeper.*

BEHAVIOR: *Living in a dark environment, where eyesight would be of little value in the murky water, these toads have small, star-shaped swellings at the tips of each of their toes. Packed with nerve endings like our fingers, these swellings are very sensitive.*

DIET: *Predatory; eats a variety of relatively large invertebrates. Must not be mixed with tropical fish, since it is likely to prey on them.*

BREEDING: *When in breeding condition, females develop a ringlike swelling of the cloaca. Mating takes place at the surface, and the eggs are released in batches. The male then uses his bulky hind feet to channel the eggs onto his mate's back, where they become anchored. A special pad of skin will grow out to surround them. After a period of 12 to 20 weeks, at the time*

when the female sheds her skin, the young emerge from the chambers where they developed as miniature, fully formed adults.

TROPICAL CLAWED TOAD

Silurana tropicalis   Family Pipidae

Although relatively small in size, this particular species displays the typical body shape of other, bigger, clawed toads, with its eyes located on the top of the head. It is dark in color, with long, relatively slender front legs ending in unwebbed digits, contrasting with the hind feet, which are heavily webbed.

SYNONYM: *Xenopus tropicalis.*

DISTRIBUTION: *West Africa, from Senegal to Cameroon.*

SIZE: *About 2 in (5 cm).*

ACCOMMODATION: *A similar setup to that recommended for other clawed toads will be required in this case as well. Filtration is beneficial in order to maintain the water quality. This will also reduce the number of times you have to strip down the tank, and partial water changes can be undertaken instead.*

BEHAVIOR: *These toads prefer relatively shallow water so they can reach up easily to the surface in order to breathe, supporting themselves on their hind legs.*

DIET: *A range of invertebrates and pelleted food can be offered.*

BREEDING: *Beware—if these toads spawn successfully, the eggs are likely to be eaten soon afterward unless they can be protected by a grid that they can fall through. Alternatively, they can be transferred directly to a separate aquarium that will serve as a nursery tank for the tadpoles.*

▲ TROPICAL CLAWED TOAD (SILURANA TROPICALIS)

KENYA CLAWED TOAD

Xenopus borealis   Family Pipidae

The coloration of the Kenya Clawed Toad is distinctive, being purplish gray over the back, with a spotted patterning on top. The legs are yellowish with purple spotting, while the underparts are white.

DISTRIBUTION: *Kenya in east Africa.*

SIZE: *Up to nearly 4 in (10 cm).*

ACCOMMODATION: *A heated aquarium, as recommended for the African Clawed Toad (Xenopus laevis), will also be suitable for these clawed toads.*

BEHAVIOR: *The muscular hind limbs allow these toads to swim quickly if they feel threatened.*

DIET: *Carnivorous; these toads eat invertebrates of suitable size, although it should be possible to wean them onto pelleted foods, which are less likely to pollute the water. There are various sizes available, and food of this type contains all the necessary vitamins and minerals..*

BREEDING: *The female's cloacal region has papillae, while the male develops nuptial pads and becomes vocal at the start of the spawning period. The tadpoles are unusual in that they have sensory feelers protruding from around the mouth.*

AFRICAN CLAWED TOAD
(XENOPUS)

Xenopus laevis   Family Pipidae

This particular amphibian once played a crucial role in the laboratory, where it was used to help determine whether or not women were pregnant. Today it is popular as a pet. Its natural color is grayish, but various color morphs have now been established, including the red-eyed leucistic form, which is often erroneously called the albino—the Golden Clawed Frog is a more accurate name.

DISTRIBUTION: *Eastern and southern parts of Africa.*

SIZE: *Up to about 5 in (13 cm).*

ACCOMMODATION: *Relatively shallow water is recommended for these amphibians, heated to about 68°F (20°C). A heating pad that fits under the tank is also useful. There is little point in planting the aquarium, because any plants are likely to be uprooted by the vigorous swimming style of these large frogs.*

BEHAVIOR: *The flattened body shape of these and other aquatic frogs allows them to swim more easily, since they encounter less water resistance.*

DIET: *Worms and other invertebrates are eaten readily. Fish also rank as natural prey.*

BREEDING: *Often hormonally induced. Mimicking rainfall as in the wild can prove a satisfactory trigger; however, allow the water level to fall and then top it up with colder water that has been dechlorinated.*

▲▼ ABOVE: *AFRICAN CLAWED TOAD* (XENOPUS LAEVIS TROPICALIS); BELOW: *AFRICAN CLAWED TOAD—GOLDEN FORM.*

TOADS

Families Bombinatoridae and Bufonidae

In spite of their name, fire-bellied toads belong to a family of frogs, the Bombinatoridae. They make excellent vivarium occupants, since they are easy to care for and will often breed in these surroundings. They are popularly known as toads because of their rather warty upper parts. Only members of the genus *Bufo* (family Bufonidae) are considered to be true toads, with approximately 150 species recognized worldwide. Of these, only about 17 are found in North America and Europe—and one-third of the family is represented in parts of Central and South America. Relatively few of the latter group are seen in the vivarium hobby with any frequency, although they are generally not difficult to maintain and can have a life expectancy measured in decades. Because these anurans have protective skin toxins, it is advisable to wear disposable gloves should you need to handle them directly.

EUROPEAN FIRE-BELLIED TOAD

Bombina bombina   Family Bombinatoridae

Grayish green coloration with variable markings is a feature of this species. The underparts are a combination of fiery orange-red markings set against black areas. The sexes are similar in appearance, but mature males have thicker forearms.

DISTRIBUTION: *Central and eastern parts of Europe, extending into western Asia.*

SIZE: *1.75 in (4.5 cm).*

ACCOMMODATION: *These toads favor an aquaterrarium with relatively shallow water. At typical room temperature, no additional heating is required. In temperate areas they can be housed outdoors in a secure vivarium through the summer.*

▼ EUROPEAN FIRE-BELLIED TOAD (BOMBINA BOMBINA)

BEHAVIOR: *Fire-bellied toads like to rest on aquatic plants, remaining largely hidden just below the water's surface, from where they can ambush unsuspecting prey.*

DIET: *Feeds on a range of invertebrates, including mealworms, waxworms and earthworms.*

BREEDING: *This species has proved to be one of the hardest to spawn successfully in vivarium surroundings. Exposing the toads to cooler conditions over the winter may act as a breeding trigger.*

GIANT FIRE-BELLIED TOAD

Bombina maxima   Family Bombinatoridae

Giant Fire-bellied Toads tend to be brownish with variable black markings on their upper parts, although their patterning is highly individual. Their skin also tends to have more of a warty appearance than in the case of other *Bombina* species.

DISTRIBUTION: *The Himalayan region into western parts of China, at altitudes above 7,000 ft (2,100 m).*

▲▶ ORIENTAL FIRE-BELLIED TOAD (BOMBINA ORIENTALIS)—UPPER PARTS (ABOVE) AND UNDERSIDE (INSET).

SIZE: *Up to 2.4 in (6 cm).*

ACCOMMODATION: *Found in pools where there is plenty of aquatic plants. A similar setup, with an easily accessible land area, suits them in vivarium surroundings.*

BEHAVIOR: *Although not commonly kept, this toad has similar requirements to other members of the genus.*

DIET: *A mixture of invertebrates, treated with a vitamin and mineral powder as necessary, will be required.*

BREEDING: *A cool period over the winter helps encourage spawning when the temperature rises again in the spring. In all Bombina species the male grasps the female in front of the hind legs rather than the front legs when spawning is taking place.*

ORIENTAL FIRE-BELLIED TOAD

Bombina orientalis   Family Bombinatoridae

This is the best-known and most colorful member of the genus, with vivid, bright green upper parts broken up by a variable black patterning. The underparts are fiery orange, again broken by black markings. Easy to maintain and with a life expectancy of seven years, these fire-bellied toads make ideal pets.

DISTRIBUTION: *Northeastern China, extending to Korea.*

SIZE: *2 in (5 cm).*

ACCOMMODATION: *Their requirements are similar to those of related species. Smooth, clean pebbles can be used to create a land area, and the water must be kept clean, with no uneaten food left here.*

BEHAVIOR: *These frogs can be tamed to take larger food items, such as waxworms, from your fingers. Beware of dropping food into a group, however, or they may bite at each other's legs. Otherwise, they are social by nature.*

DIET: *Invertebrates of a suitable size.*

BREEDING: *Similar to related species. A color food for guppies containing carotene should be powdered up into a rearing food for the tadpoles. This coloring agent helps ensure that the young frogs develop brightly colored bellies in due course. Metamorphosis takes one to two months, with maturity being reached when they are just over a year old.*

YELLOW-BELLIED TOAD

Bombina variegata   Family Bombinatoridae

Light brownish upper parts, with black markings characterize this species. As its name suggests, its underparts are yellowish in color, rather than red as in the Oriental Fire-Bellied Toad (*Bombina orientalis*). Its skin is particularly warty. Several subspecies have been identified.

DISTRIBUTION: *Central and southeastern parts of Europe.*

SIZE: *1.75 in (4.5 cm).*

ACCOMMODATION: *A tank incorporating both a land area and space for swimming is important. Like other fire-bellied toads, this species can climb well, and its quarters need to be securely covered.*

BEHAVIOR: *The brightly colored belly is used as a warning to would-be predators. These fire-bellied toads will rear up and arch the underside of their body, although such behavior is not often seen in vivarium surroundings.*

DIET: *Suitable-sized invertebrates; hatchling crickets dusted with a vitamin and mineral powder are useful for recently metamorphosed individuals.*

BREEDING: *About 100 eggs or so result from a single spawning and are scattered in small clumps among the aquatic plants in their quarters. These need to be hatched separately. The tadpoles also need to be divided into groups of similarly sized individuals as they grow, to prevent cannibalism.*

GIANT RIVER TOAD
(COLORADO RIVER TOAD; GIRARD'S TOAD)

Bufo alvarius   Family Bufonidae

This is the largest bufonid species found in North America. These semiaquatic toads are grayish in color or sometimes brownish green. They have relatively few warts on their body, and their skin appears relatively smooth overall, but they have white warts at the corner of the mouth.

DISTRIBUTION: *Southeastern California, linked with the Colorado River, extending to the southwestern edge of New Mexico and south across the Mexican border to Sonora.*

SIZE: *From 3–7 in (7.5–18 cm); there is no clear difference in size between the sexes.*

▲ *YELLOW-BELLIED TOAD (BOMBINA VARIEGATA)*

▲ *GIANT RIVER TOAD (BUFO ALVARIUS)*

ACCOMMODATION: *A spacious enclosure is necessary for these river toads.*

BEHAVIOR: *They occur in relatively arid surroundings and are nocturnal.*

DIET: *Will eat a wide variety of invertebrates.*

BREEDING: *Spawning occurs in temporary pools between May and July. It is triggered in the wild by seasonal rains, so the toads should be conditioned accordingly. Males will call loudly at this stage. The eggs are deposited in strands, as in the case of other* Bufo *species.*

AMERICAN TOAD

Bufo americanus   Family Bufonidae

Reddish brown in color, with some darker markings, these toads have prominent parotid glands behind the eyes. Their coloration varies, however, not just between individuals but also through the wide area over which they are found. The Dwarf American

▼ *AMERICAN TOAD (*BUFO AMERICANUS*)*

Toad (*Bufo americanus charlesmithi*) from the southern part of its range is significantly smaller than the other subspecies.

DISTRIBUTION: *Southeastern parts of Canada, from southeast Manitoba extending through the eastern part of the United States.*

SIZE: *2–4 in (5–10 cm).*

ACCOMMODATION: *This species will thrive in a secure outdoor vivarium.*

BEHAVIOR: *Males may utter chirping calls, which have been likened to those of birds, on a regular basis. These toads often move by ambling rather than hopping.*

DIET: *A range of invertebrates, dusted with vitamin and mineral powder.*

BREEDING: *Males call loudly at the start of the spawning period, unlike the European Green Toad (Bufo viridis). Females are prolific, often laying more than 4,000 eggs. Hatching can take place after three days, with metamorphosis taking about two months.*

GREAT PLAINS TOAD
(SAY'S TOAD)

Bufo cognatus   Family Bufonidae

Dark, often circular or oval-shaped areas on the back help identify these toads, interspersed with dull green and beige markings.
The sides of the body are paler than the back.

DISTRIBUTION: *Extends from southeastern Alberta in Canada through the
area of the Great Plains, via Texas down into Mexico. Is also found across
the western United States to southeastern California.*

SIZE: *2–4.5 in (5–11 cm).*

ACCOMMODATION: *Relatively open countryside is this species' natural
habitat. This should be reflected in vivarium surroundings, with a deep
layer of substrate provided so the toads can burrow.*

BEHAVIOR: *Burrows underground to conceal itself, emerging usually
at night or after a period of heavy rain to seek food.*

DIET: *Will prey on a variety of suitable invertebrates, often favoring
cutworms in the wild.*

BREEDING: *On average, males tend to be slightly smaller in size than females
and they have a vocal sac that often hangs down over the throat. Onset of
heavy rain acts as a spawning trigger. This can be replicated for vivarium
stock by transferring them to an aquarium with rocks and aquatic plants.
A large number of eggs are likely to be laid, and the resulting young toads
can be reared easily on powdered flake food.*

GREEN TOAD
(SONORAN TOAD)

Bufo debilis   Family Bufonidae

A colorful, small, predominantly bright green species, this toad
also has black spots over its body. The male is easily recognized
by its black throat.

◀ *GREAT PLAINS TOAD (BUFO COGNATUS)*

DISTRIBUTION: *Central-southern United States, extending from
southwestern Kansas and Colorado to Texas, New Mexico and Arizona,
across the border into Mexico.*

SIZE: *1.25–2 in (3.2–5 cm).*

ACCOMMODATION: *A fairly typical temperate setup will suffice, consisting
of a slightly damp substrate. Some retreats, such as partially buried
flowerpots, should be incorporated in the enclosure.*

BEHAVIOR: *The male has a call resembling that of a cricket, uttered
repeatedly when spawning is taking place. If the rains do not come
in a given area, breeding will not occur that year, reflecting the arid
surroundings in which these toads are found.*

DIET: *A range of invertebrates of suitable size.*

BREEDING: *Tadpoles metamorphose quickly because these toads usually
spawn in temporary pools of water. In the wild the entire breeding cycle
may be accomplished over just three weeks.*

OAK TOAD

Bufo quercicus   Family Bufonidae

This is the smallest species of toad found in North America. It is
instantly recognizable by the white, yellowish or orangish stripe
that runs down the center of the back from the snout. The toads'
body coloration is dull green, with pale reddish and beige areas.
Males can be distinguished by their vocal sacs.

DISTRIBUTION: *Southeastern corner of the United States, extending from
southeastern Virginia down to the tip of Florida and westward to Louisiana.*

SIZE: *0.75–1.25 in (2–3.2 cm).*

ACCOMMODATION: *A sandy environment with hiding places and an
area of water in which the toads can immerse themselves.*

BEHAVIOR: *These toads are active during the day, rather than
being nocturnal.*

DIET: *Invertebrates of various types.*

BREEDING: *Will start spawning following a period of warm, heavy summer
rain, which can be mimicked in vivarium surroundings. Eggs are laid in small
strands of anywhere from two to six eggs, attached to vegetation.*

CRESTED TOAD

Bufo typhonius/margaritifer   Family Bufonidae

The crest of these toads is formed by a very distinctive ridge that
is present over each eye. They are also unusual in having a rather
pointed, triangular-shaped head when viewed from above,

rather than the more rounded profile of other members of the genus. Their coloration is brownish, occasionally with a cream stripe running down the center of the back.

DISTRIBUTION: *The Amazon region of South America.*

SIZE: *3.5 in (8.5 cm).*

ACCOMMODATION: *A rain forest species, the crested toad needs to be housed in warm surroundings, heated to about 77–82°F (25–28°C). The substrate should include leaves, which is the usual hiding place for these toads in the wild.*

BEHAVIOR: *They are active during the day, hunting over the forest floor, and may climb up onto leaves to rest at night.*

DIET: *Ants are their natural prey, which may explain their unusual facial shape. In vivarium surroundings they will take other invertebrates, though, such as crickets.*

BREEDING: *Little is recorded, but they produce relatively small eggs, which are laid in water.*

GULF COAST TOAD
(MEXICAN TOAD; WIEGMANN'S TOAD)

Bufo valliceps   Family Bufonidae

Like othe members of the genus, the patterning of these toads is variable. In the Gulf Coast Toad, however, there is a dark band with a pale border evident along each side of the body. The body itself is usually a combination of brownish and beige colors. Males can be recognized by their yellow-green throats.

DISTRIBUTION: *Ranges from Louisiana and eastern and south-central parts of Texas in the United States down through Mexico to Costa Rica in Central America.*

SIZE: *2–5 in (5–13 in).*

ACCOMMODATION: *A large vivarium. In common with other members of this group of amphibians, the Gulf Coast Toad can have a large appetite, so the substrate should be cleaned regularly.*

BEHAVIOR: *These bold toads are often seen out in city gardens, becoming active at dusk.*

DIET: *A range of invertebrates of suitable size.*

BREEDING: *Varies through its range and is stimulated by rainfall. The eggs are laid in long, often rather fragile, strings and hatch about two days after laying. The life cycle is quick, with the young froglets emerging onto land about a month later.*

▲ BLACK-SPINED TOAD (BUFO MELANOSTICTUS)

OTHER TOADS

Giant Toad (Marine Toad) (*Bufo marinus*)

Range: Extends from southern Texas as far south as Argentina in South America. Introduced to various localities worldwide, including southern Florida and Australia.

Size: Up to 9.5 in (24 cm).

Habitat: Relatively warm, humid areas where cover is available.

Black-spined Toad (*Bufo melanostictus*)

Range: Southeast Asia, extending to the Sunda islands.

Size: Up to 3.5 in (9 cm).

Habitat: Adaptable, often found close to towns.

Red-spotted Toad (*Bufo punctatus*)

Range: Southwestern parts of the United States, from southeastern California to central Texas, and extending into Mexico.

Size: Up to 3 in (7.5 cm).

Habitat: Arid areas of countryside, occurring near water.

▶ GIANT TOAD (BUFO MARINUS)

LEMON TOAD
(VARIEGATED TOAD; CHRISTMAS TOAD)

Bufo variegatus   Family Bufonidae

The Lemon Toad is one of the more commonly available South American bufonids. Its coloration is variable, but the upper parts are greenish brown with a pale gray stripe running along the center of the back. The underparts are pale with black spotting.

DISTRIBUTION: *Southern South America, occurring in Argentina and Chile.*

SIZE: *2 in (5 cm).*

ACCOMMODATION: *A moss-covered floor in the vivarium with logs and similar retreats and a suitable area of water is recommended for this species. It is naturally found in areas of moist, cold forests as well as tundra and bogs.*

BEHAVIOR: *Males of this species are quiet, even when spawning, although they occasionally utter calls that sound like the cheeping of a chick.*

DIET: *A range of invertebrates, such as small earthworms and crickets.*

BREEDING: *The young toads can be reared on hatchling crickets, sprinkled with a vitamin and mineral powder, and other small invertebrates, including whiteworm.*

▲ EUROPEAN GREEN TOAD *(*BUFO VIRIDIS*)*

EUROPEAN GREEN TOAD

Bufo viridis   Family Bufonidae

This adaptable, colorful species will thrive in a secure outdoor vivarium, certainly during the summer months. Its patterning consists of blotches of pale green with reddish and beige areas.

DISTRIBUTION: *Extends widely through much of Europe, except for northwestern parts and the United Kingdom. Extends through the Mediterranean to North Africa and into Asia as far east as Mongolia.*

SIZE: *3 in (7.5 cm).*

ACCOMMODATION: *Since they occur over such a wide region, it is important to try to match the environment to the area of the toads' origins. Those from North Africa should therefore be housed in warmer surroundings than those occurring in the far north.*

BEHAVIOR: *These toads will be stimulated to breed in spring following a cooler period over the winter, provided they have been well fed in the preceding months.*

DIET: *Provide a wide range of suitable invertebrates, dusted as necessary with a vitamin and mineral mix.*

BREEDING: *Most likely to occur in small ponds, which can be incorporated in an outdoor vivarium. Metamorphosis is usually completed within three months.*

BUMBLEBEE WALKING TOAD

Melanophryniscus stelzneri   Family Bufonidae

As their name suggests, these toads are black and yellow in color. Their upper parts are dark with yellow spots, and their underparts are bright yellow. Like many other species, the Bumblebee Walking Toad produces irritating skin toxins, indicated by its bright coloration, which serves as a warning.

DISTRIBUTION: *Southern South America, in Paraguay, Argentina and Uruguay.*

SIZE: *1.3 in (3.5 cm).*

ACCOMMODATION: *A relatively warm, moist vivarium, heated to about 77° F (25° C), with the temperature being dropped back slightly at night. Because these toads are active during the day, a light should be incorporated in the vivarium.*

BEHAVIOR: *Occurs in open areas of grassland, on the pampas. If threatened, the toad rolls over, displaying its bright yellow underparts as a warning.*

DIET: *A mix of small invertebrates, with a vitamin and mineral supplement added as necessary.*

BREEDING: *This is triggered in the wild by the rains and a drop in temperature beforehand. A typical spawning comprises up to 250 eggs, with hatching taking about two days.*

INVERTEBRATES

▲ *Praying Mantis (Mantis religiosa)*

The range of invertebrates that can be kept as pets is very broad, and their requirements are equally diverse. Some can be maintained successfully at room temperature, while others require heated accommodation—equipment available for herptiles is suitable for this purpose. The invertebrates most commonly seen in vivaria are arthropods (phylum Arthropoda), although members of other phyla are occasionally kept.

Arthropods are distinguished by having segmented bodies. The most primitive group are the millipedes and centipedes. They have a head and a long body or trunk with many segments and legs. Insects, such as leaf insects, have a distinct head, thorax (with three pairs of legs) and abdomen. Many insects are also equipped with wings that enable them to fly, although not all are able to do so because of their weight—some stick insects, for example. Arachnids such as tarantulas have a cephalothorax (fused head and thorax) and an abdomen, the former possessing four pairs of legs

Land hermit crabs are also arthropods, but they belong to the crustaceans. Although they hide their bodies away in shells, their body plan is similar to that of insects. Their eyes are mounted on a very distinctive pair of antennae. The first pair of legs has typically become specialized and has developed into claws that can be used for grasping food or defending themselves.

Mollusks belong to a completely different phylum (Mollusca). Examples such as giant land snails have a shell designed primarily for defensive purposes but which also protects them against dehydration. They move not by means of legs but on their foot, laying down a carpet of slime that helps them glide over the ground more easily.

One feature that links the majority of invertebrates is their high reproductive potential. This is a reflection that they are near the bottom of the food chain and are preyed on by many other animals. Breeding them in vivarium surroundings can create difficulties because the number of offspring produced can be huge. In some cases it is not even necessary to have a pair for breeding success—some walking sticks are able to reproduce effectively by cloning themselves. Giant land snails are hermaphrodites (having male and female sex organs); keeping any two individuals together will result in the production of fertile eggs.

WALKING STICKS (STICK INSECTS)

The twiglike appearance of many species of walking sticks (order Phasmatodea) accounts for their common name, while "phasmid," meaning "ghostlike," describes the way they can blend very effectively into the background to escape detection.

Indian, or Laboratory, Stick Insect

The best-known member of the group is the Indian, or Laboratory, Stick Insect (*Carausius morosus*). It is usually a light shade of green, although sometimes it is browner in color. Mature individuals have red markings at the top of the legs. The origins of today's strains date back directly to those obtained in southern India in 1898.

The population today comprises almost entirely females, which can grow to just over 3 inches (8 cm) long. Males crop up occasionally, but they tend to be infertile. They are recognizable by their smaller size, averaging closer to 2 inches (5 cm), and with red coloring extending onto the thorax. These stick insects reproduce by

▼ *INDIAN STICK INSECT (CARAUSIUS MOROSUS)*

warm environment of about 75°F (24°C). The young are a striking shade of reddish brown and measure about 0.5 inches (1.3 cm) long. Sexual maturity is attained at about five months, and they can live for at least 18 months. Like the Indian species, these stick insects will feed readily on bramble leaves.

Pink-winged Stick Insect

The Pink-winged Stick Insect *(Sipyloidea sipylus)* has fully functional wings and can glide considerable distances. Although it is also known as the Madagascan Pink-winged Stick Insect, the origins of this species lie in Southeast Asia, and it was introduced to Madagascar long ago. Today's stock was collected on the island in 1951 and has become parthenogenetic. Females tend to be a light shade of brown, growing to about 3.5 inches (9 cm). Males are much smaller, measuring just 2 inches (5 cm). They thrive at room temperature but will benefit from gentle spraying of their food plant, which ensures a more humid environment and a source of water.

Females stick their eggs around the vivarium rather than scattering them. The young nymphs emerge after about four months, at which stage they are green in color. Be particularly careful when cleaning out their quarters, because if these stick insects try to fly, they may end up ripping their wings or catching them on any bramble thorns in their quarters.

Other Stick Insects

There are several stick insects that are not arboreal by nature. They include the Giant Spiny Stick Insect *(Eurycantha calcarata)*, which occurs on New Guinea and neighboring islands, including the Solomons. Females grow to a slightly larger size than males—up to 6 inches (15 cm)—and can also be distinguished by having a particularly sharp spine on each hind leg. The spine tends to be dark brown in color but is sometimes greenish. Unlike many stick insects, this species can be very aggressive. Do do not house them together and if you have to handle them, do so with care. They will drink readily from a shallow water container on the ground and will eat grass as well as a wide range of other plants, including rose leaves. Females will lay up to 400 eggs in a tub of moist sand on the ground, and the young hatch after about six months.

The Jungle Nymph *(Heteropteryx dilatata)* became available from Malaysia in the 1980s, soon after the Giant Spiny Stick Insect. This species is sexually dimorphic. Females grow to twice the size of males, attaining a length

parthenogenesis, with the females producing dark brown eggs that resemble seeds. They are simply dropped onto the floor of their quarters in reasonably small numbers on a daily basis over the course of several weeks. The subsequent hatching period is variable, lasting up to eight months at room temperature. The young are delicate miniatures of the adults and should not be handled unless it is absolutely essential, in which case use a small clean paintbrush to lift them up.

Giant Prickly Stick Insect

One of the most spectacular stick insects is the Giant Prickly Stick Insect, or Macleay's Spectre *(Extatosoma tiaratum)*, from Australia, where it occurs in arid areas of forest. Captive strains originate from stock obtained in Queensland. Females are significantly larger and heavier than males, growing up to 8 inches (20 cm) in length and weighing up to 1 ounce (30 g) once mature. Although they have wings, they are not large enough to allow them to fly. The lighter males, which may measure only half the size of females, have fully functioning wings that enable them to fly in search of mates. Both sexes are mostly a brownish color, but some are green.

Females can breed parthenogenetically in the absence of a mate, although this prolongs the hatching period. Eggs laid following mating tend to be more viable. The young stick insects, called nymphs, may take up to nine months to hatch. Like the adults, they benefit from a reasonably

enclosure should also be relatively tall to allow these phasmids to molt easily by hanging off a branch or the roof of the vivarium. They will be mature soon after becoming one year old, and females will lay several hundred eggs in a container of damp sand.

The length of time it takes for the nymphs to emerge is very variable and can take from just eight months to as long as three years. It is thought that in a number of species of stick insects there may be a diapause affecting the development of some of the young. By delaying the hatching of some nymphs, the likelihood of a number emerging when environmental conditions are more favorable is increased, enabling more to survive and breed. Jungle Nymph eggs must not be allowed to dry out throughout the incubation period or they will die.

of over 6 inches (15 cm). The female is a bright shade of green. Her broad body tapers along its length, and a pair of nonfunctioning wings on the back can be grated together to create a hissing sound. This acts as a warning if she feels threatened, after which she will lash out quickly with the spines on her hind legs. Males have much more spiny bodies overall and are brown, with brightly colored pinkish wings that are kept largely hidden.

Originating from tropical forests, Jungle Nymphs need to be kept warm, up to 80°F (27°C). Their surroundings should also be sprayed regularly to keep the relative humidity high, but beware of molds developing. The

A number of new stick insect species have entered the hobby over recent years, including two spectacular species from northwestern South America. The Peruvian Fern Stick Insect *(Oreophoetes peruana)* is highly colorful; females are slightly larger than males, mainly black with bright orange patches; males are a combination of black and red. They defend themselves with an unpleasant secretion, and should therefore be handled with particular care. They need warm humid surroundings, in which the temperature can be up to 77°F (25°C).

Once mature, females lay a single egg daily and they can reproduce either sexually or by parthenogenesis. Hatching takes about four months under similar conditions to those in which the adults are housed. The main

drawback of keeping this particular species is its diet of fern leaves. Shop-bought ferns may sometimes have been treated with insecticides that could kill the stick insects. However, ferns are not generally difficult to grow, and a rotation of pots will give a constant supply.

One of the most recent newcomers to the hobby, which has attracted considerable interest is the Peruvian Black Stick Insect *(Peruphasma schultei)*. It was discovered in a remote area of northern Peru in 2002. The sexes are similar in appearance, but males are smaller. They are matte black in color, with striking white eyes. They have small wings that are a deep pink color and that are displayed as a warning gesture rather than being used for flight. It is not a good idea to get too close when they use them in this way, because they are thought to release a chemical which can result in sneezing. Their care is straightforward—they can be kept at room temperature and will eat privet leaves, which are available throughout the year, even in temperate areas. Quarters should be sprayed regularly with tepid water to maintain the humidity.

Housing and Care of Stick Insects

Specially designed enclosures are now on the market for housing stick insects. However, they are not essential, and a suitable plastic container with a ventilated plastic lid is adequate. Ensure that nymphs cannot slip through the ventilation spaces; if in doubt, partially block the spaces, using plastic wrap, which can be removed once the insects are older. The enclosure must be tall enough to allow the stick insects to suspend themselves upside down and shed their skins without difficulty.

While some species can be kept at room temperature, others will require additional heating, which can be provided by a pad heater. Spraying of the enclosure, using a clean plant sprayer, is also often necessary. Regular white paper towel serves as a useful floor covering; it can be easily changed and also enables the seedlike eggs to be spotted. Overcrowding may cause individuals to nibble off the legs of their companions, although they are not cannibalistic by nature. Handle them carefully to avoid limb loss—although if a juvenile's leg is lost for whatever reason, it should regrow at the next molt. Once mature, however, stick insects stop molting, and adults will be permanently disabled by the loss of one or more legs.

The best way of providing food is to cut stems with the leaves attached and place them in a narrow-necked container of water, packing the sides around with tinfoil so there is no risk of the stick insects falling in and drowning. It is important to try to supply enough of the same food plant throughout the year in all cases, because it is often not possible to persuade them to feed on substitute plants. In addition to bramble, plants which can be tried during the winter months in temperate areas include privet, ivy and rhododendron.

LEAF INSECTS

Leaf insects (order Phasmatidae, family Phylliidae) are well camouflaged. They blend in against vegetation, their flattened body shape giving them the appearance of shriveled-up leaves rather than twigs. Their legs are also disguised, and their wings are broad and transparent. Leaf insects are present on islands off the coast of eastern Africa, where they are thought to have been introduced in the distant past, although their natural homeland is in southeastern parts of Asia, extending south to Australia.

Members of the genus *Phyllium* are usually kept in vivaria. They include the Javan Leaf Insect (*P. bioculatum*), found not only on the island of Java, but also in other parts of Asia. Males are easily identified by their slimmer shape and ability to fly well, in contrast to the females. Males are unlikely to grow much larger than 1.5 inches (3.75 cm), although the females are larger. The males' antennae are also shorter, and it is only the males that have two eyespots.

Javan Leaf Insects can reproduce sexually and, less commonly, by parthenogenesis. Males are relatively short-lived. Mating does not occur directly, but the spermatophore (a package of sperm) is passed across to the female to fertilize the eggs. The eggs are brownish and have a rough shape. It can take from four months to over a year for the young nymphs to emerge. Nymphs are red in color and very lively. They require soft-edged leaves to eat to begin with. Their color will change to green, and they grow to full size through a series of molts.

Other leaf insects kept in vivaria include *P. celebicum* and the rarer *P. siccifolium*.

Housing and Care of Leaf Insects

Accommodation similar to that used for stick insects will suffice for leaf insects, but their food preferences are more challenging. If available, guava leaves are ideal, but they can be fed on oak and bramble. Leaf insects need to be kept in warm surroundings, with a temperature of about 75°F (24°C). Relative humidity should be 75 percent and maintained by regular spraying with tepid water.

PRAYING MANTIDS

Praying mantids (order Dictyoptera, family Mantidae) have a gruesome reputation. This can be attributed not only to their aggressive feeding habits, but also to the way

▶ *ABOVE RIGHT: LEAF INSECT (PHYLLIUM SICCIFOLIUM)*

▶ *CELEBES LEAF INSECT (PHYLLIUM CELEBICUM)*

◀ *JAVAN LEAF INSECT (PHYLLIUM BIOCULATUM)*

in which males are likely to killed by the females during mating. Although there is a total of about 2,500 species, very few are available as vivarium subjects. It is only just before they shed their cuticle for the last time that it becomes possible to distinguish the sexes. Females will ultimately grow to a larger size than males, and display a much larger appetite. Some praying mantids can reproduce by means of parthenogenesis.

Always feed the female well before any mating attempt. Praying mantids will eat a variety of invertebrates, but small worms may be better than crickets. The remarkable reflexes of a praying mantid mean that these insects can strike in an instant. Regular feeding of the female should help prevent the male from being decapitated during mating. Nevertheless, courtship is often a protracted process, with the male approaching the female very carefully to ensure she will be receptive to his advances.

The eggs themselves are laid in an egg case known as an ootheca, which will set hard, protecting the eggs. Humidity is important to ensure they hatch successfully. Daily spraying helps, but take care not to saturate the egg case, and use only tepid dechlorinated water.

It is likely to take about six weeks for the young praying mantids to start emerging, lowering themselves out of the egg case on a fine mucous thread. They will need to be separated for rearing purposes. Fruit flies *(Drosophila)* or aphids are an ideal first food and will be needed in large quantities, because the young praying mantids have prodigious appetites.

Mantis religiosa is one of the most widely kept praying mantids. Its coloration can vary from green to brown, and females attain a length of about 3 inches (7.5 cm). It is a temperate species and hides its egg cases under stones. Up to 200 offspring can be anticipated.

Sphodromantis species are also often available. This is an African genus, especially common south of the Sahara. Their egg cases change color from white to brown soon after laying. As many as 400 young may hatch after a period of approximately six weeks.

Housing and Care of Mantids

The predatory nature of mantids means that they need to be housed individually. They require a temperature of 77 to 86°F (25–30°C) and a relatively tall vivarium in which they can hang upside down and molt without difficulty. A variety of branches, some with leaves, should be included in their quarters. These branches can be artificial, since the mantids do not feed on vegetation. Their quarters should be sprayed two or three times a week to maintain a reasonable degree of humidity.

◀ *Praying Mantis (Mantis religiosa)*

▶ *Rhinoceros Beetle (Dynastes hercules)*

BEETLES

A huge number of beetles (order Coleoptera) exist, but only a tiny percentage are popular in vivaria. In many cases identification can be difficult, but among the most commonly seen are various fruit-eating chafer beetles (family Scarabaeidae). Their appeal is based largely on their coloration—they are often shades of luminescent green or yellow, and may have striking markings. They are not particularly large, averaging about 1 inch (2.5 cm).

Ripe fruit such as bananas, occasionally laced with a vitamin and mineral powder, is recommended for these beetles. It needs to be removed from the vivarium before it can turn moldy, and so should be offered only in limited quantities. Thawed frozen peas are another feeding possibility. Some rotten wood should also be included in their quarters, since it is an important source of food for the larvae. Male chafer beetles tend to be larger in size than females. Once mature, females lay a small number of eggs in the ground each day. These will hatch within six weeks. The young larvae remain in the soil and pupate after three months or so, before emerging as adults about a month or two later.

Another popular group (Dynastinae) includes the rhinoceros beetles. Although invariably dark in color, these beetles have "horns" on their head, giving them a spectacular appearance. The horns can grow up to 3.5 inches (9 cm) in the case of the South American Hercules Rhinoceros Beetle *(Dynastes hercules)*. As a group, their dietary needs are similar to those of chafers, and dry leaves are an important food source for the larvae. Some species prefer to live in trees rather than on the ground as adults.

Housing and Care of Beetles

Reasonably warm, moist surroundings, with an average temperature of 77°F (25°C), will suit these beetles. There should also be a deep humus substrate in the vivarium, incorporating leaves, rocks and branches at the surface, under which they can hide away. Chafer beetles will not remain permanently buried but will climb around their quarters. Spraying in the vivarium two or three times every week will help maintain the relative humidity.

CENTIPEDES AND MILLIPEDES

Despite their name, centipedes (class Chilopoda) generally have fewer than 100 legs. A pair of legs is present on each segment running down the body, and they therefore have about 50 legs in total. *Scolopendra* species are most often kept, and this genus is found in both temperate and tropical areas. They can grow up to 12 inches (30 cm) long but are larger in the tropics. They need to be handled very carefully, since bites can have serious effects in humans. Avoid picking them up directly, because contact with their skin can trigger allergic reactions. Centipedes are predatory, preying on slow-moving invertebrates such as slugs.

Millipedes (class Diplopoda) are more popular as pets, although they too possess an ability to defend themselves by releasing a toxic spray. This can cause blistering on human skin and is likely to be particularly serious if it enters the eyes. If they are overcrowded, millipedes may react in this way to each other, with deadly effects. They can grow up to 12 inches (30 cm) in length. Although it is often difficult to distinguish the species, it is important to be aware of their origins to meet their care needs.

▼ *African Giant Black Millipede (Archispirostreptus gigas)*

Small "pill millipedes" are available occasionally. They reach a maximum size of about 2 inches (5 cm) and have requirements similar to larger species. They also burrow underground when molting. Millipedes are vegetarian, but they will feed on dry dog food and similar items, which will supplement their vitamin and mineral intake.

Sexing is possible, since males develop little hooks on the first and frequently the second pair of legs. A more obvious sexual indicator is that males have longer antennae than females. A plug of sperm is transferred to the female at the time of mating, although a few species replicate by parthenogenesis. The eggs are laid over the course of a month or so. They are hidden, often in the ground, and are likely to number several hundred. A millipede that has burrowed into the soil must not be disturbed because this is a sign that she is likely to be laying. Young millipedes emerge after about six weeks and have only a few pairs of legs at first. They develop rapidly, but it is likely to be at least two years before they are sexually mature. Individuals can live for over 10 years.

Housing and Care of Centipedes and Millipedes
An acrylic vivarium with a lid is ideal for accommodating these invertebrates. The base should be filled with several inches of vivarium soil, and the surface covered with

dry leaves and some logs, which serve as hiding places. Ensure that the substrate remains moist and is not allowed to dry out. Spray part of the floor area regularly for this reason. Warmer surroundings may be required for those species originating from tropical areas. They can be housed as part of a mixed collection, in the company of arboreal stick insects.

TARANTULAS AND OTHER SPIDERS

Not everyone is enthusiastic about large spiders, which are all often described, misleadingly, as tarantulas. Tarantulas (order Araneae, family Theraphosidae) can give a painful bite, and their body hairs can cause irritation. Like most invertebrates, they are pets to admire from a distance rather than to pick up, because their bodies are extremely fragile and they can be fatally injured as the result of a fall. Some tarantulas are terrestrial, living in underground burrows from where they ambush prey, whereas other hunt off the ground in trees and bushes. In almost all cases, however, individuals should be housed on their own, with pairs being brought together only for mating purposes.

The first species of tarantula that became popular in the pet trade was the Mexican Red-kneed (*Brachypelma smithi*), which grows to just over 3 inches (7.5 cm) long. It is a brightly colored combination of red and black. Its vivarium should be heated to at least 77°F (25°C). As many as 1,000 spiderlings may hatch from a single egg sac after a period of about three months. Captive-bred young Red-kneed Tarantulas are therefore now widely available, but it can take five years or more for them to attain maturity.

◀ *Mexican Red-kneed Tarantula (Brachypelma smithi)*

▼ *Red-rumped Tarantula (Brachypelma vagans)*

Another tarantula from the same part of the world is the Mexican Red-rumped *(B. vagans),* also known as the Black Velvet. It too lives in burrows, and its distribution extends from Mexico to Guatemala and Honduras. There are slight regional variations in the depth of black coloration, with some being more brownish than others. This species tends not to be quite as prolific as the Red-kneed when breeding, producing no more than 500 offspring.

The Palomino, or Blonde, Tarantula *(Aphonopelma chalcodes)* also occurs in Central America, ranging across the border from Mexico to Arizona. It is typically a shade of golden brown. It inhabits burrows and requires a vivarium temperature of about 82°F (28°C) and dryish conditions, with a relative humidity of about 70 percent.

The blackish brown color of the legs, banded with creamy white stripes, accounts for the common name of another Central American species, the Costa Rican Zebra Tarantula *(A. seemanni).* It requires a similar temperature but higher humidity than the previous species. Some variations in coloration among different populations have been recorded, but when they undergo their final molt, males become entirely blackish brown. The hatching period for the young in this case is about two months.

The South American rain forest is home to a number of bird-eating tarantulas, so called because of their potential to trap tiny hummingbirds in their webs. There are about 35 species in the genus *Avicularia,* of which the Pink-toed Tarantula *(A. avicularia)* is the most commonly kept. Adults are basically black, except for their distinctive pink feet, and can grow to nearly 2.75 inches (7 cm). They need a spacious vivarium in which they can spin a large web. Flying insects are their preferred prey, but crickets can be provided as an alternative. It may be possible to house more than one of these spiders together, providing each has sufficient space around its web to avoid them coming into conflict, but the spiders must all be of the same size.

The requirements of the similar Yellow-toed Tarantula *(A. nigrotineata)* match those of its pink-toed relative, and the genus also has representatives through the Caribbean. The islands of Martinique and Guadaloupe are home to the Antilles Pink-toed Tarantula *(A. versicolor),* which undergoes a remarkable color change from nymph to adult. The young are bluish at first, with a grid pattern on the body. As they mature, reddish gray areas develop on their legs, and the body becomes blackish with a purple suffusion. Regular spraying in their quarters is important, because these spiders will drink droplets of water.

The Goliath Birdeater *(Theraphosa blondi)* is the largest of all tarantulas—with its legs extended it is capable of achieving the size of a dinner plate. It is resident in the Amazon region of northern South America. It is rather unremarkable in terms of coloration, ranging from dark brown to black. As well as being kept warm, these spiders must have a high relative humidity in their quarters of around 80 percent. They will hide beneath the substrate, under cork bark. Breeding is commonly achieved, with the spiderlings being up to 0.75 inches (2 cm) on hatching. They can be reared on small invertebrates

The Chilean Rose Tarantula *(Grammostola cala)* originates from farther south on the continent. By nature a burrowing species, it requires housing similar to that of the Mexican Red-kneed Tarantula. Its pale brown and pink coloration makes an attractive combination, and it is not a particularly aggressive species. This spider should not be confused with the Chilean Pink Tarantula *(G. rosea,* formerly known as *G. spatulatus),* however, which occurs in the same part of the world but tends to be more terrestrial in its habits. It is lighter in color than the Chilean Rose Tarantula, and can be identified by red bristles apparent on the pedipalps. In the case of both species development of young spiderlings is slow, although they can be bred without too much difficulty.

▼ *ANTILLES PINK-TOED TARANTULA (AVICULARIA VERSICOLOR)*

▼ *CHILEAN PINK TARANTULA (GRAMMOSTOLA ROSEA)*

There are some 14 species in the genus and they require an arboreal enclosure, with holes cut in cork bark and boxes behind, into which they can retreat. They feed on moths in the wild, and it is possible to replicate this by giving them waxworms that have completed their metamorphosis, although these tarantulas will feed on crickets and other similar invertebrates. A relative humidity in their quarters of about 75 percent should suffice. Young spiderlings hatch in six weeks, with up to 150 emerging from a single egg sac.

Housing and Care of Tarantulas

Heated accommodation is usually necessary for tarantulas, depending on location, and the design of the vivarium should reflect the spider's natural environment as far as possible. Those found in arid areas should therefore have a sandy substrate, with a broken flowerpot set in it to replicate the entrance to a burrow. In contrast, tarantulas occurring in tropical forests require an arboreal setup, with plenty of branches fixed securely in place for climbing purposes. The relative humidity is very important in all cases, since tarantulas are susceptible to dehydration. Spraying of their quarters, and a shallow pot of water, are both recommended to guard against this problem.

SCORPIONS

As a group, scorpions (order Scorpiones, family Scorpionidae) have a reputation for being even more deadly than spiders. As a result, many are subject to legal restrictions concerning ownership. One very interesting species that is suitable for the terrarium, however, is the Emperor Scorpion (*Pandinus imperator*). It is large, growing to about 6 inches (15 cm) overall. It has particularly fearsome pedipalps and relies more on these to defend itself than on the sting at the tip of the tail.

Originating from West Africa, where its distribution extends from Mauritania to Zaire, the Emperor Scorpion is a rain forest rather than a desert species. The temperature in the vivarium should therefore be from 77 to 86°F (25–30°C), and relative humidity should be maintained at approximately 80 percent. These scorpions will feed readily on invertebrates such as waxworms and mealworms, but take care not to overfeed them, since this will cause the scales on the back to start lifting up.

Males tend to be smaller and slimmer than females. They drop a packet of sperm on the ground during

Baboon Spiders

Although there are no tarantulas in Africa, this continent is home to baboon spiders, which can attain a similar size. Unfortunately, they have a justifiable reputation for being aggressive and are also very quick. Their venom tends to be more potent, too. Some are arboreal by nature, while others are terrestrial. Accommodation similar to that recommended for tarantulas suits these spiders well.

The genus *Pterinochilus* comprises about 20 species of baboon spiders, all of which can be distinguished by a stellar marking on the front part of the body, and other markings on the abdomen. They build webs beneath cork bark and similar objects on the floor of the vivarium, where they then lurk and wait for prey. Baboon spiders prefer a slighter drier environment to that of many tarantulas. The relative humidity in their quarters should be about 70 percent. Baboon spiders also differ in having their egg sac incorporated into their web, rather than being separate. Each sac produces up to 150 spiderlings; females may lay three egg sacs over a six-month period following a single successful mating.

Asiatic Tarantulas

A number of strikingly patterned tarantulas originate from Southeast Asia, and these are now being kept more widely. Unfortunately, they are not especially docile, and careless handling is likely to result in a painful bite, which will be more severe than in the case of New World species. A typical example is the Indian Black and White Tarantula (*Poecilotheria regalis*), which grows up to 2.75 inches (7 cm). In spite of its name, it also has some yellow markings on its legs, like other members of the group. These marks are used to warn off would-be predators.

courtship, which will be retrieved by the female. A year later she will give birth to up to 25 white offspring, each measuring just over 0.5 inches (1.5 cm) long. The female is a dedicated mother, carrying her offspring around on her back for at least a week and retrieving any that fall off. The young will be slow to mature, and will not breed for the first time until they are about six years old.

HERMIT LAND CRABS

Scavenging along the shoreline rather than living in the sea is typical of the lifestyle of hermit land crabs (subphylum Crustacea, order Decapoda, family Coenobitidae), which means they can be accommodated easily in a vivarium. As they grow, they will seek out larger shells in which to live, favoring those with broad openings. A selection of shells can often be purchased from curio shops or specialized stores, some of which advertize on the Internet. There is no guarantee, however, that when your crab sheds its existing shell it will choose your favorite! High humidity is particularly important at this stage, to prevent the crabs from becoming dessicated. They may burrow in the sand for a period at this stage.

Feeding these instinctive scavengers is straightforward; thanks to their popularity there are several specially prepared foods available. Alternatively, fish foods can be used. Beware of overfeeding, however. When picking up crabs, take hold only of the shell. This is partly to avoid being nipped by the large pincer, but also because their body is extremely fragile, and a fall could be fatal.

Healthy crabs will usually withdraw into their shell if picked up. If a crab appears inactive, it may be that it is dehydrated, so place it in a saltwater solution. Breeding in the vivarium is impossible, since these crabs only breed in the sea, and it is not possble to distinguish visually

▲ *HERMIT LAND CRAB (COENOBITA PERLATUS)*

between the sexes while they are in their shells. Their life expectancy can be up to 20 years.

A converted aquarium can be used for housing, with a thick layer of sand as a floor covering to replicate a beach. Driftwood, pebbles and shells will create a natural landscape. An area of seawater should be provided in a non-metallic container; seawater substitute can be made using marine salt as sold for saltwater aquaria. The sand should be sprayed regularly with this saltwater. The crab's enclosure needs to be kept warm, between 70 and 78°F (21 and 26°C) during the day, falling back slightly at night.

GIANT LAND SNAILS

Giant land snails (phylum Mollusca, order Stylommatophora, family Achatinidae) are banned in some areas, including the United States, because of fears that escapees could become established in the wild. However, elsewhere they are very popular as pet invertebrates, particularly with children, since they are easy to keep. *Achatina fulica* originates from West Africa and can grow to 8 inches (20 cm) long and weigh over 8 ounces (225 g). These "megamollusks" require humid surroundings and heating if necessary, to maintain the temperature in their vivarium at between 70 and 75°F (21 and 24°C).

Feeding is straightforward—they will eat a wide range of vegetable matter and fruit. This should be sprinkled with a vitamin and mineral supplement. In addition, a piece of cuttlefish bone (as supplied for budgies) should be included in their quarters so the snails can rasp at the soft side with their mouthparts. If deprived of calcium, they can develop a soft shell. Breeding is simple because the snails have both male and female organs in their body. If two of these snails are kept together, fertile eggs will result and will be deposited in jellylike masses around their quarters.

▼ *EMPEROR SCORPION (PANDINUS IMPERATOR)*

GLOSSARY

Words in SMALL CAPITALS refer to other entries in the Glossary.

activated carbon Filters out chemical pollutants from water in a vivarium by adsorption.

airstone A way of breaking up bubbles of air drawn into an AQUATERRARIUM, forcing them out through a fine nozzle, so they create less of a current and improve oxygenation.

algae Primitive, usually green, organisms that can develop on the sides of a tank or on rocks. They photosynthesize under well-lit surroundings but they do not flower and flourish only in moist, preferably wet, conditions.

alkalinity Water conditions that exceed a reading of 7.0 on the PH scale. *See also* pH.

amphibian A vertebrate that spends time on land, generally returning to water to reproduce.

amplexus The way in which male frogs or toads grip females during courtship and mating.

aquaterrarium Accommodation for HERPTILES or invertebrates that largely, if not exclusively, consists of water rather than land.

basking Behavior in which reptiles seek out a warm place and remain there for some time to raise their body temperature.

biological filtration A "natural" means of filtration using beneficial bacteria to maintain favorable conditions.

brackish water Water containing approximately 10 percent seawater.

C.B. Captive-bred; describes a HERPTILE or invertebrate bred in a VIVARIUM or similar enclosed surroundings, where its parents are well established.

C.F. Captive-farmed; a HERPTILE raised from collected eggs. *See also* C.B.

carapace The upper surface of a CHELONIAN's shell.

chelonian A reptile of the Order Testudines (formerly Chelonia), consisting of turtles, tortoises, and terrapins.

cloaca Area around the VENT; can be used for sexing newts.

color morph A change in the coloration of a creature as the result of a mutation, which is then often developed by selective breeding.

ectothermic A species that cannot control its body temperature by internal means and is therefore reliant on an outside source of heat.

feeding stick A device used to hold food; it can be moved around in front of the animal to encourage it to strike.

femoral pores Hollows down the underside of the femur.

filter medium A substance used, especially in an AQUATERRARIUM, to remove or break down waste matter.

food stick A type of formulated food, typically used for CHELONIANS and so called because of its length, to distinguish it from a PELLET.

green food Plant matter used as food.

heaterstat A unit combining a heater and a thermostat.

heat spot Warm area beneath a VIVARIUM spotlight, where the temperature will be warmer than elsewhere in the tank.

hemipenis Male reproductive organs of lizards and snakes, consisting of two "half" penises.

herpetology The study of REPTILES and AMPHIBIANS.

herptile A term sometimes used as a collective description for REPTILES and AMPHIBIANS.

hygrometer A device for measuring relative humidity in the VIVARIUM.

live foods Invertebrates fed to HERPTILES and other invertebrates, bred specially for the purpose.

mulm Fine particulate matter that may cloud the water in an AQUATERRARIUM if disturbed.

nuptial pads Swellings that develop on the limbs of some male frogs at the outset of the spawning period; used to grasp females when mating.

nymph An immature arthropod; commonly associated with stick insects.

ovovivipary The process by which eggs are retained in the female's body and develop here without being nourished directly. *See also* VIVIPARY.

pH A measure of relative acidity or ALKALINITY; the scale ranges from 1 (very acid) through 7 (neutral) to 14 (very alkaline). Most aquatic HERPTILES and invertebrates require a neutral pH.

parthenogenesis Reproduction without transference of sperm; the eggs produce what are effectively clones of the female.

pellet Formulated food presented in a small ball.

photoperiod Length of time the VIVARIUM lights are left on or the amount of daylight exposure a HERPTILE encounters in the wild, which can change with the seasons and may be a breeding stimulant.

plastron The underside of a CHELONIAN's shell.

power filter A filtration device in the form of a canister that draws water into the container and expels it once it has passed through FILTER MEDIA.

reptile A creature with scales on its body; reproduces sexually by giving birth to live young or laying eggs; is unable to regulate body temperature independently of environment.

sexual dimorphism A means of distinguishing between the sexes by their appearance.

spawning The part of the reproductive process that involves egg fertilization. May be external—occurring outside the body, as in frogs—or internal, as in tortoises.

species-only setup A VIVARIUM used to display a single species rather than a group of species.

spermatophore A packet of sperm transferred during mating by a male newt or salamander to the female.

subspecies A localized population of a species with recognizable features.

substrate The floor covering in the VIVARIUM.

terrarium Housing for land-dwelling HERPTILES.

thermoregulation Ability to maintain a comfortable body temperature.

tortoise table An indoor open-topped enclosure for tortoises.

undergravel filter A method of filtration favored in AMPHIBIAN tanks, in which the gravel acts as a filter bed, removing potentially harmful impurities from the water.

vent The urogenital opening, present at the base of the tail in many species.

vivarium Covered housing for HERPTILES or invertebrates.

vivipary Reproduction in which young develop and are nourished inside the mother's body. *See also* OVOVIVIPARY.

water change The volume of water (usually up to a quarter) that needs to be removed from the AQUATERRARIUM on a regular basis to maintain a healthy balance here; it should be replaced by fresh dechlorinated water.

FURTHER READING

Alderton, D. *A Step-by-Step Book about Stick Insects* (TFH Publications, Neptune, NJ, 1992).

Alderton, D. *Turtles and Tortoises of the World* (Facts On File, New York, 2004).

Ballasina, D. *Amphibians of Europe: A Colour Field Guide* (David & Charles, Newton Abbot, Devon, UK, 1984).

Bleher, J. L., and F. W. King. *National Audubon Society Field Guide to Reptiles and Amphibians—North America* (Alfred A. Knopf, New York, 2000).

Branch, B. *Bill Branch's Field Guide to the Snakes and Other Reptiles of Southern Africa* (New Holland, London, 1988).

Brock, P. D. *A Complete Guide to Breeding Stick and Leaf Insects* (TFH/Kingdom, Havant, Hampshire, UK, 2000).

Christenson, G., and L. Christenson. *Day Geckos in Captivity* (Living Art Publishing, Ada, OK, 2003).

Coborn, J. *Snakes and Lizards: Their Care and Breeding in Captivity* (David and Charles, Newton Abbot, Devon, UK, 1987).

Cogger, H. G. *Reptiles and Amphibians of Australia* (Reed Books, Sydney, NSW, Australia, 1986).

Conant, R. *A Field Guide to Reptiles and Amphibians of Eastern/Central North America* (Houghton Mifflin, Boston, MA, 1975).

Ferri, V. *Turtles and Tortoises* (Firefly, Buffalo, NY, 2002).

Frye, F. l. *Captive Invertebrates: A Guide to Their Biology and Husbandry* (Krieger Publishing, Melbourne, FL, 1992).

Hancock, K., and J. Hancock. *Tarantulas: Keeping and Breeding Arachnids in Captivity* (R & A Publishing, Taunton, Somerset, UK, 1992).

Heselhaus, R. *Poison Arrow Frogs: Their Natural History and Care in Captivity* (Blandford, London, 1992).

Highfield, A. C. *Practical Encyclopedia of Keeping and Breeding Tortoises and Freshwater Turtles* (Carapace Press, London, 1996).

Mattison, C. *Keeping and Breeding Amphibians* (Blandford, London, 1993).

Mattison, C. *Keeping and Breeding Lizards* (Blandford, London, 1991).

Mattison, C. *Keeping and Breeding Snakes* (Blandford, London, 1996).

Smith, H. M. *Handbook of Lizards—Lizards of the United States and Canada* (Comstock Publishing, Ithaca, NY, 1946).

Staniszewski, M. *Mantellas* (Edition Chimaira, Frankfurt am Main, Germany, 2001).

Stone, J. L. S. *Keeping and Breeding Butterflies and Other Exotica* (Blandford, London, 1992).

Vetter, H. *Turtles of the World Vol. 1: Africa, Europe and Western Asia* (Edition Chimaira, Frankfurt am Main, Germany, 2002).

Vetter, H. *Turtles of the World Vol. 2: North America* (Edition Chimaira, Frankfurt am Main, Germany, 2004).

Vetter, H. *Turtles of the World Vol. 3: Central and South America* (Edition Chimaira, Frankfurt am Main, Germany, 2005).

Vetter, H., and P. P. van Dijk. *Turtles of the World Vol. 4: East and South Asia* (Edition Chimaira, Frankfurt am Main, Germany, 2006).

Wright, A. H., and A. A. Wright. *Handbook of the Frogs and Toads of the United States and Canada* (Comstock Publishing, Ithaca, NY, 1949).

WEB SITES

GENERAL

http://www.demogr.mpg.de/longevityrecords/index2.htm

http://www.eurorep.net/retail/

http://www.herper.com/

CHELONIANS

http://www.austinsturtlepage.com/

http://www.chelonia.org/

LIZARDS

http://www.beardeddragon.org

http://www.chameleonnews.com/index.html

http://www.leopardgecko.com/

SNAKES

http://www.buddhaboa.com/

http://www.reptimania.co.uk/

AMPHIBIANS

http://www.amphibian.co.uk/

http://amphibiaweb.org/index.html

http://www.caudata.org/

http://www.livingunderworld.org/

PICTURE CREDITS